SAINTS + SINNERS
2020

NEW FICTION
FROM THE FESTIVAL

SAINTS + SINNERS
2020

NEW FICTION
FROM THE FESTIVAL

edited by

Tracy Cunningham and Paul J. Willis

SAINTS+SINNERS

2020

SAINTS + SINNERS 2020:
NEW FICTION FROM THE FESTIVAL
© 2020 BY SAINTS & SINNERS LITERARY FESTIVAL. ALL RIGHTS RESERVED.

ISBN 13: 978-1-63555-797-8

THIS TRADE PAPERBACK ORIGINAL IS PUBLISHED BY
BOLD STROKES BOOKS, INC.
P.O. BOX 249
VALLEY FALLS, NY 12185

FIRST EDITION: APRIL 2020

CREDITS
EDITORS: TRACY CUNNINGHAM AND PAUL J. WILLIS
PRODUCTION DESIGN: SUSAN RAMUNDO
COVER DESIGN BY TIMOTHY CUMMINGS

Acknowledgments

We'd like to thank:

The John Burton Harter Foundation for their continued support of the fiction contest and their generous support of the Saints and Sinners Literary Festival program.

Radclyffe, Sandy Lowe, and Bold Strokes Books for their talents in the production of our anthology and their sponsorship of the Saints and Sinners event.

Timothy Cummings, cover artist for the 2020 Saints and Sinners Literary Festival anthology and program book.

Amie M. Evans, whose editorial contributions over the years have informed and shaped the quality of these anthologies.

Everyone who has entered the contest and/or attended the Saints and Sinners Literary Festival over the last 17 years for their energy, ideas, and dedication in keeping the written LGBTQ word alive.

Our Past Contest Winners

2019
J. Marshall Freeman "The Grove of Mohini"

2018
Jeremy Schnotala "Sand Angels"

2017
J. Marshall Freeman "Curo the Filthmonger"

2016
Jerry Rabushka "Trumpet in D"

2015
Maureen Brady "Basketball Fever"

2014
Sally Bellerose "Corset"

2013
Sandra Gail Lambert "In a Chamber of My Heart"

2012
Jerry Rabushka "Wasted Courage"

2011
Sally Bellerose "Fishwives"

2010
Wayne Lee Gay "Ondine"

CONTENTS

Introduction
Don Weise, 2020 Finalist Judge

Some years ago while out at New York Pride, I came across a gay couple in their thirties, both good-looking men with big smiles, and if that weren't enough to draw attention, a small blonde girl sat on the shoulder of one of the men, also smiling and, okay, good-looking too. I then noticed the T-shirt worn by the man carrying the girl; on it were the words "Family Is the New Gay." *Alright*, I said to myself, *that takes care of that*. As a single gay person who never intends to marry or become a parent, I was, as of that moment, no longer gay apparently and without the aid of conversion therapy. Nor were most of my gay friends nor the scores of men I hook up with, also single, unmarried, and childless for the most part; despite all the man-on-man sex that would usually qualify them as bona fide homosexuals, they, too, could hang up their gay hats and head to the exit, safely out of the way of this not-so-brave new world of normalcy advocated by this smiling, shining family.

I share this incident because it came to mind as I read the stories in this anthology. Not that any of the stories exactly shares the outlook expressed on that T-shirt's slogan; rather, most of these contributors go in the opposite direction, offering depictions of gay life that are realistic in the sense that, for the most part, they're not about fitting in. I wouldn't necessarily say that anyone is outright challenging the general shift of the gay community toward the mainstream that's been happening for decades. However, I would argue that these authors are writing "from where they live," as writing instructors like to say. And with that comes a kind of authenticity that says, in so many words, "This may or may not be the world you live in, but it's the world my characters and I live in." As such, I, the reader, am essentially welcomed in, whether I'm familiar with the setting or not. No one herein declares that any one thing is the new gay, or even the old gay, but just *their* gay. Take it or leave it. In this, I find liberation.

I'll start with "Big House," the contest winner. There's so much going for this story that I almost want to say nothing and let readers see it for themselves unbiased. But I will say that if you're not grabbed from the first line, "Kasper and I dug the grave with the butts of our guns and buried the fox," you might as well stop reading because you likely won't appreciate how good the rest of the story gets. And if your idea of gay fiction is writing where the queer content is front and center, this probably isn't the story for you either. In fact, I found this to be one of the appealing aspects. Nothing jumps out at the reader to tell us that the narrator is queer, but at the same time, it's so present under the radar throughout, which immersed me in the storytelling even more. It's told by a disenchanted Marine who describes his tense relationship with a sadistic superior named Casota, whom he's hated, he tells us, since the day he met him. Yet Casota improbably mesmerizes this young soldier who confesses, "Sometimes, often when I least expect it, I find myself saying his name in a low voice. I say it over and over, in a kind of mantra. It makes a susurrus of sibilant wind against my tongue, with only that one T near the front of my mouth to stand above the tidal wave of his name." You tell me, but if this isn't a guy who's deeply turned on by his commanding officer, I can retire as an editor right now. Hold the applause.

To be sure, readers in search of openly queer content won't be disappointed. In "Mesopotamia," for instance, a group of fifty-something, San Franciscan gay men lament the loss of their youth: "…What happened to us?" the bewildered protagonist asks his friends. "When did we become middle-aged?" Says one of them in reply, "It just happens. It creeps up on you. One day you're out and about, running around, thinking about the future. And the next you're counting gray hairs in the mirror." The author depicts gay midlife so realistically (to me, anyway) that I'm not sure my therapist didn't ghostwrite it based on our sessions.

Another stand-out is "Jingle-Jingle-Pop," about a young transwoman of color working on the rough streets of Los Angeles, which is about as far removed from the environs of "Mesopotamia" as you can get, yet I found this story equally powerful. When her friend, another young transwoman of color, also a sex worker, asks, "Where'd you be right now if not here? Tell me, Lalo," I get choked up, because who hasn't been stuck "someplace" they didn't want to be and with no way out in sight? For Lalo, it's the dream of taking her man, someone she hasn't even yet met, home to meet her mother on Thanksgiving, wearing "sensible sandals, no heels." Perhaps surprisingly, as a gay man, I see myself as clearly in this character as I do in the gay men discussing midlife. Since all submissions in this anthology contest were submitted to me without names attached, I can't say whether either of these authors is writing autobiographically, but I don't think it matters after all. These two stories simply feel authentic regardless and should connect not just with me but with any reader with a heart.

One of the elements that I wasn't expecting from this batch of stories is that many of them are set in locales not typically seen in LGBT fiction; more specifically, many of them take place outside the familiar, big-city gay meccas depicted endlessly in gay writing. Take "What Covers the House Is a Roof." It's the story of Small Man, an obese, thirty-year-old gay man who plays music in a cocktail lounge in Hawaii. The author writes with profound and impressive insight into the lonesome predicament of a sexually "undesirable" queer person, not exactly a staple of gay fiction. When approached by a drunken, playful straight friend who gets sexy and asks, "What, no can be affectionate because you gay?" A despondent Small Man replies, "Just no can," as he tries "not to think about how he is built to love but maybe not to have affection." As if this moment weren't moving enough, the friend, on leaving, turns and calls out, "Big Boy. Remember, you beautiful." Words needed maybe now more than ever before in the often brutal, virtual realm of gay sex apps, the same ones that leave Small Man wishing that some man out there "might not see his body but see his love."

In terms of overall craft, I'd also like to make mention of "Life and the Theater," "Une Tranche de Vie," and "Forgive Us Our Trespasses." One of the hazards of singling out stories in an introduction is that it implies that the stories not mentioned somehow don't measure up. That's not the case, needless to say; there's much to admire throughout this book. But it's inevitable that some stories will appeal to a judge of such contests more so than others, and this can easily be as much about personal taste and preferences as craft. Yet if nothing else, these stories, when taken as a whole, show us that the so-called "new gay" isn't dramatically different from the old gay. Despite the many political and technological advances in our lives, we are, all of us, when you get right down to it, still seeking love, connection, understanding, and to be embraced for who we are rather than who we are supposed to be. It sometimes takes a good short story to remind us of that.

MADE MAN
MORGAN RAE HUFSTADER

I t's just a cat."
The white pool ball flew across the green fabric and sunk straight into the side pocket, which was how Alex knew he was in trouble.

Vince was a pool aficionado. Pool was to Vince what bowling was to The Dude. Vince never missed a shot.

Alex had his hip against the pool table, Miller High Life in hand. When he dared to lift his eyes, he saw Vince glaring at him, cue stick still in hand. He approached and, for a second, Alex thought his uncle might hit him over the head with it.

"Just a *cat*?" Vince repeated, his voice pitching with rage. When Alex tried to look away—to the fat guy playing video poker or the group of jocks doing shots at the bar—Vince jabbed his finger in chest and forced Alex's attention back on him. "You listen to me, you hopped-up little shit—this isn't *just a cat*. It's the Capo's cat. You know what that means?"

Vince's eyes were red-rimmed; he always got sloppy-intense when he was drunk. Alex wet his lips with the tip of his tongue. "It's a big responsibility—"

"You're goddamn right!" Vince barked, spit hitting Alex in the face. "It's a big responsibility! The Capo tells you to watch his cat, or change his lightbulb, or wipe his ass—you do it, no questions asked. Capiche?"

The bar smelled like stale piss. His beer was lukewarm. And Vince was drunk beyond the point of it being fun for anyone. Alex didn't want to watch a cat. Mostly, he just wanted to go home.

But that wasn't an option.

He'd given up that right at the start of the summer when he'd been booted from boot camp and his mother wouldn't take him back in and his uncle Vince had been generous enough to let him sleep on his couch (after wiping the tiny mouse turds from the mattress). Vince lived in a shitty shotgun in the Seventh Ward that took Alex twenty hours to get to on the Greyhound. It didn't matter that Vince was a drunk most of the time, that he slept all day and stayed out all night, or that he'd been in and out of jail more times than anyone could count. He had a place to sleep, and that was fine for now.

They lived on different time schedules for a couple weeks— Alex applying to every service industry job he could find during the day, Vince lumbering out of the bedroom at sunset in nothing but his boxers to stand in front of the box fan in the kitchen. Then, finally, Vince invited him out. "To meet the guys," Vince said. "If they like you, you might get a job out of it."

They'd gone to a Cajun restaurant with the neon sign blaring CLOSED. The side entrance led them to a small, dark room, where four different men crowded around a crimson table. Bottles of wine on the table, along with a basket of crawfish and cornbread. They were all older—Vince's age, in their forties, maybe. With thick cheeks and tailored suits.

Alex—in his torn jeans and t-shirt—wished he'd got the memo.

When Vince and Alex entered, the men got quiet and all their eyes turned to Alex.

That was when Vince put his hand on Alex's shoulder and said, "This is my nephew, Alex."

Not: my niece.

Not: my sister's dyke daughter.

Not: Kathryn.

This is my nephew, Alex.

The other guys bobbed their heads, greeted him to the crew. Meanwhile, Alex quietly broke apart every double-helix in his body and bonded it to Vince.

At that moment, he knew he'd do anything for his uncle. Anything.

So far, "anything" included:

• Attending frequent cigar-smoke-filled meetings

• Jacking a car

• Driving an Impala to Joe's Lot to get crushed

• Pretty sure there was a body in the trunk

• Like, really sure

But that didn't matter. Because Alex's loyalty was limitless. Because his uncle *saw* him. The crew saw him. When everyone else turned away from him, they saw him and they didn't give a shit.

So he'd do whatever his uncle needed. Even if that meant watching the Capo's cat.

His uncle's hot breath hit him with every pant—wet and sticky.

"Yeah," Alex said. "Capiche."

Vince took his beer from him (asshole) and chugged it. Then he threw the empty in the trash—it bounced off the edge and crashed on the floor, spilling sparkling shards. No one seemed to notice.

"Go feed the fucking cat before I turn you into cat food," Vince hissed, and Alex made his exit.

His bike was chained up to the fence and Alex had to crouch down and fight through an overgrown patch of ivy to get it unlocked. He tossed the bike chain and lock in his backpack and threw it over his shoulder. He put the address in his phone's GPS, hooked an earbud in his ear, and kicked off. The bike was a loaner—a rickety thing he'd dragged out of Vince's shed—and the brake screamed bloody murder every time he squeezed it.

The night was damp, the fog turning street lights and gas lanterns into a watercolor smear.

The air tasted like metal. Sewer. Hot garbage. And then when he rode over the street car track, into Uptown—jasmine. Lavender. Honeysuckle.

People drove like crap this time of night. Everyone was drunk. Swerving home.

The fantasies kicked in. He dreamed about tilting too far to the side. Hitting asphalt at just the right moment. Letting his bones twist with bike metal and tire rubber.

But then he'd think about how his mom would fuck up his obituary and it sobered him up. He turned left, down a quieter road.

He hadn't met the Capo. *Capo Gene*. Not officially, anyway. He'd seen the other man through the frosted glass of his office windows, though, when Vince went to visit him in the warehouse and came out with wads of hundreds.

It paid to be made, Vince told him. He believed him.

Alex wasn't there—not yet, anyway. Maybe never. Did trans men get to be made-men? Until he found out, he had to earn his way doing the crappy tasks no one else wanted to do.

Like babysit the Capo's tabby cat while the man was out of town for the weekend.

The Capo's house sat on the corner of Soniat Street, surrounded by a large stone wall crisscrossed with ivy. The wall was maybe ten feet high and reminded Alex of a prison. Alex dug into his pocket and pulled out a key ring, fished around until he found the right one, and swung open the Capo's gate. His mailbox was full, so Alex grabbed the mail as well. He closed the gate behind him and leaned his bike up against the wall inside.

The house itself was a goliath. Two stories with a red, fish-scale roof. The second floor windows were closed with heavy storm shudders. On the ground floor, an amber light glowed.

Alex unlocked the front door. Inside, it opened up to a wide living room that was clearly meant to impress. Bookshelf stuffed with thick hardcovers, fireplace (who the fuck needed a fireplace *here?*), and a flatscreen that nearly took up the whole wall.

He took a step inside, put the mail on the foyer table, and then stopped. The floors were sleek wood and the polished coating gave them a shine. He looked down at his boots. He'd already trailed in clumps of dirt. He knelt, undid the laces, and took them off, making them stand like little soldiers by the door.

A clicking sound caught his attention. When he looked up, he saw the orange tabby strutting towards him. It stopped a couple paces from him, tail switching, and meowed.

He shrugged his backpack off his shoulders, reached out, clicked his tongue. The cat cautiously approached, velvet nose knocking against the backs of his fingers, and then pushed its head against his hand. He hooked his fingers underneath its chin, to the soft throat and chest, and rubbed.

"Hey, buddy. Are we friends now?"

His fingers curved underneath the belly, to its soft stomach. In a flash, the cat grabbed his hand between his paws, dug its teeth into his knuckle, and then launched away, scampering down the hall.

Alex swore, turning his hand to see the damage. Small, thin lines of red.

"He's a bastard, isn't he?"

Alex jerked upwards so quickly he had to drop his hand to the floor to hold his balance.

A woman stood in the arched open doorway between the living room and kitchen. He noticed her legs first—bare, long— that tucked into a long, white top. She raised her hands above her head. An easy smile. "Whoa, don't shoot."

He didn't shoot. He did have a piece—a crappy 9mm that Vince loaned him. It was sitting in his backpack. He'd have to unzip it, rummage through the junk in there, flick off the safety and take aim.

In hindsight, not a great place to store it.

Alex blinked. "Who are you?"

"Virginia." Alex went through his mental rolodex. Nothing. She sighed. "Gene's daughter?"

"Oh."

She looked about the right age to be the Capo's daughter. Late twenties. Tanned skin, dark hair in a long braid. The kitchen light put a halo around her hair. Showed off all the little frizzy bits that poked out.

Slowly, Alex rose to his feet. "Sorry. I thought the place would be empty."

She pursed her lips and folded her arms over her chest. "Can you keep a secret?"

"Sure."

"I'm not supposed to be here."

"Where are you supposed to be?"

"Rehab."

"Ah."

She leaned against the wall, cocked a hip. "It's not like serious addiction, like life or death, intervention style shit. Just a bad habit Daddy isn't really crazy about. But I can quit anytime. Speaking of. You got any cocaine?"

"Uh—no."

She smiled. "I'm kidding. You want water or something?"

"Please."

She straightened up, pivoted, and vanished into the kitchen. Alex followed.

The kitchen was delineated with white-tiled floors, separating it from the rest of the house. The house seemed devoid of doors and the open floor plan made Alex feel like he needed to keep checking over his shoulder.

Virginia opened a cabinet, closed it, then tried another. "Found them!" she announced. "Pesky things always running away."

"Pesky," Alex repeated. He wondered if she was high right now.

She reached up and plucked a glass out. When she reached, her shirt rode up, exposing a slice of black boy shorts underneath.

Alex looked away. His lips felt dry, but he didn't dare lick them.

"What's your name?" she asked as she pressed the glass to the dispenser built into the fridge. The purified water hummed as it trickled out.

"Alex."

"Do you work for my dad, Alex?"

"Sort of."

"Sort of?"

"He asked me to feed his cat."

She smiled. "So *you're* the cat whisperer."

"I guess."

She handed over the glass and he thanked her. It felt cool in his hand and cool down his throat. New Orleans summers were a bitch—no relief from the heat, not even in the blanket of night. The ride over had left him splotchy with sweat.

Feeling grimy, he lifted the edge of his shirt and used it to wipe his face. Out of the corner of his eye, he saw her gaze drop to his bare stomach.

Let her look. He'd worked hard for the flatness of his stomach, the bulge of his biceps, for all the parts of him that screamed *call me by the wrong fucking pronouns, I dare you.*

But then her fingers reached out, and everything inside him clenched when she touched his hip. "You in the military?"

She was tracing the eagle tattooed across his hip, wings spread wide.

"Uh. I got through boot camp. But…didn't get deployed or anything."

They'd forced him to make a choice—pretend to be someone he wasn't or get discharged.

Made the tattoo a big fucking embarrassment, now.

He dropped his shirt, she dropped her hand. She remained close, though, her elbow on the counter. Her eyes were green, with little flecks in them, and they swept over him, sizing him up. "You barely look old enough to enlist."

"I'm 25. So. In army years, I'm grandpa."

She laughed at that. It was a dumb joke. She didn't have to laugh, but she did.

Alex was getting comfortable around her. Too comfortable. The swallowing warmth of a bed and a body and a lazy morning. Time to make an exit.

He jabbed his thumb over his shoulder. "I should head out."

"You have somewhere to be?" She took a seat at the round kitchen table. When she crossed her legs, her shirt rose over her knee.

Alex thought about the saggy pullout couch and the air conditioning that never worked.

He shrugged. "Don't want to take up your night."

"You're not. Distraction is good for me. Keeps me from feeding bad habits. Have a beer! There's plenty in the fridge."

She pointed to the chair across from her. The tabby trotted in and, in one leap, made it onto the counter. Its yellow eyes dared him, tail swishing.

"Uh. Sure. Thanks."

He peaked into the fridge. Dixie. Yuengling. St. Pauli Girl.

He took the Yuengling and cracked it. The teeth bit into the flesh of his palm. He set the cap on the counter and took the seat at the table across from her.

"Are you from here?" she asked.

He shook his head. "Minnesota."

"Did you float down the Mississippi?"

"Something like that."

"Why'd you leave?"

"Just…a lot of toxicity. People trying to tell me who I am. How I should act. What I should do."

"How do you like it here?"

"It's fine."

He put the beer bottle to his lips.

"So!" She smiled wide. "Have you killed a guy yet?"

Beer sloshed down the wrong tube. He choked. "Have I *what*?"

"You know. For the cause. That's how it works, right? You're not a made-man until you've killed someone. Daddy's rules."

"No. I haven't…done that."

"Awww. A virgin." Her fingers tiptoed up his arms. He didn't like the cloying sound in her voice when she said it. He jerked his arm away.

"Yeah. Well."

She dropped her head in her hand. Her fingers left little dimples on her cheek. "I bet you would, though. If you had to."

"Wouldn't anyone? If they had to."

"Not *anyone*."

"Okay," Alex reasoned with her, "a guy breaks into your house. He's got a knife. What do you do?"

"Go belly up and die."

"I don't believe that."

"No, you're right." She smiled, her teeth too-white. "I'd call Daddy."

"And if Daddy doesn't get here on time?"

She shrugged.

He filled in for her: "You'd grab the lamp and beat him to death. Survival instinct."

She lifted a finger. "That's self-defense. Not the same. That's doing what you have to in order to survive."

"Depends."

"On?"

"How you define *surviving*."

She propped her head in her chin. "I like the way you make small talk."

He snorted on a laugh. Eyes ducked down. "Sorry. We can talk about something else. What's it like growing up with a Capo as a father?"

She bit her lip. Her blasé attitude was unnerving. Like tiny shards of glass stuck under the skin. "People make assumptions about me. They think they know me because they know my father."

"What kind of assumptions?"

"Like I'm spoiled. And a slut."

"Are you?"

She grinned. "What do you think?"

"I don't know you."

"What if I told you I've been thinking about kissing you since you walked in?"

His laugh was a low, nervous bark. "You're—uh."

"I'm what?"

"Gene's daughter."

"Aren't you the one who said we shouldn't let other people define us?"

"Yeah...but."

"So...if I was any other girl. Not the Capo's daughter. What would you think of me?"

Her hands were folded together at the center of the table. He leaned forward and traced his fingertips over the backs of her knuckles. "I think you have nice eyes."

She smiled. "Now we're getting somewhere."

His heart pummeled in his chest. "I'm not...uh. Like other boys."

"I know." She reached forward. Her fingers curled through his short hair, tracing underneath his ear. "You're different. You're an angel."

She drew closer. Too close. If he leaned in, just an inch, he'd be able to feel her breath on his face. The softness of her lips.

"I've gotta...um. Mind if I use your bathroom?"

"Sure. Down the hall to the right."

Alex rose, avoiding eye contact, and followed his feet out of the kitchen, down the hall, and into the hallway bathroom.

It had a toilet. Sink. Mirror. Vanity. Towel racks with such fine, imperfect detail in the metal work they looked handcrafted. Even the Capo's bathroom was extra.

Alex ran the faucet. Cupped some cold water and wiped dried sweat off the back of his neck. Off his face. Underneath his shirt. He popped open the button of his jeans, reached in. Adjusted his packer so it fit more naturally at his pelvis.

He met his reflection's gaze. Immediate thoughts that crossed his mind:

Does she know?

How far can I take this?

How far should I take this?

What if she finds out?

What if the Capo finds out?

Holy fuck. What if the Capo finds out?

His pocket vibrated. He reached in to see Vince's name blaring across the screen.

"Hey, shithead." Vince's voice was clipped. "You feed that cat yet?"

"I'm here." Alex lowered his voice. "His daughter's here."

"Who?"

"Capo's daughter."

"His daughter is in rehab."

"Yeah. Not anymore."

"You dumb shit—of course she is. That's where the Capo is. He's visiting her in Italy."

"She...uh." A pile of clothes in the corner. A shudder-stop in his chest. Alex felt the blood rush to the front of his face.

"Alex," Vince's voice was a thin, annoyed whine. "Are you fucking high? You better not be fucking some girl in his house, I swear to Christ—"

Alex disconnected the call and pocketed his phone.

The pile contained: a blazer. Nice pants. He started opening drawers. Found what he needed in the vanity drawer, turned on its face. A framed picture of the Capo, his ex-wife, and their daughter.

Dark hair. Crooked smile. Aquiline nose.

Not this girl. Not this Virginia.

Adrenaline rushed through him. The kind of high he got from taking a slight swerve in a busy street.

He put the picture away. Closed the drawer.

Not-Virginia was where he'd left her: sitting at the kitchen table. Her smile was too wide. "Everything okay?"

He nodded.

"So. Tell me more about your uncle. Why kind of work do you do for him?"

"Normal."

"Normal work? What does that mean?"

Questions that before seemed innocently inquisitive now felt prying. Blood thumped in Alex's temple.

"I need another beer. You want one?" He crossed to the fridge. Hadn't noticed the note on the door before. He opened it up, scanning his options.

His piece was in his backpack. Why the fuck had he left it in his backpack? Dumb. Such a rookie mistake.

"No, thanks," he heard her voice drift in behind him. "Rehab, remember?"

"Right. They don't let you drink there?"

"No. Sort of the whole thing."

He plucked out another Yuengling.

"So what's that flight like?"

"The flight?"

"From Italy."

He let the fridge door snap closed. When he turned around, he was staring into the eye of her pistol.

"Beer down, hands up," she said. She'd lost her smile.

Slowly, Alex set the beer on the counter and lifted his hands behind his head.

"Turn around," she ordered. "Face the cabinets."

So he did. He stared at foggy pane that housed all those uniform glasses. He heard movement—in the bad reflection, it looked like she'd set the pistol down on the table. Then he felt her hands make their descent: first at his chest, his back, and down his waist.

"I don't have any weapons on me," Alex said.

He almost added: *my gun is in my backpack because I'm a dumbass*, but he didn't.

She stalled at his hips when she felt the buckle of the harness there.

"That's not what you think," he muttered.

"I know who you are," she said flatly. "You think we don't do workups of every family that falls in Gene Guiseppi's orbit? We know all about your uncle, Vincent Marsh. And we know all about you, Kathryn—"

He had a perfect angle, and he took it: in one swift movement, he swung his arm down and back and cracked her face with his elbow. She let out a yelp of surprise and went flailing backwards.

The cat yowled and scattered. Virginia grabbed her gun off the table and swung it towards him, but Alex maneuvered close and blocked her arm. A shot rang out by his face, glass exploded behind him, and his ear drum burst in a pitched squeal.

Her body hit his and then they hit the floor. A chair went crashing. The scramble was quick—twenty seconds of nails and knees and tight breath.

And then he had it. Alex got to his feet, her pistol in his hands, and aimed it at her.

She didn't look small or cute now. She looked feral, pushing herself to sit up against the wall. Her shirt was lopsided on her shoulder and he could see it now—not a bra, but a shoulder holster.

"You're a cop?"

Slowly, she lifted her palms. "Yes," she said plainly. "I'm a cop."

"So, what. You just break into Gene's house when he's not around?"

She seemed to chew on her words for a moment before she finally answered. "We bugged his house," she said. "It's been bugged for years. Every now and then, someone has to come swap them out."

"So that's what you're doing?"

"Yes. And they're active. I was about to leave when you walked in. Do you understand what that means? We have agents listening in. Right now. Put the gun down."

"Why should I believe you?"

"Because you're a good person. You don't want to go to jail for the rest of your life for a mobster like Gene Guiseppi." She wet her lips. "Alex. Look at me."

He did. Those green eyes swam.

"You left Minneapolis because you didn't like people telling you who to be, right? What do you think these guys do? They're using you. Trying to change you. Don't let them tell you who you are."

"Who am I?" he asked.

She shook her head. "Not this. You're better than this—"

He pulled the trigger. The bullet didn't go through clean. Her face splattered wetly across the tile and the walls. It hit him, Van Goghing his arms, his clothes.

Okay, he thought. And then exhaled.

Okay.

He set the gun to the side. Took off his socks. Walked barefoot through the house, checking.

There was a bug under the lamp in the living room. Another under the fire place mantel. Under a chair in the kitchen.

The cat watched Alex with yellow, suspicious eyes from underneath the Capo's bed.

When he'd collected them all, he shoved them in his backpack. Then he went to the kitchen and unmagnetized the note from the fridge.

When it's done, call me.

And a phone number.

Alex dialed it, putting the cell to his good ear. As it rang, Alex rummaged around until he found the cat food and peeled back the tin.

"Hello." The Capo's voice on the other end was low, smoky.

A hot sting in his left eye. Alex blinked it away. "It's Alex," he said.

"Who?"

"Vince's nephew."

"Ah." A stretch of silence on the other end. "And is it done?"

"I fed your cat."

"Good." He sighed and Alex felt the sound, like a spider crawling up the back of his neck. "Welcome to the family, son. Here's what you'll do now."

EATING THE CHRYSANTHEMUM
RICH BARNETT

Jaybo had never fainted before but he felt certain he would soon unless he could extract himself from beneath his date Sarah Margaret and her big boobs, perfumed fuzzy sweater and mane of blonde curly hair. The two of them had almost finished off a pint of Sloe Gin and Sarah Margaret was quite loopy. For a girl who claimed never to drink except on special occasions, she'd downed most of the bottle herself.

What had he been thinking in suggesting they climb into the small backseat of his Volkswagen Beetle? In all honesty, he thought it'd be nice to mix up another Sloe Gin and Sprite and gossip some more about the Homecoming game and dance earlier that night. Sarah Margaret, on the other hand, had gotten a very different idea when he parked the car by the old millpond outside of town.

Now he was sweating and gasping for air, as Sarah Margaret pressed up against him in all her fluffy femininity, staring at him and swaying back and forth like a cobra, plump pink lips perfectly pursed. Before she could lunge, someone flung open the front doors of the little black car. Bobby Jack and his date Rita jumped inside.

"C'mon," they yelled in unison, banging their hands on the front seat headrests, clearly inebriated. "Everyone's going to Ray's for free hamburgers."

Hallelujah! Jaybo cheered to himself, saved by the bell, or in this case, by the burger. His heartbeat slowed as Sarah Margaret retreated to her side of the backseat and finished off the last of the

Sloe Gin. Romantic evening foiled, she transitioned quickly from kissy to pouty and demanded to be driven home.

When the foursome arrived at her house on Church Street, Jaybo escorted her—dragged her was how Bobby Jack would later describe it—from the car up onto the big wrap-around front porch. He rang the doorbell and ran, leaving a drunk Sarah Margaret slumped and slack-jawed in a rocking chair. Jaybo knew there'd be hell to pay for this cowardly deed because nobody wanted to get on the bad side of Sarah Margaret's father, the esteemed Reverend Smith of St. Paul's United Methodist Church where Jaybo and his family worshipped every Sunday morning. He'd deal with the Reverend's wrath later. For now, he was free! He jumped in his car and drove off quickly while Bobby Jack and Rita kissed in the backseat.

Sure enough, Ray's was hopping when they arrived. It was as if the entire Homecoming Dance had migrated from the high school gymnasium to the local burger joint. The manager of Ray's gave out free hamburgers when the Maroons won a home football game, which they seldom did these days. Tonight, though, on a crisp October evening, the George Wythe High Mighty Maroons blocked a punt late in the 4th quarter and returned it for a touchdown to defeat the Radford Bobcats for the first time in ten years. The gridiron upset set off much celebrating in Wytheville and a lot of teenage drinking.

The free burgers were a draw; however, the real lure of Ray's was its location as eastern terminus of the cruising circuit. Every Friday and Saturday night a steady progression of pickup trucks and cars filled with kids from the high school and the local community college drove up and down Main Street between Ray's and the Pizza Hut on the western side of town. Ridin' around was how romances were born and died, how friendships grew, and rivalries played out. Besides high school sports or a movie at the Milwald Theatre, ridin' around was the only entertainment in town.

Bobby Jack grabbed free burgers to go and Rita procured some more beer from her older sister who was hanging out in the parking lot. Provisions in hand, the trio joined the slow-moving caravan on Main Street, which was still going strong at 11:00 p.m. Horns were honking. Kids were yelling and jumping between cars at stoplights. It was wild. From his vantage point behind the steering wheel, Jaybo sipped a beer and watched his friends nuzzle and eat hamburgers in the back seat. Oh how he envied the easiness of their perfect romance, the handsome football player and the cute majorette, the king and queen of Homecoming 1978. His right hand instinctively gripped the VW's stick shift when Rita's hand slipped between Bobby Jack's meaty thighs.

Once Rita was certain the hamburger had disguised the smell of beer on her breath, Jaybo and Bobby Jack dropped her off at home a few minutes after her curfew. She popped a handful of Tic Tac mints, gave Bobby Jack a kiss and left the boys to the rest of their evening.

"Let's drive up to The Ridge," Bobby Jack suggested, squeezing his big frame into the front seat of the VW. "No curfew for me on game nights!" Jaybo looked at his friend who was grinning and holding a six-pack of beer.

Jaybo nodded and started driving, past the Pizza Hut and the Kroger shopping center and then up Pine Ridge Road where eight identical houses perched like hawks atop Pine Ridge on the west side of Wytheville. There was a wide turnaround at the end of the road, a place where the kids gathered and the police seldom bothered to patrol. The Ridge was popular with couples wanting to park and make out while overlooking the town. Jaybo usually avoided the spot for that very reason.

Because of the dance, the turnaround was busy. He recognized a few cars, most notably Dale Staley's cherry red Chevy Duster. The car's windows were fogged up. No doubt he was in there with his steady girl Dreama Dawn. Dale was one of several boys in the senior class whose tight threadbare jeans always had a perpetual Skoal tin ring imprint on the back pocket. Jaybo hated how he found this trapping of redneck style so erotic.

"Perfecto," Bobby Jack exclaimed when Jaybo parked the Beetle away from the other cars. "Lookie what I've got." He pulled out a fat joint from the shirt pocket beneath his sweater.

"Where'd you get that?"

"Rita's sister. It relaxes me after games. We suck this season and I'm gettin' real banged up." Blonde Bobby Jack with his sexy smile played center for the Maroons and was a team co-captain this year. Though he was one of the better athletes on the team, he had neither illusions nor desire to play college ball next year. His plan was to enroll at Virginia Tech and study engineering.

"So, uh, what was going on with you and Sarah Margaret tonight?"

"She was hammered."

"She was pissed." Bobby Jack looked at his friend. "What'd you do?"

"I dunno. She's been so moody all fall…I guess I don't wanna be around her."

Jaybo felt bad lying to his friend and slandering Sarah Margaret in the process when he knew darn well the problem was what he didn't do. One could play the role of proper Southern gentleman but for so long. A girl, even a straight-laced girl like Sarah Margaret, wanted to be kissed and to fend off her boyfriend's roaming hands from time to time. Jaybo recognized her confusion and growing frustration with his lack of passion because it had happened before with other girls he had dated.

"Why do you still go out with her? There are lots of fun girls you can pick from."

Bobby Jack was still staring at him, fishing for information it seemed. The two boys had been friends since Jaybo's family moved to Wytheville when he was in 8th grade and they were paired up as science lab partners for the year. If Jaybo were ever to confess his deepest secret to anyone, he wanted it to be Bobby Jack. "I dunno" is all he said.

"Rita is hinting about getting engaged when we're at Tech next year. I'm not so sure. I love her, I think. It's just… Well, I've never dated anyone but her. Maybe I should meet new people?"

"I know exactly what you mean. That's why I've studied so hard to get into UVA. I won't know a soul there. It'll be a true tabula rasa…if I get accepted."

Bobby Jack nodded his head. "You'll get in and then we'll be arch enemies."

"I suppose so. Wahoowa!"

"Hokie Hokie Hokie Hi!" Bobby Jack punched his friend on the shoulder and opened another can of beer for both of them. "How 'bout we fire up this doobie?" He pressed and started the cigarette lighter on the VW dashboard.

Jaybo cringed. He tried to stay away from pot. The few times he'd smoked he'd been scared of how it made him feel. Alcohol loosened his inhibitions, but not like pot did.

Bobby Jack lit the joint, took a few puffs and then passed it to Jaybo, who faked a drag and a cough while Bobby Jack leaned back in the Beetle's bucket seat and held in the smoke to intensify the buzz. Jaybo handed it back to his friend and popped in a cassette tape.

Bobby Jack finally exhaled in a quiet whistle. "Good tunes. Loves me some Meatloaf." He turned up the volume and the two boys sat in the car, not speaking, just listening to the music. Bobby Jack smoked. Jaybo drank. The lights of Wytheville twinkled down below. Bobby Jack finally broke the silence. "Ever tried a shotgun?"

"A beer, sure, a couple of times," Jaybo answered, starting to sweat.

"No douche bag, I mean with a doobie... I'll show you... Open your mouth."

Bobby Jack took a deep, long drag from the joint and pulled his friend's head in close. Jaybo was powerless to resist. Bobby Jack blew the warm smoke into his friend's mouth. They were eye-to-eye, chest-to-chest. Jaybo inhaled. When Bobby Jack didn't pull back, Jaybo realized his friend was not only stoned, but might even want to kiss him. Holy shit! He'd be lying if he said he hadn't dreamed of this many times, but there was no way he could let it happen. It was too risky. He exhaled softly, yet he didn't try to pull away. What if he was reading the situation all wrong? Their friendship and everything he'd worked so hard for—golf team, yearbook, and teacher recommendations—could literally go up in smoke. And though his parents weren't as conservative as most in Wytheville, he believed they'd have a hard time accepting a gay son.

What he did next was silly, but it was the only thing he could think to do. He grabbed the white chrysanthemum wrist corsage that Sarah Margaret had left behind and he took a bite. "Blimy, she don't taste too bad," he exclaimed in an outrageously fake British accent, "She's sweet and a bit floral, which I wasn't expecting when eating a mum."

The antic caused Bobby Jack to giggle and immediately join the improv bit. "Who's mum you talkin' about eating, you perv?" He grabbed the corsage.

"Your mum."

"Me mum's mum or me's mum?" Bobby Jack swatted Jaybo on the nose with it; then he took a bite. "By jolly, you're right, old sport, me mum is quite tasty." He giggled again and washed it down with beer.

A sense of humor was one of the traits Jaybo relished most about Bobby Jack. That and a fondness for comedy was the glue that held their friendship together. Study hall was their stage, the place they replayed out their favorite skits from *Saturday Night Live* and invented new ones instead of doing their calculus homework. Bobby Jack was the first person Jaybo had confided in about his dream—some of it at least—of reinventing himself at college and then moving to New York to be around irreverent and witty people who read books, drank cocktails and ate dinner at 9 p.m.

Bobby Jack flicked the remains of the joint out the window. "Let's roll, I'm thinking my mum will have some leftover spaghetti in the fridge." The munchies had doused any flames of desire that might have been still burning in the big boy's belly.

Jaybo drove his friend home and watched with relief, affection, and disappointment—but mostly relief—as Bobby Jack went inside without attempting any sort of awkward good night. He sat for a while in his car and pondered whether or not he should call it a night too. The clock on the dashboard now read one o'clock in the morning. Despite the beer and the pot, he was too wired up from the incidents with Sarah Margaret and Bobby Jack to go home yet. He'd practically had to fight them off. And unlike most of his friends, Jaybo didn't have a curfew so long as he kept his grades up and stayed out of trouble. He decided to drive down to The Gates, another popular hangout, to see what was going on.

There were about a half dozen cars when he arrived. He parked the VW, grabbed a beer and started walking over to the metal gates that closed off access to the Wytheville Golf and Country Club at night.

"Yoo hoo, Jaybo, over here!" Flo Pendleton was waving at him. "Be a sweetheart and bring me a beer," she yelled. He went back and grabbed the remaining not-so-cold beer and headed over to where Flo and some other girls were smoking cigarettes. Flo Pendleton was a year ahead of him and in her first semester at Mary Baldwin College. She was back in town for Homecoming and sporting the latest in collegiate fashion—a plaid kilt and a Fair Isle sweater—and an overly breezy new demeanor. Flo's family lived across the street from Jaybo's family. They'd been close when they were younger but had grown apart the last couple of years.

"Aren't you a saint? I'm absolutely parched." Flo gave him a peck on the cheek and grabbed his arm tightly. "Get me the fuck away from these nitwits," she hissed in his ear. "I don't know what I ever saw in them." She steered Jaybo back toward the VW and then turned and gave a big wave to the girls. "Y'all have fun," she yelled. "Prince Charming will take me home."

They got in the car. "What's this sorry looking thing?" Flo held up the white wrist corsage.

"It's a long story. Sarah Margaret left it behind."

"Jaybo Valentine, why are you messing around with that silly Farrah Fawcett wannabe?" Flo laughed and tapped her finger on his chest. "You, my friend, are going to appreciate college girls so much when you get out of this hole-in-the-wall town. As cute as you are, they'll be fighting to get in your pants."

Oh no they won't, Jaybo said to himself. When he got to the University of Virginia he was finally going to be rid of restrictive small town social norms. He could stay up all night reading and drinking and then sleep all morning if he wanted to. No more church on Sunday. And he wouldn't have to pretend to like girls. Of course, he didn't say any of this to Flo.

"College girls are open minded and adventuresome," she continued, lighting a Virginia Slims cigarette. "Of course, you need to get rid of this old tin can. It won't be good for your image."

"I like the Bug. Nobody else has one."

"Darling, that's because nobody else wants one. I see you more in a little two-door tan Beemer or a sporty green MG like all the cool W&L boys drive."

Flo smoked and went on and on ad nauseam about the boys from Washington & Lee, the all-male university not too far from her girl's college. He tuned out until she asked if he wanted a blowjob. Or at least that's what he thought he heard.

"What?"

"You heard me. Don't make me ask again because it's not polite." She put her hand on his thigh.

Dear God, not her too… He had to quickly nip this craziness in the bud.

"Um, don't you think we need more booze? I know where to find the extra key to the golf club bar," he proposed in a singsong voice.

"Darling, that's a fabulous idea! Let's have a late night cocktail, just the two of us. This beer is too warm." She tilted her head back and drank down the last bit.

"Okay then. Put on your seatbelt," he instructed, relieved Flo was up for liquor instead of love. "And hold onto the passenger strap cuz we're gonna jump the ditch." With the gates closed, the only way onto the golf course was over the drainage ditch running alongside the road and separating it from the 9th hole green. Boys jumped it all the time in order to joyride on the golf course. Because the VW was a light car, Jaybo felt certain he could do it even though he'd never attempted such a stunt. Flo egged him on.

He started the engine and gave it a little gas to rev it up, then drove toward the gates. He veered to the left away from the small crowd cheering him on, shifted into neutral and then popped the clutch into first gear as the car approached the edge of the road. The little car bucked. Flo screamed. And Jaybo drove the VW off the road and head first into the ditch.

Once the group by the gates stopped laughing, a couple of boys ran over to help. One had a chain with a hook and he attached it to the back bumper of the VW. With his pick up truck, he easily pulled the car out. Seems Jaybo hadn't been driving fast enough to pull off the jump, even over the shallowest part of the ditch.

They were lucky, however, that neither of them had been hurt. Flo, it turned out, would have a little bump on her forehead, which she wore for a couple of days with great pride. Jaybo would wear his shame for much longer as the story spread like wildfire through the halls of dear old George Wythe High. A headlight was busted. Mud covered the front of the car. But there was no serious damage.

Jaybo and Flo hatched a cover up plan on the drive home. He parked the car close in against a bushy Hemlock hedge along the driveway so his parents wouldn't be able to see the front end. Early in the morning, he'd get up and take it to the car wash and then over to Bubba Houseman's repair shop. His folks would be none the wiser. Flo ground her cigarette out on the driveway, gave him a kiss on the cheek and slowly sauntered across the street to her house.

What a crazy fucking Homecoming! Jaybo tilted his head back and took a big whiff of the night air, wondering half seriously if there might be something in it making everyone horny but him. He picked up the mangled white corsage from the car dashboard and slipped it on his wrist. Had eating it been a smart or a dumb move? Sure it helped keep his secret intact and his plan to get out of Wytheville on track, but what had he forsaken? Remembering Bobby Jack's warm breath and the closeness of his lips, Jaybo took another bite. This time the mum tasted bitter, not sweet so he spit it out. Then he removed the corsage from his wrist and threw it as far as he could over the Hemlock hedge. He kicked off his shoes and went inside quietly so as not to wake up his parents.

LILY, ROSEMARY, AND THE JACK OF HEARTS
(Loosely based on the song by Bob Dylan)
GANIA BARLOW

Intro

J♥—*An unselfish relative. A sincere friend*

The Jack of Hearts, they say, is a man of many talents. He can pick a lock like it's a knotted rope. Charm women like they're snakes. Rides like a centaur, drinks like a whale. The sharpest shooter, the coolest bluffer. The quickest, the quietest, the boldest. His deeds murmur through prairie grasses and gallop down horse-shoed trails. His name keens around campfires like the loveliest heartbreak and drifts as smoke up into the hills.

But the Jack of Hearts is not what she seems to be.

She is a red card dressed in black. She knows the way of the gun. The warm thick taste of smoke on her teeth. Horse sweat and leather, trail dust in her hair and her mustache. The smell of dynamite on her fingers. She watches you from under her hat, through her mask, behind trick mirrors. She'll learn all of your secrets and never give up hers. She has the key to your dearest treasure pressed in wax.

The Jack of Hearts is always in disguise.

Verse I

9♦—*A roving disposition, combined with honorable and successful adventure*

It is perpetually fall. That bleak, dirty quality clings to everything—twines around the steeple, hitches itself to hitching posts, hangs from the scaffold. It is the autumn of this life. The West is no longer exactly wild. The buildings are all still mainly wood and nails, but the railroad is coming and things will change. You can feel it in the air, like dust suspended in a beam of sunlight. See it, rumbling up over the horizon, dark in the east.

But tonight it is warm and clear. The lights are coming on in the cabaret and men are fluttering toward it like moths.

Jack pauses in the doorway of the whiskey-smoked barroom. She cuts a figure, dark against the orange and pink sky.

No one looks.

There is tension in the moment—like water bulging at the lip of a glass. But it goes unnoticed by the rough men within. They've drained so many glasses down that one more tipping cup is of little interest. But Jack feels it. This is, after all, her line of work. She knows what's at stake. Knows exactly what is swirling at the edge of the cup: the stranger at the door of the bar, the women dressing, the rich man fingering his knife, the outlaws lying in wait.

The water breaks itself and spills over. Jack moves into the honey lamplight of the low-slung room.

Verse II

8♥—*Pleasure. Mixing in society*

The Jack of Hearts sidles up to the bar, lays some money down, and projects her voice, husky and sly.

"Set it up for everyone," she says.

This stranger is noticed, sized up. They see her as a young man—cocky, struck it temporarily rich. Wiry and smallish. She is slapped on the back, she is toasted, and she is forgotten. This is just what she wants.

Because she knows to listen for it, she hears the muffled sound of a drill, the thud and creak of movement in the tailor shop next door, which shares its other wall with the bank. She is the only one who hears it.

She asks the bartender, with a wink, what time the show begins, and dissolves into a corner.

Verse III

Q♦—A fair woman, fond of gaiety & a coquette

Backstage the girls are deep in their pre-show poker game. Lily has two queens—diamonds and hearts—and is pretty sure she can expect a third. She watches the backs of the other girls' hands and listens for the quiet signs, for the breath, the heartbeat, the murmur of the cards. Lily rarely loses.

Queen of spades.

She stuffs the bills into her brassiere. It'll all go back to the other girls in loans and presents anyway. She doesn't need to bother about money. The new coat of paint in her room (robin's egg blue, brought all the way from Boston) will attest to that. She's got Big Jim somewhat literally wrapped around her finger. He'd like to think it's some kind of agreement, some kind of contract—that, if not love, there is some similarity of temperament, some style or idea that binds them to each other. But Lily knows rings can just as easily be taken off as put on.

She prefers the cabaret life. The smoke and perfume. The late night poker games. Girls slipping into her room to cry on her shoulder. Kissing away their tears. The lace and paint to cover rough wood, and smooth skin. Silk, cigarettes and brandy. And singing.

Lily deals. The game catches the pace of the footsteps in the street outside. Catches the rising tremor of the barroom. Catches somehow, inexplicably, the lonely, gentle moan of the twilight breeze through the open window.

Lily draws the jack of hearts.

Verse IV

K♠—A man of dark complexion, ambitious & unscrupulous

Big Jim makes his usual entrance into the cabaret with a tip of his hat, brandishing his silver cane as though he's come to lead them all to battle.

He doesn't have to pay for his drink, but he does. He overpays. That's the kind of guy Jim is. And he wants you to know it. He wants you to know that not only does he have connections to that far-off diamond mine you hear so much about, he's got Boston connections too and they're always begging him to come out there, but love of this town and its fine citizens keeps him right where he is. Jim wants to be sure you know that he is truly the only thing that holds this town together. That without him the church-going folk and the whiskey-drinkers would have eaten each other alive by now and all that would be left is the bones for the buzzards. Just so you know what you owe him.

Jim orders another drink. His squint-blue eyes sweep the barroom. Noticing who is noticing him. A nod or a frown where it's due.

And then he sees the stranger.

Verse V

Q♠—*A widow*

Across town, in the largest house, high-ceilinged rooms holding empty air. Rosemary sits at her mirror.

Her black hair shimmers under the brush like a river. Like the sound of a river rushing over her head. She can hear it. If she closes her eyes, she can hear the blue green rushing all around her.

She traps and twists the river. She pins on her brooch.

Rosemary sits alone at the table set for two. As the gravy slowly settles into mud.

Rosemary. Fingers trailing along the hallway, eyes on the grandfather clock (dark cherry, brought all the way from Boston). Struck eight. Fingers scratching along over paper walls, over picture frames, like she can hardly feel her way.

At the hallway mirror. Pale and disembodied. The bruise on her neck from his mouth. Struck nine.

There is something in the wind tonight. Her hair slips out of its pins and crackles live around her head. There is something in the wind. Some whisper, some dark magic. She watches it in her eyes, watches it moving through her eyes like storm clouds riding the gale.

Rosemary pinches the blood into her cheeks and puts on her coat.

She knows there will be a scene. Jim will try to send her home. The cabaret is not for ladies. And the other men will laugh into their cups. Because Rosemary is not a lady. If she's a lady, where's her ring? You'd think, with all of Jim's diamonds, that he could give her a ring. So Rosemary will not be sent home. Not tonight.

She enters the cabaret by the side door, face in shadow. She stumbles into the poker game, and through it. She does not look at any of the girls. She is at least more respectable than that.

But Lily watches her go, watches Rosemary fleeing toward the man-smoke of the barroom. She studies the shape of Rosemary's movement. Breathes the wind of her wake. Roses and night air trailing off of her like a train. Rosemary *is* a lady—her fear gives it away. Rosemary is a queen in exile.

Verse VI
4♥—*Domestic troubles caused by jealousy*

Big Jim sizes up the stranger. He seems to be a young man, and cocky. Wiry, smallish. Nothing particularly special. Except that he looks familiar—Jim is sure he's seen that face somewhere. But a hand slips up Jim's leg and slides around his waist with the thick smell of flowers and warm breath in his ear, drawing his attention away.

"Sorry darling," Rosemary murmurs, "I guess I'm late."

Rosemary and Jim put on a spectacular fight. He calls her crazy and she calls him cruel, and their hands twist and slip over each other, trying to find a place to hold, to pull toward or push away. And in the middle of the growls and whines, Jim's left-hand clamping both of Rosemary's wrists, Rosemary sees the stranger seeing her.

Rosemary steps out of her body for a moment to watch the scene.

The stranger looks at Rosemary like she is a sorry sight, the way her mother looked at her when she came home with her ears full of river water. The stranger looks at Rosemary like she is Somebody and she thinks he must have her mistaken for somebody else. Rosemary is dimly aware of the desire to ask the stranger who he thinks he is that he should be bothered about her.

Jim has Rosemary almost by the throat now, shaking her and yelling. The stranger stands and begins to approach. Rosemary lifts an arm to touch the stranger, to pull him to her maybe, or to push him away. But it is only her ghost arm that rises, and it reaches across the room and pushes through the stranger's body—through the shirt, through the breast. All the way through to the living heart.

And just as suddenly as the fight began, it is over. Jim is defeated by timing. The barroom lamps are being turned down and there's a rustling behind the stage curtain and the crowd has started to stamp its feet in anticipation. Jim pushes Rosemary into a chair.

In the fading light, Jack is the last one standing, a dragging step behind the crowd, eyes still on Rosemary. Jack stands out a moment too long. Rosemary looks over again, her own heart now pounding in her ears. Jim looks up and sees Rosemary seeing the stranger. Sees the stranger seeing them. And then the music starts.

Verse VII

Q♥—*A faithful, prudent & affectionate woman*

In a spotlight, descending: a butterfly. Orange, red and pink, bright as flame. Above the heads of men like a wind-borne goddess. A butterfly—with a sweet, round face like a child, but a smile like the devil. Lips stained the color of blood, faux jewels in her fiery hair, a chest full of dollar notes, and cards tucked into her garter. She is everybody's dream. She is better than real. She opens her mouth and sings.

Lily's charm is her wildness, her evasive mystery. It's in her blood.

She was a girl between places. In the gypsy wagons, set between barrels and boxes like so much cargo, or, when she was a little older, driving while her father slept. In her father's tent, hung with extra fabric so the light could not shine through. Sweet, thick smoke of incense. Lily learned to read the cards and the stars before she learned her letters.

Lily used to dream she was a pioneer instead. In Oregon there would be gold and honey, milk and the sea. She would be a farmer and wear ribbons on Sunday.

Then, Lily at fifteen, up on a hillside with her new best girlfriend for the season—for as long as the wagons are parked nearby. Lily's little fingers quick with the cards. They laugh until they can't breathe, face down in the grass gasping in the sweet bitter smell of it. And then Lily stands up and throws the cards into the air, and the wind catches them and spins them like whirling leaves around the pair.

Lily always was the type that could do what needed to be done, and in that moment, there was one thing that she felt the need of as strong as gravity, as sure as the sun, as sweet as a psalm on Sunday. Lily took the other girl's braids in her hands, right there, out in the June-flushed hills, and she kissed her on the lips.

But as the cards settled around them, Lily read a journey. Lily read separation and disaster. She turned her face out of the wind, away from her friend whose own face was already changing. Below them, through the trees, Lily could see the afternoon sunlight glazing the shifting creek. And something dark moving in the water.

Verse VIII

5♦—*Unexpected news*

The Judge enters in the middle of the song. He is an inauspicious character, but goes unnoticed by the crowd.

They have eyes only for Lily. Her voice and the liquor. The smoke and song. The room wavers, quivers, melts away from itself. The flickering lights and whiskey-spinning music take snapshots, silver tinted.

Jack with her hand against the wall, the only one in the room feeling the beat beneath the beat—the quiet, quiet mumble of the drill. Her eyes now also trained only on Lily.

Rosemary kissing Big Jim's neck with tongue and teeth. Eyes open.

Jim, full and slick, in his cups. Eyes on one woman while his hand moves up another's leg.

Lily in the spotlight, in flame, diamond on her finger.

The flash of light in Rosemary's eye. She turns to the stage. To Lily. Diamond on her finger, diamond on her finger.

Lily suspended above the crowd, the teeming hunger. Above the darkness. Swinging through the light, in song. She tosses her head, carried by her voice and the arc of her movement, and for a moment, in a mirror, she sees Jack's face. Jack's face. And she swings away.

Jim with his hand on Rosemary's thigh. Watching the faces of the men, hungry. For his woman, his Lily. Cut and set for him there, sparkling only for him. Diamond on her finger.

Rosemary turns away from the stage, not breathing. Not caring to breathe. And for a moment, in a mirror, she sees a face. That face, which she is sure she's seen before. The stranger does not look at her, does not open his mouth, but he calls her name. That voice. She breathes again, gasping, like she has finally come up for air.

Kaleidoscope dark: flashes of gold, smudges of black, the occasional shine of a glass, held against the light. Lily and Rosemary search the mirrors, search the shadows, for what is lost and found, what is just out of reach. Kaleidoscope sound: the tinkling melody, the quick notes of the song, the moans and shouts in the drunken crowd. The music crescendos like the toppling of a tree and then the curtain falls.

When the curtain comes up again other girls are on stage. The scene has changed and some of the characters are missing.

Verse IX

8♣—*Danger from covetousness*

Big Jim has Rosemary on his lap now, like a chorus girl. His sloshing head sinks between her breasts. The cabaret bends around her and reshapes itself into a new world. A new world whose sun is a single stone, sparkling onstage in spotlight. On someone else's finger.

Jim puts his hand on her breast and there is laughter. All around her, the bar is full of laughter. Everyone knows. Rosemary is a whore and the cabaret girl has Jim's ring. She pulls Jim's head back by his hair.

"I need a drink."

"Money in my coat," he mumbles.

The coat pocket also contains a handkerchief she mono-grammed for him, scented with her perfume. A receipt of deposit from the bank. And Jim's pocket knife—mother of pearl, studded with diamonds and as long as her hand.

The bartender hesitates and glances toward Jim, where he's slumped half out of his chair, before pouring the two glasses Rosemary ordered. When he turns his back she opens the blade. Jim keeps it shiny as a mirror. The knife flashes in her eye and she flashes in the eye of the knife—her image distorted, like she is seen through water.

She looks up into the face of the Judge, leering at her. Grinning like a skull.

She reaches for the whiskey. It feels like drowning. The burn in her chest, in her lungs as she chokes on it, and sinking her head in her arms, the steady crash of the music, rushing over her head.

Just as Rosemary, at sixteen, lay down in the water to die. The creek water around her head was finally quiet. The hush of slow movement—ever, ever, forever. The blue green light, and the grey of the stones. Small fish flickering like sunlight through the water. The gypsy charm in her fist—for binding love. She was bound now to a dead boy, to death.

Jeremiah. Whose touch had been shy and sweet as a mouse, but whose love held her like an eagle in its claws—bore her aloft, up from the prairie, up from the dust of life into the cold air of heaven. Waiting only for the right moment to devour her heart and the soft places of her body—to scatter her bones back down among the grasses from which she came. Jeremiah, who made promises that he could no longer keep. Whose whispers still lived in the hollows of her ear.

She was cold and then warm. She opened her mouth and it filled with water. She opened her throat and it burned. But she would not let go. The quiet rush around her. She closed her eyes. She would not let go. Of death, of love, the water, the sunken log.

Two hands took her shoulders and she turned to embrace him in death. But instead she was lifted from the water and saved. An aching burst of yellow white sound. The world—bright and dry and screaming.

"Don't tell mother, Meg. Please, please don't tell mother."

There is something in the wind tonight.

Rosemary lifts her head from the bar and something like fear rushes at her in a flood wave. For a moment she is lost. But then the water calms. It finds its level, filling her up, tense at the lip of the glass.

Verse X

2♦—*A clandestine engagement*

The stairs slink past Lily, out of her way. She opens the door and Jack is already there, sitting in the chair at Lily's dressing table like she belongs there.

There is the slightest pause. And then Lily laughs, full of theatrical sparkle. Her stage voice.

"Well has your luck run out?" she asks. She locks the door behind her. A dramatic turn, her eyes on Jack's mouth. "I guess it was bound to one day."

"Nice ring," Jack says, just as casual.

"I hope you've been careful in here, the paint's still fresh."

"Robin's egg blue?"

"You know what I like."

"Does Jim?"

It is an accusation.

Lily's face doesn't change, but her right hand goes to her throat where her collarbone stands out sharply from tense shoulders.

"Don't be stupid," she says, turning away from Jack. Her voice now is edged, careful. "Drink?"

She pours brandy from a crystal bottle. The little luxuries she has come to expect. She takes a breath and draws herself up like she is preparing for battle.

Jack moves up behind her. Touches her back where the costume leaves it bare. Lily shivers. It was not the move she was expecting.

"I'm glad to see you're still alive," Lily says sharply, putting a glass into Jack's hand. "What's it been, two years?"

"Nearly."

"Why are you here?"

The words come out too fast and then settle slowly into the room.

Jack's voice is soft as the pelt of a wolf. "Why do you want to ask a question like that?"

Lily downs her drink. She does not want to play nice.

"Last time you saw me," she says, her jaw tightening with each word, "you said if you were lucky, you'd never lay eyes on me again."

They stare at each other for a long moment.

"Will you go away with me?" Jack asks. It is not really a question, just another move in the game. It always comes around to this, and the script is always the same: Jack asks, and Lily answers.

"No."

The familiar words stand in the air for another long moment, caught in the static tension between them.

"Why are *you* here?" Jack asks.

Lily laughs sharply. "I like the sunsets," she replies, waving her left hand toward the dark window.

Jack catches Lily's hand and fingers the gold band on her ring-finger. Lily twists her arm, but Jack holds her firm.

"Is this meant for me or for Rosemary?" Jack asks, feeling the edges of the stone on her thumb. Her voice too, is cuttingly edged. "This display?"

"I don't mean to hurt her." But she knows she has.

"Then you could help her!" Jack's voice trembles slightly with sudden emotion.

"That's not my job, sweetheart," Lily says, each word an iron nail. "You have to take care of your own problems."

Jack's jaw twitches and trembles. She squeezes Lily's hand hard for a moment like she wants to crush it, ring and all. And then she loosens her grasp and looks away.

"Look," Lily says, softer now, but raw. "It's not like I care about him. But he's never going to marry her."

Jack's voice is fierce and quiet. "Is he going to marry you?"

Lily looks into Jack's eyes, red with dust. They are so tired. Lily gives in. "Don't be stupid," she whispers.

Jack releases her hand, but Lily does not retreat. Instead she reaches up and rips the false mustache off. Jack's face swims to the surface. Lily cups Jack's smooth cheek in her hand, runs a thumb along the pink new skin of her upper lip.

"Sometimes," Lily says, her hand moving down the short ends of Jack's hair to her neck, "sometimes I still want to reach for your braids."

Jack pulls Lily against her and they kiss like starving men.

They unwrap each other slowly. Lily's butterfly wings and spangles. On Jack's chest, a long white cloth like a bandage. Jack is pale and crushed next to Lily's butter skin. It has been two years. Lily takes Jack's breasts in her hands and warms them, bringing the blood back. And Jack is a woman, pants around her ankles, shivering in the night air.

Lily laughs and it catches on tears in her throat. "You look like a saint."

Lily's little fingers along Jack's scars—the old ones, a new one. Along the landscape of her back, strong and pale, bunches of freckles like wildflowers. Lily presses herself against Jack's back, arms around her, against Jack's breasts. How they fit together.

Lily is calm now and strong, and she holds Jack against her. They find each other's mouths. And Jack sobs. Jack sobs as they touch each other. As they move in darkness. Across and through each other's bodies. Thin shifting candlelight. Low sound of sob, of moan. Fingerprints in blue paint. And their bodies, known to each other like an old song. They move and fall together, worn, in a tangle, in shifting light. Jack cries and sleeps. And Lily holds her.

There is the dream—almost, just the dream—of a kiss. And Lily pretends to sleep as Jack rises to leave her.

Bridge

A♥—*The house of the person consulting the decrees of fate*

In a picture frame. In sepia.

Two girl-children in rough gingham. Rosemary and Margaret. Two sisters holding hands in the brown wind smell of the fields.

The rustle and creak of the wooded hills. The taste of sap, bitter sharp between your fingers. The itching of thistles in your sleeves.

Two sisters. One lovely and tall like their mother, pale-browed, lips stained dark and sweet with blackberry—an icicle catching the sunlight, trembling in the push of wind. The other skinny, smudged with dirt, pollen in her wheat-gold hair—the branch of a tree.

For a time they were all there was of the world. Two girl-children arm in arm in the sundust and sweat. Under the blankets, whispering crystal breaths into the winter night. Walking in a line, toes in the creek, arms full of wildflowers or apples or air.

Two sisters. Born pulling in opposite directions. East to ballrooms, to love poems and silver on the table. West to the open plains, to songs unwritten, to ore still in the ground.

And then came the summer that the gypsies settled nearby and Jeremiah Mason drowned in the creek. One sister's eyes swelled shut with tears. And one sister's eyes opened, stinging in the great, wide wind of the world, straining west toward the horizon.

West.

West.

Or the *idea* of west.

When it came time to go, the girl who would be Jack actually went north first, because it was the opposite of the direction she wanted to go. The gypsies went south. But they'd stolen her all the same. It was the fortune-teller with his deck of cards. With his art of illusion and his gift for dealing out fates. It was the fortune-teller's daughter, bright and strong like amber. Her little fingers, quick with the glue. This is how you'll make a mustache with horsehair—when you're a little older. This is how you'll bind your breasts—when you have them.

A kiss, a breath. And then she was gone. Never a backward glance.

And Rosemary was alone in the brown autumn fields. Widowed and empty. That great, wide wind rushing over the prairie like an endless flood. Like the river that had not taken her life for her. Her dark hair blown loose around her face like a mourning veil.

Verse XI

9♣—*Danger caused by drunkenness*

The stage is empty for too long. And Jim's lap is cold. He sits up and looks around.

"Where's Lily?"

The Cabaret Manager wrings his hands and paces at the foot of the stairs. He peers up into the darkness to Lily's closed door. There's something funny going on. He can feel something in the air. There's a smell of fear, there's a pulsing of held breath, there's a crackle of thunder.

His knees wobble as Big Jim stumbles through the door, and he can't help another glance up the stairs. "Where's Lily?" Jim growls.

"Almost ready, I'm sure," the other man says, voice too high.

Jim turns back towards the bar and bumps into Rosemary, hard on his trail. For some reason, this reminds him of the stranger, and he glances across the dim bar to the corner the stranger had been occupying all night. But no one is there.

He pushes past Rosemary and thunders up to the Judge, slumped against the bar. "Wake up, Judge. Something funny's going on." Jim shakes him until the Judge slips off his stool and lands in a heap, snoring dead drunk.

"Jim. Let's go home," Rosemary says. But Jim doesn't answer. He's looking down at the Judge. At the Judge's revolver.

"Jim. Leave her. Forget it. Let's go home."

Rosemary sounds the part now—a terrible queen, exiled for terrible deeds. It is a voice that should have startled Jim. He should have realized it was like nothing he'd ever heard from her before. If he had been listening.

A door opens and shuts upstairs, and the Cabaret Manager rushes forward. At the same moment Jim bursts back in with a purpose, Rosemary still right behind him.

"Be careful, Jim," the other man yelps, not even sure what to be afraid of.

Rosemary grabs Jim's arm. "I want. you. to take. me. home. Now." Each word is a revelation. A stone dropped in a river. The Cabaret Manager at least has the sense to shiver.

The stairs creak and, almost before they can react, someone is rushing by them, dressed in a billowing brown monk's costume, hood pulled low over her face.

"You seen Lily?" Jim hollers at the retreating figure.

The Cabaret Manager is puzzled, counting his girls in his head, trying to recall if they'd put the monk bit back in the show. "Is Lily up there?" He asks, uncertainly.

"Don't know," the strange woman replies, escaping through the barroom door in a cloud of perfume.

Bridge

A♣—*A letter*

The cabaret, empty as a stage, except for one card table in the middle. In spotlight. Lily, Jack, Rosemary and Big Jim are at the compass points, girl, boy, girl, boy. But Jack, you might notice, has the long straw hair of her youth, and is for the moment clean-shaven.

Lily deals out one card each and they all raise their cards to their chests. Jim, the King of Spades, and Rosemary his Queen. They are both yelling now. She wanted Hearts and he had every reason to expect Diamonds. For Jack, of course, there is no question. But Jack smiles strangely at Lily, and so she looks at her own card. The Queen of Hearts.

"I told you," Lily's father says, from the chair where Jack was a moment ago, "You always chose the wrong card."

Jim has a gun in his hand. He points it at Lily's father and pulls the trigger.

Verse XII

A♠—*A duel*

No one, when asked later, could tell you the exact circumstances. It happened pretty quickly. Even the Cabaret Manager doesn't quite remember Jim ascending the stairs. He just knows that he was alone at the stage door when he heard the explosion. And he, along with everyone else, ran outside. It wasn't until at least a half-hour later that anyone found the body.

The story though, goes something like this:

The door to Lily's room bursts open and Jim pulls the trigger of the Judge's gun, and the bank safe two doors down explodes. Lily awakes with a scream. She and Jim both know she's dead. They stare at each other, waiting.

But she is not dead. The revolver isn't loaded.

And just when they realize this, just when Lily's face is tightening into disgust, and Jim's quivering loose into fear, something else happens. A lightning bolt hits Jim. His body jerks and spasms and he frowns at Lily like she is somehow responsible. He opens his mouth as though to speak, as though to give one last soliloquy before the curtain falls. But instead it is he who falls, flat on his face, a diamond studded knife handle sticking out of his back.

Rosemary alone in the doorway behind him, bright with his blood.

Verse XIII

10♣—*Unexpected wealth through the death of a relative. A fat sorrow*

Three men wait on their bellies in the dry creek bed. They are a perfect set—maiden, mother and crone: the sharp-shooting dream-eyed boy, trembling still from the heist; the hardened facilitator, already adding and dividing, rubbing at the inked sketch of the escape route on his arm; the quiet, mysterious safe-cracker, eyes on the silver moon.

Crone is first to hear the whistle in the trees, and he purses his lips to answer it. Maiden jumps to his feet and is pulled roughly down again by Mother who swears under his breath. Whistle. Response. They lie still, listening through the night. Whistle again, closer. And then a rustle and crunch and a figure moves out of the darkness. The Jack of Hearts. Divested of her fraternal robes and re-mustachioed.

"Well," Mother says with a sniff, "If the boy here's noise don't put them on our trail, they can't help but miss that stink on you, Jack."

Maiden hoots with laughter, slaps Jack on the back. "What have you been up to anyway? You smell like about seven gallons of French toilet water."

"All in the line of duty, boys," Jack says. She pulls a hand out of her pocket and it flashes full of diamonds in the moonlight.

Between the bank's safe and the safe in Rosemary's house (which wasn't discovered burgled until several days later), it's said the Jack of Hearts Gang got upwards of $50,000 that night. Of course, a lot of things are said about it. They say that both safes were as clean and tidy as if they had just been asked politely to open. They say Rosemary was a part of the planning all along, that she'd been seduced by the outlaw like so many others and then left to take the fall. They say that Jack did it all single-handedly and caught the show at the cabaret while the fuse was burning down. They say, eyes darting, face reddening, leaning in and hushed, they say, there's something not quite normal about the whole thing. They say the Jack of Hearts is…not quite normal, not entirely… human.

Verse XIV

10♠—*Death on the scaffold*

The next day the sky is black and heavy. There was rain before dawn, but it has stopped now. The scent of wet earth rises thick, stronger than the smell of smoke, of perfume, of blood, of the trail.

The characters are gathered in the little one story stone building that serves as Law in the town. All but one. Even Jim is there, covered up, waiting burial. The funeral is scheduled for directly after the hanging. The Judge is hung-over and eager to execute justice, and Rosemary makes an excellent candidate. She is unrepentant, unmoved. They've already begun calling her Stinging Rose and by the time the tale gets back around to Jack it will be almost unrecognizable and, at first, she will just smile.

Lily stands at the bars for a moment before Rosemary notices her.

"Did you find it?" Rosemary asks.

Lily hands her a package.

"The safe was broken into, but all the jewelry you wanted was still on the dressing table."

"That's Jim's safe," Rosemary says. "Nothing in there was mine."

Their eyes meet briefly, shyly, tinted with an almost amused understanding. Nothing needs to be said, not about Jim at any rate. Yet there remains a certain tension humming between them. The little room is thick with words unspoken.

Rosemary shakes out the dress that Lily brought, heavy with lace, and lays it across the small cot in the corner. She pours the jewelry into her palm. "These were my mother's."

Lily shivers and wraps her arms around her stomach.

Rosemary moves slowly, taking off her diamond earrings and replacing them with the small pearl drops that her mother wore on her wedding day. She stands still a moment, arms hanging limp at her sides, her eyes seeing through the floor to another place.

(To the unlit stove and cold candlelight on her mother's drawn face. To the dark of her childhood bed. Waking to find the other half empty. Waking out of a dream, drowning, gasping for air and reaching out to find her sister gone. Night after night, still gone.

And calling out—with all that was left of her heart—for her sister, or for her sister's ghost, wherever it ran, stretching like a jackrabbit through the wide world.)

And then—so quietly that Lily sees the word on Rosemary's lips more that she hears it—Rosemary says the name, like a sigh, "Meg."

Lily catches her breath as though she has heard a terrible secret. She exhales slowly to keep from shaking. "Maybe…" she says, clutching her cold fingers in her cold hands, "Maybe I can… talk to somebody…try to go and get…help."

Rosemary frowns and shakes her head. For a moment she is so like Jack that Lily's heart leaps.

"I'm not afraid to die."

It is just as well. You can't find the Jack of Hearts by looking for her. Lily knows this better than anyone.

Rosemary looks up at Lily and her face softens into a smile at the sight of Lily's tragic expression. "You think I don't remember you, Lily, but I do. I remember everything. Help me with the buttons."

She backs up to the bars so Lily can reach her, so Lily does not have to respond, so Lily can hide the thick tears that are welling in the corners of her eyes. Lily's little fingers tremble against the other woman's straight back.

The dress is still smeared with Jim's blood, in a dark crust across Rosemary's chest and belly. As it slips off her shoulders, she presses her palm against the stain, against her heart. But it is not Jim she is thinking of.

At ten minutes to noon the Judge comes in. Although righteous and fiery to the crowd outside, he is suddenly strangely embarrassed before the two women. "No rain, but there's thunder in the east," he says. As though this was the purpose of his visit.

"I only wish it would rain," Rosemary murmurs, beginning, for the first time, to look distressed. She looks up at Lily. "I always loved sound of it."

"It's time to go," the Judge says, taking out his keys.

Rosemary reaches through the bars and grabs Lily's hand.

"Just one thing," Rosemary whispers as the Judge rattles the lock open. "When you see her—tell her for me. Please?"

The Judge pulls Rosemary's hand back and ties her wrists together. Somewhere outside a drum begins to beat.

Rosemary.

Rosemary.

In her unworn wedding dress, standing on the gallows.

Across the empty prairie around her the long grasses float west on the wind like her hair. The long grasses, twisted into a rope, at her throat like a jewel.

(Rosemary. Submerged. Breathing in gasps the heavy water. In the wind of the current, flying east. Feet among the river stones. Water through her fingers and in her mouth. Rushing in her ears like a storm, the drumming of the water.)

She didn't even blink.

Verse XV

3♠—*A journey by land. Tears*

In the hush of the empty cabaret, Lily bathes, carefully washing all of the red dye out of her hair, scrubbing herself as clean as she can. She puts on a plain grey dress, ties her tired brown hair out of her face, and looks for all the world like an ordinary woman.

From the back of her closet comes the large brown carpet bag that has been her sole traveling companion more times than she can count. She fills it, picking at random through her wardrobe, through her small pile of possessions.

When she opens her own jewelry box she discovers, with a weary smile, that Jim's diamond ring is gone. Her stash of money, however, is in its proper place, rolled up in a glove at the bottom of a drawer, alongside her other, less valuable treasures: A hat pin that had belonged to her mother. Her favorite deck of cards. The little charms her father had made for her the last time she'd seen him, for safe travels, money, and good health. A faded, old hair ribbon with the end of a cut braid still tied up in it. And her newest treasure, taken from Rosemary's house, a small, blurred photograph of two young sisters hand in hand.

Lily takes the cards out of their box. She shuffles as her father taught her, seven times. And then she cuts.

The Jack of Hearts.

With a sob-scream that folds her body in half, she throws the cards across the room, and they flutter to the ground like snowfall.

When her eyes are dry, she carefully collects the deck again and puts it in her bag.

The town itself seems hushed, but only because everyone is up at the church, attending Jim's funeral. A sign on the cabaret door reads "Closed for Repair," although with its chief patron being lowered into the ground, its shining star slipping out the side door in her traveling clothes, and the minister pointing out the evils of sin over two new corpses, the cabaret, it turns out, will never reopen.

Coda

2♠—*A removal*

It was Lily who saw Rosemary go into the water that day long ago, from up on the hill where she and Jack sat planning their escapes. But it was Jack who flung herself down the steep slope, rolling and falling and tearing her skin. It was only Jack who could have pulled her sister out of the water and back into life. No other hands would have had the power.

And Lily had waited this day, at the back of the crowd, for her to do it again. She closed her eyes as they put the noose over Rosemary's head, and through the darkness she listened for galloping hooves, for the gunshots and the yells of the crowd and the thwack of the rope being cut. She waited for the feeling of those hands around her waist, pulling her up onto the back of a horse, and carrying her and Rosemary both away to safety.

She opens her eyes in the train station.

Rumor has it that the gypsies are traveling in the north and that the Jack of Hearts gang has been spotted to the south. But the trains run east and west.

Lily waits to see which one will come first.

Winner

BIG HOUSE
MATTHEW CHERRY

Kasper and I dug the grave with the butts of our guns and buried the fox at dawn.

We had been in Iraq for less than a month, and Casota had been away on assignment so much that I had seen almost none of him since arriving in-country. I'd been foolish enough to miss him. The fox taught me better.

Tough, tall plants ran in a wide strip down the center of the wadi. I learned later that they were a kind of wild corn. We filtered through them four abreast, rifles relaxed, cursing at the absurdity of mosquitos in the desert.

Patrol was even less eventful by night than by day. By day, you sometimes ran across a good-sized viper or a local taking a shit in the weeds. It broke up the monotony.

Casota was the first one to see the fox. He laughed and the animal startled. It ran right over my boots in its terror. Casota came after it like a kid at recess. He slid on stones, barreled through the corn. He clapped me on the shoulder as he went by and told me to come on, or I'd miss all the fun.

We made a game of herding the fox before us. I'm sure it could have escaped—we were spread wide, thrashing the corn grass into a frenzy—but it went forward in panic. The sides of the wadi must have been too steep for it. It was a small, sleek thing, nothing but a streak of tufted white fur moving like liquid through the grass. I knew we were terrorizing it, but we were bored.

That's my excuse. We were bored.

In the disorder of the chase, I got separated from the others. I had just come out of the corn when I heard the shot. I ran down the bed and found Kasper and St. George standing back from Casota.

The fox had tried the bank, after all. The loose stone had slowed it down, making it an easy target.

Casota lowered the rifle, and we all watched the little body tumble back to the wadi floor. I didn't see that it was still alive until Casota drew his knife. "Hey, little guy," he said. He walked forward. The blade of the knife was a dull length of shadow in his fist. "Hey, there, fella."

The fox raised itself up on its front legs and tried to scramble back up the bank, but Casota had hit it somewhere in the back, and it could only drag itself along. I saw no blood.

"Hey, buddy." Casota slung his rifle behind him and out of the way. "Hey, buddy buddy."

"Casota." This was Kasper, whose neck and cheeks still hadn't quite lost their dewlapped look from boot camp.

Casota turned. Kasper said nothing, but his rebuke was plain.

"Aw, c'mon," Casota said. "They don't have foxes where I come from." He was the estranged son of an illiterate dock worker from New Jersey. He told us once that he had joined the Corps because if he was going to get beaten, he at least wanted to get paid for it. "I want a pair of fox socks." He started, maybe liking the sound of the phrase, and giggled. "Fox socks!" He turned back to the animal, which had ceased its struggles and lay still, watching us with inkdrop eyes. The fur on its muzzle was a shade darker than the rest of its coat. It looked fine as silk.

"I will not wear you in a box," Casota said. He went forward. "I will not wear you over rocks."

I raised my rifle and shot the fox in the chest.

Casota whirled. His knife was raised.

"Come on," Kasper said. He didn't outrank any of us, but his basset-hound features gave him a grave air that had a way of getting through to people. "Let's finish our route."

For a second or two, Casota just looked at me. Then he laughed. He sounded the same as before. He sheathed the knife and walked away.

I followed. A few hours later, Kasper and I came back and buried the fox among the roots of the desert corn.

I would say I hated Daniel Casota from the day I met him if I could remember exactly which day that was. I've never been very good with dates, which hampers my ability to return library books or to develop and catalogue life-long enmities.

Casota was a believer. By the time I realized what the Corps was and that I wanted no part of it, it was too late; in the way of shared dirt, we had become close. I would go to bed at night with sand in my ass and machine-gun nomenclature rattling in my ears and swear that in the morning I would not smile at his charisma as all the others did. Then the morning would come, and I would smile.

I enlisted and went to boot camp after my sophomore year. A lack of funds kept me from finishing college, which in turn meant I couldn't go out for officer. Yet I knew myself to be better than the men I was signing up with. I had always been smarter and more competent than my peers, in quality if not in execution.

We flew into San Diego International from across the country and stood in line outside the USO terminal all afternoon and long into the night. Late spring in southern California means heat around the clock and a mugginess that makes the world slick to the touch. The arc sodiums along the highway put a pink glow on the palms and on the roofs of government housing. The overpass beyond the airport gates sloped up and away in a promise of dewy, light-glossed asphalt. It looked sleek and flawless as a woman's raised thigh.

Even then, I was already becoming obsessed with roads and airplanes and horizon lines. Already I wanted two degrees in hardwood frames on the wall behind a desk. Already I wanted a way out.

Around midnight, a red school bus pulled up to the curb. It was covered in Marine propaganda, an infantilizing thing, and I think we all felt slightly ridiculous piling into it. We spent about 40 minutes driving around and at last came to the recruit depot, which I later learned shares a fence with the airport. I don't know if the ride was obfuscation or incompetence, but it says pretty much everything I have to say about the Corps.

In the military, you spend a surprising amount of time on buses. I remember that first trip clearly. The driver was silent. The moon followed us like a prop in the sky. I did not feel fear, not then; I think I was still dumb enough and enough in love with my own sense of destiny to feel nothing worse than a kind of blank, nervous enthusiasm.

We arrived at the recruit depot. Yelling and running ensued.

Part of the Corps' effort to dismantle your personal identity is a reinvention of language. I am sure Saussure or Baudrillard would have something to say about this, but I always think of Orwell when I remember the military doublespeak that replaced our civilian tongue. The strangest change of all was the reduction from first to third person. For thirteen weeks, I was not I or me; I was "this recruit."

Processing took all night. We did not sleep, although they did give us peaches with breakfast.

After the first week, we were sifted into our training platoons. That was when I met Franz and Kasper, Kasper whose entire body had the deflated look of a man who has cut ninety pounds in six weeks in order to make weight. I thought the instructors would give him hell for that—they pounced on almost any idiosyncrasy—but they didn't. They treated Kasper with a kind of offhand reverence, like a disciple who has gone out into the desert for forty days and come back changed.

I must have first seen Casota around that time, but I don't remember it. I remember Gohn, who was selfish and stupid, and whose simulacrum of innocence when called to account for his antics sometimes made me wonder what it would feel like to strangle a man with my fingers. I remember Davenport, whose Kansas cock I one day saw flopped out over the lip of his underdrawers when the whole platoon, partway through our morning dressing routine, froze at the command of our drill instructor.

But Casota, like so much of what becomes meaningful in our lives, came into mine almost without my noticing.

This is what I remember:

In Marine Corps boot camp, you have to be loud and fast. It almost doesn't matter what you do, so long as you are those two things. (Once, when DI Patino—in some kind of weird reverse imperialist joke, all five of our DIs were as Mexican as refried beans—was briefing us for our martial arts test, he told us that when the examiner called, "front leg kick," we could throw a rear-hand punch into the sky, so long as we shouted at the top of our lungs as we did it. I did not test this advice.) My first memory of Casota is of him looking at me as our platoon stood in formation outside the mess hall one morning. Second or third week, this must have been. DI Rocha had just called me out for not responding loudly enough to one of his instructions.

Several recruits turned to me. Casota was the one who struck me across the arm and chest with the back of his hand and said, "Speak the fuck up, Robinson!"

My name isn't Robinson. But I've wanted to be a Robinson ever since I read *Robinson Crusoe* in sixth-grade Advanced English. I can't make my stories from the Corps about living on a tropical island or enslaving herds of cats and goats, but I can make them about a guy named Robinson. So:

"I was," I said to Casota. It's possible I said it with the unconscious indignation of an educated man confronted by proletariat scum. It's possible some other aspect of my personality made Casota rear back and punch me in the jaw, but I think it was probably that one.

Someone with better reflexes than mine saw Casota broadcast the punch, which is why I didn't end up in Medical with a broken jaw or missing teeth. Such an injury would almost certainly have led to both of us being expelled from the platoon and held back for a number of weeks. This, in turn, would have led to me never knowing Casota—aside from the one right hook—and thus never having the chance to cry his name as I tackled him to the ground before he could shoot several Iraqi men on bicycles.

No fewer than three recruits grabbed Casota away from me as he went in for a second blow. Someone else caught me as I fell, though this was probably more geographic proximity than philanthropy. The platoon, so recently a neat grid of columns and rows, dissolved into a noisy tangle of men.

Rocha waded in, not so much pushing men aside as gliding through them without apparent effort, the way a wedge of magnetized aluminum might glide through a pile of iron shavings with the same polarization.

"What the fuck? What the fuck, Robinson?"

The man holding me let go and stepped away as Rocha came in range. I started to slump, and the drill instructor caught me by the collar and raised me to my feet by main force. I would have thought this impossible—even my best civilian attire is, I think, not so hardy as to withstand a full-fledged collar-hauling—but it happened. For one frightening second, I thought Rocha was going to hit me. I had no immediate reason for believing this, save that drill instructors give the impression of impending violence on general principle.

"What happened to you, Robinson?"

For a second, I merely gawped at the man. His brown cheeks were so free of stubble that they gleamed. His teeth looked strong enough bite the tines off a fork. I have a false memory—false, I know, because it is impossible for anyone who is nose-to-nose with a DI to look anywhere but forward or down—of looking sidelong at Casota, who stood glaring at me. The depth of that glare was hate, though concern moved across its surface like light on water. I know I did not look at him, and yet I remember it, all the same. His eyes on mine.

Sometimes, often when I least expect it, I find myself saying his name in a low voice. I say it over and over, in a kind of mantra. It makes a susurrus of sibilant wind against my tongue, with only that one T near the front of my mouth to stand above the tidal level of his name. Years later, after I had left the Corps and was in Guyana on sabbatical from a graduate fellowship, I met a Guatemalan short-order cook named Quezada and was so startled by the same sound coming from another mouth that I made the man write his name down for me, so I could look at the two spellings side by side. I often think of the names of my boot camp mates, or of the other men of my unit, or of the men with whom I went into the desert, but his is the only one I speak aloud. Casota, Quezada. Quezada, Casota.

"Robinson?"

"This recruit cut himself shaving, sir."

If there is a safety razor somewhere the misuse of which will produce a bruise on the left cheekbone identical to that generated by a smart right hook, it is not sold at Marine Corps boot camp. My understanding of Rocha's knowledge of safety razors and of his general faculties remains incomplete to this day, but I guess he knew that I had not, in fact, cut myself shaving.

Another second passed, during which Rocha's face, normally severe as his mowed hair, softened almost imperceptibly. It could have been the sun, striking through the clouds along the horizon and brightening his features. It could have been the passing urge to murder me for impertinence.

"He cut himself shaving, sir. This recruit saw him do it this morning."

It was Casota. He looked about as afraid as a man waiting for a bus.

At first I thought that Casota was saving me. Then I thought that he must be saving himself.

Rocha looked back and forth between us. I don't know why he didn't report us. Maybe he thought that Casota's willingness to lie for a man he clearly didn't like spoke to something deeper, something men like Rocha have been training boys like us to develop for generations. Maybe, in our truculence and anger, Casota and I had discovered some crucial root of what it meant to be soldiers.

I met Casota's anger in that first punch, but I came to know it in all parts of him. I came to know it in the precision of his posture at mess, and in the speed with which he reassembled a rifle while sitting cross-legged in the sun coming through the squad bay doors.

I came to know it in his respect for the Corps, something he felt not blindly like so many but because he understood the essential despotism and cruelty behind it: traits necessary to find the part of a man willing to do harm and to bring that part to the fore.

I recognized these parts of Casota in part because I shared them. We all had anger; why else the Marines, instead of somewhere useful, like the Air Force or the Navy? Why not the civilian sector? Nobody who is good at everything he does enlists in the military— all of us felt the shape of some failure beneath us when we lay down exhausted each night.

I wanted to get away from boot camp—I wanted to leave it almost every day I was there—so let me tell about the last important part. Let me tell about the only time I made Casota laugh.

I've always been funny. For a person who's funny, making someone laugh is even more important if you hate that someone. The ability to manipulate humor at will is one of the last magics left in the world. Comedy is a kind of power, and laughter is a form of obedience.

Every Sunday, we scrubbed the squad bay floor on all fours with big wooden brushes.

Rocha stood in the center of the bay. "Scrub!"

"Faster, sir, faster, sir!"

"Scrub!"

"Harder, sir, harder, sir!"

Fraught with homoerotic subtext, I know. I suppose debasement is part of teaching a man how to be a finely tuned engine of discretionary destruction, but I can't figure out why that should be.

One Sunday toward the end of June, one of the recruits slipped and fell. He slid for ten feet in the suds before crashing nose-first into a footlocker. We laughed. Rocha laughed and snarled at us to shut up all at once. He went to the guy. Overeager, the kid snapped to his feet as Rocha approached, flinging a froth of blood and grey water across the DI's pristine shirtfront. Rocha looked down at himself, then took the kid by the ear and dragged him from the room. To escort him to Medical? To dismember him behind the building? Who could know?

Casota elbowed me in the ribs as we waited for Rocha to return.

"What was it you were saying?"

"I didn't—"

He nudged me again. "Not about that." He raised his brush and waggled it back and forth. Sudsy water flipped off the ends of the bristles and stippled his cheek. "During the scrubbing."

Without looking away from Casota, I reached behind me and found a handful of Franz's shirt.

"Franz," I said, "tell me to scrub."

"Scrub?"

Still looking at Casota, I let go of Franz and twirled a finger in the air: *go on.*

Franz paused for a moment, and then gave a passable impression of Rocha's voice: "Scrub!"

"Heineken, Heineken."

Casota grinned. I twirled my finger at Franz again. "Scrub!"

"Foster's, sir, Foster's, sir."

Casota laughed. He was coldly handsome, but the laugh warmed his face and made him beautiful.

The evening air came through the long hopper windows along the squad bay. I smelled mesquite from the pebbled yard and lemon detergent soaking into my raw knuckles. Laughter was an offense worth a sleepless night, and here was Casota, laughing in the sun. Franz and I laughed with him, and for a time I forgot how much I hated Casota, hated our country, hated the whole damn mess.

What did I see in him? What did I want to get out of all this? I was jealous of Casota. I can admit that. He was good at everything that I professed not to care about. He was one of those men in whom intellect, leadership, and the pursuit of violence have come together so neatly as to make him unstoppable.

After graduation, our boot platoon went in a million directions, but Casota proved amazingly difficult to escape. When we were assigned to the same artillery battery out of Nebraska,

Casota was promoted within a month because of his exceptional boot camp scores. He ran our squad during combat training. In the field, his plans were the only plans, and one either adhered to them or was mowed under. Having been punched into reason earlier that summer, I never tried to challenge Casota, but I watched man after man—if the Corps is good for nothing else, it produces men who are willing to challenge those in charge—go up against him and fail, sometimes in spectacular or bloody fashion. I once saw him fling an entire extra-large meatball pizza into the face of another corporal who had the bad grace to question Casota's tactics after a five-day field exercise.

He reminded me of all the bullies I had known in high school. Somewhere in Casota's charmed rise to leadership, I saw some cousin to the meanness I remembered from back home.

Though we were an artillery unit, nothing would do for Casota but infantry. What was otherwise the recourse of knuckle-draggers became, in his hands, a noble profession. There were winter days when I watched from the safety of my truck as Corporal Casota drilled his fire teams until the ice storms drove half the men indoors with either frostbite or pneumonia. For the frostbite, Casota got a commendation; for the pneumonia, he got another promotion. Two members of our little infantry squad spent Christmas having their lungs pumped, but nobody complained. I don't know how Casota did it. Maybe he gave them peaches for breakfast. Maybe he taught them to say, "Heineken, Heineken," as they lay in their white paper beds.

❖

The third-best Tuesday of my life came just two weeks before we shipped out for the Persian Gulf. We spent most of our last month stateside on paperwork, which meant that Eleanor Roosevelt and I got to spend a lot of time together.

For the sake of context: The second-best Tuesday of my life was the day I got out of boot camp. The first-best was the Tuesday of Legendary Truancy Week, which was also the week I dated Katie Hendriksen, a Dutch exchange student who spent our senior year of high school studying zoology and sublimating her anger at her abusive father into acts of breathtaking promiscuity.

Eleanor Roosevelt was my truck. Our first sergeant encouraged us to name our vehicles, as though we were heroic B-52 crews going into action over Nazi-held France instead of grunts on our way to a corner of Iraq that Anderson Cooper had never heard of. He turned down my first three prospective names for AMK37 number 519519, which were Oprah Winfrey, Emily Dickenson, and Batwoman. He suggested I go with something more patriotic. I suggested that nothing could be more American than Batwoman. He suggested that I might enjoy cleaning toilets for the entirety of our deployment. We compromised.

The third-best Tuesday came late in an unseasonably cold April. The week had been a perfect misery of ice and wind. Casota thought it prime marching weather, and at his order, his little band of infantrymen threw on packs and set out down one of the ranch roads that ran for hundreds of miles across the Nebraskan plain. Eleanor and I followed them, creeping along at three miles per hour while the drenched squad of men trudged down the hard shoulder. During one of their rare halts, Casota came back down the line and banged on my driver's door.

I opened up.

"What the fuck are you doing?"

I sipped my latte. "Have you ever noticed that we use that word a lot?"

"What?"

"No, not that one."

"Robinson."

"I've been thinking," I said, "of doing a linguistic analysis of the most commonly used phrases in the Marine Corps." I put the latte back in its cup holder and held my hands over one of the dashboard heating vents. I wasn't cold, but I enjoyed the gesture.

"Robinson, get the fuck out of here. We're trying to train."

"There's that word again."

He looked at me.

I put up my hands. "Okay, okay. I've been assigned to follow you as your safety escort."

"By whom?"

He said "whom." I confess I was impressed.

"First sergeant said it was important to give you motorized support so you don't get hit by passing motorists."

"Bullshit. You're enjoying this."

"Yeah."

Casota looked up at me for another moment, and then he turned and went back to his shivering men. I followed him, keeping Eleanor at his heels. I cranked down the driver's window and leaned out. "I could play some music!"

Casota was calling his men back into formation. He tried to look dignified, but only managed to look wet.

I reached across the bench seat, opened the passenger window, and then hit a button on the boom box that I had wired into the cigarette lighter on Eleanor's big dashboard. The opening riff to "Hungry Like the Wolf" blared out into the grey morning.

Casota gave me a final, wary look, and then spun on his heel and marched forward.

I followed, singing along.

❖

In Iraq, we got shuffled around frequently, and Casota spent a lot of time away from our base.

I spent the first two months of the deployment in a fugue of depressed anxiety. At the time, I thought this was just normal deployment shit. Beer; women; the Internet; being in a country where no significant portion of the native population wanted to kill me before sunrise. But looking back I think at least half of it came of not having the chance to ruin Casota's day. I hadn't yet come to understand the value of having an enemy conveniently at hand; without one, all the banality and frustration of one's circumstances, all the low rage we cultivate against the world for not recognizing us as the superlative creatures we know deep down we are, has nowhere to go.

Casota wasn't around to excel at our expense. I no longer smelled success waiting to occur when I happened to go into the showers after him. He was a bitter light gone from the long night of that summer, and without him, the clarity with which I had begun to see myself faded like a shape in a sandstorm.

At six weeks out, our unit regrouped in preparation for our exodus homeside.

With no more artillery missions to occupy us, we trained on light weapons. We mounted the big Browning M2s onto the turrets of our Humvees and drove off-base to make use of a crude machine gun range about two miles out in the desert. It was just a string of burnt out vehicles: the remains of bombed or decommissioned trucks. Our Humvees drove parallel to the targets about three hundred yards out while we fired. I stood near the exit line of the range and watched man after man plow the earth with bursts of fire. One man opened up with the .50 just as his driver hit a bump. His barrel dipped, and I saw the red flash of tracers as rounds struck the sand not fifteen feet in front of him. Spumes of dirt flew up in a jagged line.

Casota stood beside me. He saw the gunner rake the sand and laughed. It was a mean laugh, a Casota-laugh, nothing like the sound of unfettered joy I'd heard that summer afternoon in the squad bay at San Diego.

I grinned. Meanness, the Marine Corps taught me, is as quietly contagious as a yawn. I grinned with Casota as though we were in on a secret. We both knew our own good shooting was as much luck as skill. That he knew it and laughed anyway was part of why I hated him; most men of meanness are incapable of better, but Casota should have been good enough to make the sharp edge of his meanness count for something.

I saw a sudden flash on the desert floor to the east, out where the sun beat against the emptiness. I touched Casota's arm. He looked at me, and I pointed. "What is that?"

"What—" he said, and then a second flash came.

"Where the dead tree gives no shelter," I said.

"What?"

I shook my head. "Nothing."

Casota had seen the flash. He stepped forward, tugging at the strap of his rifle. I wanted to dismiss him, but he was in place. Every piece and aspect of his being was arranged to conduct war, despite our coming out here to discover that there was no war, that the only thing left to shoot was a line of blackened chassis in the sand. His eyes, like mine, were hidden behind the polarized lenses of ballistic sunglasses, but I had seen in the California hills the way they leapt over terrain, scanning for threat. The desert had washed some of the fiery green from those eyes, but the eagerness remained.

I looked at the place of the flash. For an instant, I saw nothing, only a confusion of dark color on the face of the land. Then my eye deciphered what it saw, and I swore.

Five or six men were approaching at a hard run. Two more were on bicycles, standing on their pedals to negotiate the uneven ground. They were locals in rags. Over their shoulders, I saw a second group, perhaps a dozen more.

None of them appeared to be armed, although several were carrying big sacks that billowed out behind them. They moved with incredible energy, as though they had only a score of yards to travel and so could throw all their effort into a short sprint. It was October and we were safe from the suicidal belligerence of summer, but still the afternoons could go upwards of a hundred degrees. I never met an Iraqi who didn't respect the heat, yet here these men were.

Other men with us were seeing them now. All of us were hot and bored and wanted to do what we had been trained to do.

Our first sergeant came up beside us. Indecision was plain on his face, and I saw the brink of old age beneath his sunburn. Then he saw me looking at him, saw others looking at him. Saw Casota looking at him.

"Get on line," he said. He turned to the men coming from the trucks. "Get on line!"

They glanced at the oncoming natives and obeyed. There were about thirty of us. We drew abreast and faced east.

The natives came on. I saw more, now; they made almost a horde of disheveled men, all of them with bags or rucksacks or buckets.

"This is it," someone said. I turned to my left but could not tell who had spoken. I could see one man and the leading edge of the man beyond, overlapped by his nearer neighbor. Each man was like that, a chain of cutouts stretching toward the horizon.

"Advance!" The first sergeant went forward. The rest of the men followed, holding the line. I saw Kasper to my right. His face had lost most of its baggy lines since boot camp. It was darker than it had been.

I hesitated, but not for long.

"Weapons on safe." This was Casota's voice. I looked over and saw him beside me, as close as he had been since boot camp. That was untrue, of course; he had come and gone, much more out of my days than in them. Yet on that afternoon, it seemed no time at all had passed between the shine of the squad-bay floor and these guns in the desert.

My finger slid across the safety. I could feel the tension in it. I wanted to push it over from Safe to Semi. I wanted the satisfying click that choice would make.

Down the end of the line, I heard the drumming of diesel engines. I craned my neck and saw a pair of Humvees with men at their guns push into our midst. The long barrels of the .50 calibers shone in the white glare of the day.

I don't think I said, "Jesus." I don't think I wondered what we were doing. I think a part of me that had been filling itself on dreams ever since I had seen the moon slip along the windows of that absurdly-painted school bus was now wide awake.

"Brass. Brass."

The call came down the line. For a moment, the word sat in my mind, heavy as a shell, its sound and various meanings so unrelated to reality that I could not make sense of it. Then I understood: the natives were here for the brass. Brass casings were valuable, especially in bulk. We had expended thousands, perhaps tens of thousands, of shell casings that afternoon, and we wouldn't bother cleaning up after ourselves in the open desert.

I glanced over my shoulder at the range behind me, and even at a distance of a hundred yards I could see the glitter of brass casings in the sand. The sun came off them in a violence of light that hurt my eyes.

I turned back around. The enemy was close now. I could see the imperfect line of one Iraqi's beard where his razor had bit too deeply along his jaw. His canvas sack flapped like a white flag in a hostile wind. Some of the shells behind us were little 5.56 from our M16s, but most of them—the overwhelming majority—were .50 cal brass, casings ejected from the M2 Brownings mounted atop the Humvees. You could pour a shot of whiskey into one of those things.

"The brass," I said. "They're just here for the brass." I took my hand off my rifle and let the weapon hang against my chest so I could wave down the line. I saw a few faces turn towards me, their expressions anxious and wanting relief. I felt relief myself. I also felt disappointment. For some reason, I thought about the white fox in the wadi.

One of the men down the line—Banks, I think it was, a skinny kid from Kentucky who sounded like Foghorn Leghorn—smiled at me. I smiled back, and that was when Casota raised his rifle and fired.

I flinched away from the sound. I happened to turn my head toward the oncoming men as I did so, and I saw the one opposite me fly back in a full-body sprawl. I could not see if he had been hit or was just diving for cover.

Casota's rifle was a black finger pointing out at the desert. How many men would follow his example, now that the levee had broken? I thought of the way 60 recruits moved in formation during close-order drill: a single stroke of falling heels as we marched across the parade ground at dusk.

"Casota!"

I can't put into type how his name sounded coming from my mouth. I want to fill the word with As and Os, even though my scream couldn't have been very long and even though the sound of his name doesn't have any Os in it; it's Americanized, and the middle syllable is the same "ah" you might make when the dentist tells you to open up or when a lover bites the lobe of your ear.

I threw myself at him. He saw me coming. For a fraction of a second, the barrel of his gun tracked my way, and then he relaxed and went down beneath me.

Casota was screaming something. It might have been, "Get the fuck off me!" I held him there, pinned to the burning land, until someone pulled me away. It was the first sergeant. Behind him, I caught a glimpse of the eastern hardpan across which the natives had come in their frenzy to beat one another to our brass. The sand in that direction had cleared as though by magic; I saw the distant shapes of men, already half a mile away, retreating at full speed. The one who had fallen at Casota's shot was among them.

Casota could have missed. Perhaps even on purpose. I didn't think a man shot seriously enough to do mortal damage could move like that, even with adrenaline fueling his legs.

I didn't know if I had saved the man. I didn't know if I had saved anybody.

❖

By week eleven or twelve, we were all coasting toward graduation. I was on my way back to bed from the head one night when Rocha came into the squad bay drunk as a lord. He was swinging his Smoky Bear hat in one hand and singing "Escape," the Rupert Holmes song about piña coladas and making love at midnight. It was such an unbelievable vision that I froze.

Rocha nearly ran me down before he saw me. When he did, his eyes narrowed.

"Where is your pillow?"

"This recruit was going to the head, sir. This recruit doesn't have his pillow."

"No," Rocha said. He swayed slightly, as though caught in a mild breeze, but his voice was clear. "I said, where the fuck is your pillow?"

"This recruit—"

"No!" Rocha's index finger came out of the shadows and found my solar plexus with the accuracy of a guided weapon. "Where...the fuck...is your pillow?" Jab, jab, jab. I fell back a step and came up against my footlocker. If he prodded me again, I'd go tumbling over it and likely whang my head on the metal bed frame.

Recruits do a lot of weird shit in Marine Corps boot camp, but so far as I know, carrying around one's pillow when making a midnight head call isn't on the list. Nonetheless, I looked around to see if either one of the pillows on the bunks behind me was in grabbing range. Neither was.

"You fucking answer me when I'm recording at you." He said 'recording.' He moved in. His bulk was monstrous in the dark bay. I smelled breath mints, last call, the unique odor of Mexican sweat absorbed by a khaki service uniform.

Something soft struck me in the chest. At first, I was so certain Rocha had lunged at me that I nearly went backwards over the footlocker in shock, and then my hands, trained to the sharp rim of reflex by three months of fear, shot up and clutched the white case of a government-issue pillow.

Rocha spun. Casota stood not two feet away. He was naked. His shoulders, half of one hip, and a wedge of thigh were visible in a bent bar of moonlight that found its way in through the windows at his back, but the rest of him had been truncated by shadow.

"This recruit borrowed Recruit Robinson's pillow, sir. It's this recruit's fault that Robinson didn't have it."

Rocha looked at Casota for what seemed like a long time. He seemed totally equanimous to Casota's nudity.

"What were you doing with Robinson's pillow?"

"This recruit was masturbating with it, sir."

There was no pause this time; Rocha threw back his head and bellowed laughter. I heard recruits stirring down the bay. It was the sound of animals awakening to the sudden presence of a predator among them.

"You're funny, big house." At first, I thought Rocha had misspoke again, but then he looked at me. "That's what his name means, Robinson. Ca-so-ta. Big house." He said it the Spanish way: with an O in the middle instead of the silken "ah" I knew so well.

"Yes, sir. He's a big house, sir." I had no idea what I was saying. I clutched the pillow to my chest. My arms were cool with sweat.

"Big house." Rocha went past me. The smell of Wild Turkey followed him.

"Good night, sir," Casota said. He stood beside me between the beds and we watched the DI walk down the bay.

Rocha whirled again. I drew in a breath. "No. That's, 'good night, pig.'"

Casota and I looked at each other.

"Good night, pig," Rocha said again.

"Good night, pig," I said.

Rocha didn't move. I elbowed Casota. It was like elbowing an oak banister.

"Good night, pig," Casota said.

Rocha turned. "Good night, pig," he said to the squad bay.

All around him, the squad bay feigned sleep.

Casota said, "What in the blind blue fuck was that?"

"Beats me." I passed him his pillow. "Thanks, big house."

That surely wasn't the last time I spoke to Casota between boot camp and our work-up to Iraq, but when I comb my memory of the Corps, it seems like it. It has the right combination of nostalgia and sheer terror, and has taken on sepia tones in my mind. I never asked him why he was naked. He wore the moonlight across his hips in a glittering sash.

FORGIVE US OUR TRESPASSES
DAVID HOLLY

When I was young, but old enough to remember, our rooster Hotspur gave me a flogging. It happened on a hot Thursday in July, and Mom had dressed me in nothing but cotton shorts and sneakers. I was walking hand in hand with her toward the chicken coop when Hotspur beat against my bare back, knocked me face down in the chicken run, and drove his talons into the flesh below my shoulder blades.

Hotspur was insanely protective of his hen harem, but his masculinist instincts would prove his undoing. Still, he enjoyed a momentary triumph. Mom swung a bucket at Hotspur but missed. While Hotspur flew onto the roof of the coop and crowed victory, Mom got me to my feet and rushed me into the house. Blood was streaming in twin rivulets down my back to the ruin of my shorts.

Mom stood me under the hot shower before she disinfected and bandaged the two deep holes under my shoulder blades and stopped my squalling. "You've cried enough, Harry. Stop now."

When Dad got home at six, Mom demanded that he kill Hotspur. But Dad was reluctant. "The hens lay better when there's a rooster, Mattie. Just keep little Harry away from the coop."

Two days later when Dad was carrying water and chicken feed to the coop, Hotspur flogged him in the calves of both legs. Dad thundered into the house with blood leaking into his socks.

As Mom cleaned Dad's legs, her eyes flamed with retribution delayed. When she had his leaking veins plugged, she asked coyly, "What do you want for Sunday dinner, Jack?"

Dad gave her a look I've never been able to describe. "Chicken! Fried!"

I was kept from the facts of life on our farm, but that didn't stop me from spying out my bedroom window while Dad caught Hotspur in a sack and took him to the top of the well housing. I laughed as Dad cut off our rooster's head with a single stroke of a hatchet. I watched the plucking and cleaning that Hotspur got, and the next day I ate my attacker. How tasty is the flesh of vengeance!

Hotspur had been digested thirty years previously, and I couldn't deal with my lover Bradley in the way Hotspur had been dealt with—even though Brad deserved to be plucked. Brad was back at my house, packing up his belongings I hoped, while I was taking a long walk that I didn't feel like taking. I hurt physically and emotionally, and somewhere in my chicken-scarred psyche I felt that something terrible awaited me at home.

Yet it was a fine day in mid-July, the path dry and the woods green and flourishing with the mix of birds, insects, and small animals. I'd hiked this path many times over the past years. I knew it well, so I was surprised to find blackberry canes blocking my passage. I gingerly pulled some thorny canes aside, but a thicker tangle beyond left no way through.

As I turned back, I touched my face, which was swollen where Bradley had punched me. My lip was split, and the vision in my right eye was blurred. He'd been wearing his ring.

Back a short way, I discovered a narrow side path I'd never seen during previous hikes. It was no more than a bunny trail with brush thick on both sides. The way led downward until it was crossed by a mountain stream. Alive with minnows, the creek burbled over stones.

I splashed across, the chill water filling my sneakers and climbing my bare ankles. From there the path led steeply upward until I came to the crest of the rise. The hilltop was cleared and had been planted with poppies.

Among the poppies waited a country church such as might have been known in a more quixotic past. It was tall and square, with windows of stained glass. A four-story steeple with a rusted bell stood locked in time, although the wind blowing through gave a melody of sorts.

The wooden boards of the outer walls were eerie in their pristine whiteness as if they'd been freshly painted. Perhaps the spiteful painter had added the faintest hint of blue to accentuate the chill. There was no parking lot, no road, no evidence that either buggy or automobile had ever been driven to this church.

I walked through the poppies toward the double front doors expecting they'd be locked. To my surprise, when I pulled on the right-hand handle, the door swung to with only a weak screech. The light inside was the product of the windows, the sun casting the shapes intended for the enlightenment of tormented souls, stories told in many-colored sun and shadow upon the unvarnished floor and thirteen pews in the nave.

As I walked toward the altar, the boards gave forth with mild complaint. I stopped before the varnished altar with the pulpit and choir section behind. With a feeling of expectation, I sat to rest in the front pew. While there was no indication that any living soul had stepped foot into that church for a century past, there was the contrasting sense of recent tenancy.

I cast about until I let my gaze rest upon the tall window in the apse. I blinked, closed my right eye, and looked again. The young boys being torn apart by bears for mocking Elisha's bald head was too accurate, and I shrank from the grisly scene. There were five stained glass windows in all, each one picturing one of the ghastlier events recorded by old testament prophets.

Was I hallucinating? Had Brad's final punch addled my brain? I'd always thought that churches should offer hope to their congregants. Here the observer was edified by the grimmest passages of Holy Writ. What manner of people worshipped here, and what did they worship?

It was time for me to be on my way. Perhaps I'd delayed long enough for Brad to pack his belongings and move out of my life. Up until that moment, I hadn't wept. Then sitting in that sinful church, I sobbed out my breaking heart.

I'd really loved Bradley, but he had his moments. The mother of all understatements! Fits of anger for no reason. Resentment and offense over trivia. Yet he was the most terrific lover I'd ever known. He could bring me to the edge of pleasure and keep me there until I begged for release. He was my lord and master, I the slave to his lusts and my own.

He could be witty and thoughtful, and he was a gourmet cook. I'd met him at a signing for my bestselling novel, *Love Must Kill the Swan Alone*, and afterward we hit the gayest bistro in town for a drink together, which turned into a late supper and many more drinks. The evening ended with me taking him back to my house. We'd been together for nearly three years.

Still, there were the unexplained rages, the anger that had no limit, no reason, no control. He'd hurt me before that day. Once while I was concentrating on getting a paragraph just right he'd punched the back of my head in a fit of inexplicable temper.

There hadn't been any violent incidents for the four months before that morning's eruption. I'd been sipping my morning coffee and studying a sheaf of page proofs. Tastefully attired in skin-hugging shorts, Bradley had been cooking our breakfast and looking as delectable as his honeyed corn fritters and the eggs he'd been scrambling with chives. "These will be ready in just a minute, Harry." He left the stove to pick up Wilson's translation of *The Vishnu Purana*, which I'd left on the far end of the table. He idly leafed through the book until he found an inked icon left by the original owner. Brad stopped with a gasp. "This is a swastika!"

I'd gone back to my proofing while he was looking through the book, but his voice was so sharp that I looked up startled.

"You have a book with a fucking swastika. Not printed. A hand-drawn swastika."

"It's a symbol for good luck, Brad. There were no Nazis in 1840 when this book was printed. Back then nobody had any idea that the symbol would be adopted by people of monstrous intent."

Bradley slammed down the book with such fury that coffee sloshed onto my page proofs.

"Hey, Brad, have a heart. I paid $1,500 for that book." As yet I hadn't realized that he was utterly out of control. Working at sopping up the spilled coffee, I could see that my proofs were beyond salvage. How much effort had gone to waste? Then the rest of my coffee went when Bradley shoved me.

It finally dawned on me that Bradley had descended into one of his mindless rages. I made one futile plea. "Get control of yourself, Brad. I warned you last time that one more attack would mean the end."

I didn't have a chance to say anything else because he punched me hard in the mouth. I fell back against the wainscoting. Bradley stooped and drove his fist into my right eye, slamming my head hard into the wall. "You fucking Nazi," he kept saying. "You fucking fascist."

He moved away and into the kitchen where smoke was rising from the frying pan. I struggled to stand as Bradley rummaged in the drawer for some kitchen utensil. I started for the bathroom to examine my face, but Bradley stopped me.

That had to be the end. I'd taken too much. "You're out of here today, Brad. Out of my house. I don't want to see you again."

Those were my last words to him ever. I turned off the stove, tossed the burning breakfast pan into the sink, and turned on the water. He must have hit my nose too because I saw blood going down the drain. There was more blood on my hand and arm. I washed carefully, keeping my back to Bradley. I didn't want to look at him. He made some whimpering noise, but I went into the bedroom without a glance behind. I dressed in khaki shorts, pulled on hiking shoes without socks, grabbed my Panama hat, and went out the screen door.

I just had to walk away, and I took a familiar path until the blackberry canes set me on a different trail. As a result, I was sitting in a strange church, perhaps the strangest church in Christendom, and grieving deep.

I saw something I hadn't noticed before. There was a loaf of steaming bread and a large chalice sitting on the altar. Curious, I went forward to investigate. The bread had been placed on an earthenware plate, and it smelled as if it had come out of the oven minutes before. The hand-thrown clay chalice was brimming with dark red wine.

When I picked up the bread knife, I shivered as if a host of ghouls were digging at my grave. In some past time, I must have handled a knife in such a manner that this innocent blade evoked a shadowy memory of sin. Was it when I'd cut into Hotspur's flesh at that long-ago Sunday dinner? That could not be for Hotspur had been fried, so we'd eaten him with our hands along with Mom's French fries and ears of corn cooked in the husk in a hot oven.

Hazy memories aside, my hand held the bread knife firmly, and it felt right there. I carved off a third of the loaf and broke off a piece to taste. Was it a broken body in my mouth, just as Hotspur's body had been, or was it merely bread? Nevertheless, the taste was delectable with nothing of the sacred. Profane bread on a holy alter and profane wine. I sipped and found the wine to my liking.

I took my bread and the chalice back to my pew. I'd missed breakfast, so my hunger gave the bread such flavor and texture to be orgasmic to the taste buds. I took a long draught of wine and savored it in my mouth before I swallowed.

Presently the church grew brighter. I smelled something that hinted of blood. "This cup is the new testament in my blood: this do ye, as oft as ye drink it, in remembrance of me." The images in the stained glass appeared to move. I drank more wine to kill the remembrance.

I was unsteady as I went to cut another third from the loaf. The bread had begun to hiss, but the wailing voices rising in the steam left me unfazed. I had to sit carefully because the pew was a writhing serpentine and even the boards of the floor wriggled and twisted into obscene shapes. I slouched in my pew as I ate bread and drank down the dregs of the chalice.

I was lethargic in body but my mind was aflame. I could've written *Don Quixote* or *Huckleberry Finn* or *The Brothers Karamazov* right then. I could have painted the *Mona Lisa* and composed *Symphony No. 9* before lunch. All my senses were heightened so that I knew that I should have heard the scratching of a quill upon parchment.

I hadn't noticed the side door until then. It stood unobtrusively to the left of the altar. I wobbled to my feet, approached, tapped lightly, waited. The answer was almost alarming. "Come in, Harry."

The name plate on his desk read Pastor Lott. Sitting behind his desk and wearing a suit the color of ketchup, Pastor Lott sneered as if I were the prodigal son or the fatted calf. "Did you enjoy our communion wine?"

"Uh, yeah. I drank it all. Sorry."

"Was the communion loaf to your taste?"

"Sorry." Was he suggesting I'd committed a profanation? A blasphemy? "Sorry."

He dismissed my apologies. "You don't belong here, Harry. Church isn't the right place for you."

My regret turned to anger. "I don't belong in a church? Why? Because I'm gay?"

Reverend Lott snorted. "You can't guess how broken you are. What of Jester? Killer? The others? Even I am a part with you."

A horrible feeling traveled up my spine. "I don't know what you're babbling about, Reverend. Jester is a fictitious person, merely a name I call myself when I don't want to be serious. As for being a killer, I am not. I am a man of comity." A ghastly supposition intruded. "Are you suggesting that I crucified Christ afresh because I ate holy bread and drank holy wine?"

"Holy wine, indeed. It took two bottles of expensive pinot noir to fill that chalice, Harry, but even that much wine couldn't fill you. Only the Most High knows the abysmal emptiness of your soul."

I wanted to tell him that my body had been broken in a breakfast nook rather than on a cross, and that my blood had spotted my kitchen linoleum. The abysmally empty soul belonged to my lover and abuser, and it was his broken body that... No! No! Let that not be!

"Thanks for that jolly insight, Reverend," I said. "I'll just shuffle off now and leave you to your charming windows."

He dismissed Jester's flippancy. "Prior to departing, you should express some gratitude to my wife for your purloined buffet." He pointed toward a side door in a wall where I should have known that there would be a side door. "She's slaving over a hot stove in the kitchen."

Feeling wine drunk and worse, I staggered toward the door he'd indicated. Silver circles were sliding along the wall, leaving musical traces with each beat of my heart. The door opened onto a landing with stairs that plunged down to the church basement.

At the bottom of the steps, thirteen long tables were arranged with unpadded folding chairs to numb the congregants' buttocks. A narrow kitchen stood along the front with a long pass-through so food could be served. A woman wearing an out-of-style pants suit of a carmine hue was washing her hands in the double sink. She'd been gorgeous once, but time and church suppers had made her stouter than her polyester garment could conceal.

"Excuse me, Pastor Lott told me where to find you."

"Somebody has at my porridge been, and has eaten it all up!" she quoted.

I was tempted to ask where the three bears fit into this nightmare, but I didn't dare. "Yes, I ate the bread you left on the altar." I hiccupped drunkenly. How much wine had I consumed?

She waved her hand over a row of hot loaves. "One more or less is nothing. You are welcome, but you should know that we have a congregant who grows wheat in conditions for ergot. The fungus heightens the experiential quality of our services."

I'll bet it does, I thought. You're baking bread laced with LSD. The congregation is all tripping. So that explained my hallucinations. Then I thought to question the wine. "What do you put in the communion wine?"

"Just a little opium. Our poppies make all dreams happy."

I wasn't sure what to say. I was drunk and doped to the gills. Still, I was feeling less pain. Bradley's attack seemed years ago, and my grief had been temporally stayed. "I ate and drank your sacraments, but I can't apologize. I've never eaten better bread nor drunk better wine."

"Thank you, but, Harry, you must know that you don't belong here. You've delayed too long already. The body is chilling and the blood is congealing. You should go home now."

Was she a raving whacko? Whose body? "What are you talking about?"

"Go back to your house. The path is long and the time is short." Was she implying that I was *dead and passing through the afterlife*? Had Brad killed me and sent me into a Dantesque limbo in a crazy church that was unlike any church that could possibly be except within the dominion of nightmare?

Without a word of farewell, I rushed back up the stairs. The church office was empty. I sprinted over the creaking floor boards and into the poppy field. One look back showed me the old church standing cruelly white in a circle of dusky Sitka spruce and Douglas firs and under a pellucid sky of eternal blue.

The hike homeward was faster than the trail outbound. I came out of the invasive English ivy and the Himalayan blackberry bushes to find my house standing with two cars in the driveway, one mine and one Bradley's. The front door was unlocked. Good because I'd run off without my keys.

My house was silent. Though it was not yet noon by my reckoning, I went first to the sideboard. Somebody had been hitting my wine hard. There were two empty wine bottles, both pinot noir, and an open cabernet sauvignon. I poured a full glass of the cabernet and drank it down as if it were a tumbler of water. Then I stripped down to my briefs and hit the couch for a nap.

Even in whatever stupor I'd fallen, some voice kept screaming in the treetops of my consciousness. *Bradley is still in the house, Harry. Wake up. Find out where he is. See what he has on his mind. Your very life may depend upon your knowing.*

I awoke drooling onto the couch pillow. Attempting to rise, I discovered that I was the victim of a wino's hangover. "Coffee," I managed with a gasp. "Strong coffee. That's what I need now."

On my way to the kitchen, I bumped into a bookshelf and dislodged three books. With exaggerated care, I replaced the books before I turned toward the ghastly display. Bradley was half-propped against the cupboard, his eyes wide and glazed, his hand gripping the butcher knife that had pierced his abdominal aorta. A thick pool of his life's blood had spread around him like a war-surplus curse.

I stepped barefooted into the thickening blood. How foolish was that? Then I pulled the knife out of Brad's gut, sealing my stupidity. It hardly mattered. He'd beaten me, but he'd loved me. He'd been true, a loyal partner. Now someone had taken him from me. Yes, he was dead.

I found my phone after some difficulty. 9-0-9. No. 9-1-9. Get it right, Harry. 9-1-9-1. Not yet. -9-1—1—1… Hit the green button.

"9-1-1: what is your emergency?"

"Someone broke into my house and murdered my boyfriend." Why did I put it so bluntly? So unfeelingly?

The police came, but not before I'd got the coffeemaker working. As the first squad car pulled into my driveway, I remembered that I wasn't dressed. I'd found my T-shirt and was looking about for my shorts when the cops started pounding.

"Coming. Just a minute. Coming." I jerked open the door. There were two, a man and a woman. I guess they were used to finding homeowners in their underwear because they didn't appear surprised. "This way." I led them toward the kitchen.

The female cop was tougher than the male. He retched when he saw Bradley. She stopped and slowly turned her head. Her eyes took in every detail, imprinting the crime scene on her mind like a camera.

"I made a mess of it," I said. It sounded like a confession. "I mean that I stepped in the blood and I pulled out the knife. I messed up the crime scene."

I distinctly saw the female cop mouth *homocide* to her partner.

By then other cars were arriving, along with paramedics and an ambulance. Then the paramedics went away and the medical examiner arrived along with other police scientists.

One detective pointed at me. "He's not exactly broken up about it."

No more so than when I ate Hotspur.

All during that time, they didn't let me dress or shave or brush my teeth. I was permitted to use the bathroom—with the door open while an annoyed cop supervised. Otherwise, I had to sit on the couch in my sweaty briefs and T-shirt until they finally handcuffed me.

They told me that they were arresting me for murdering Bradley and quoted all that other nonsense cops do when they arrest people innocent of the crime.

❖

My lawyer asked Judge Bird for a psychiatric evaluation, and the judge agreed over the prosecution's objections.

"Why'd you get a shrink involved, Lance?" I asked when we were safely ensconced in a private chamber. "Don't you believe me?"

"No, Harry, I don't," Lance Tumbril, my dubious defender, admitted. "Your story makes no sense."

I picked at my orange jailhouse jumpsuit, which was all I'd been permitted to wear to the preliminary hearing. "I'm not making it up."

"The police investigated. I investigated. There's no path such as you describe, and there's no church."

That's when I began to see the depth of the conspiracy arrayed against me. "Pastor Lott and his wife can confirm my story. Part of it anyway. Did you talk to them?"

"No such people, Harry. They don't exist in any public record."

Could my own lawyer be helping to frame me? I'd known Lance for ten years and had always thought him the best and gayest attorney on the West Coast.

"You think I killed Bradley?" I drew a breath to fight the rising nausea. "Is that what you believe, Lance? That I'm a murderer?"

The look he gave me was unreadable. "I'm certain that you killed him, Harry, but it couldn't have been premeditated first-degree murder like the prosecutor claims. I think you killed him in self-defense. Your life or his."

Self-defense? Where did Lance come up with that conclusion? I was as tender-hearted as they come. I wouldn't step on an ant. "I didn't kill Brad. I loved him—most of the time. Everything I told you is the truth. Person or persons unknown entered my house and murdered Bradley." To my own ears, my theory sounded farfetched. "Bradley had a past, Lance. He's hurt people before, and one of those must have come after him." I hesitated. "He could be a violent motherfucker, but he had the heart of a bodhisattva."

"Bod-hee whatsis?"

Why aren't lawyers educated in the classics? "A compassionate being. Someone who will sacrifice time and effort to help others." That explanation would suffice.

"Harry, do you truly believe that abusive asshole was a saint?" He held up a hand to stifle my protest. "No, never mind it. I'll let you know when the psychiatric evaluation has been scheduled."

"Wait, Lance. What about bail? I can't stay here." I pointed in the direction of my present accommodations. "That cell is squalid. It's not fit for a self-respecting hog."

"There's no bail for first-degree murder, Harry. Not for a capital offense."

"Capital! You mean I could be executed?"

My spine froze as if I'd been goosed with the products of Lucifer's popsicle cart. Yes, Jester was determined to get out, and I couldn't stop him. I could only watch and listen.

"It won't come to that, so you can stop fidgeting," my attorney said, answering too glibly for comfort. "You're vibrating like a washing machine, Harry. Judge Bird denied bail pending your mental evaluation."

Jester pushed me aside and took control. "Meaning both you and the judge think I'm having trouble with the old coconut." I laughed and pointed toward my throbbing head. "The prosecutor thinks that lethal injection for me is being soft on crime. In the meanwhile, I'm incarcerated in the one place where I'm most likely to be driven around the bend. End up crackers. One brick shy of a load."

Lance must have thought Jester was joking because he chuckled in a chummy fashion. "You're privileged with a private cell, Harry. You don't have to share a pod with the reprobates."

"Maybe I'd meet some stimulating companions in the pod."

"No doubt you would." My lawyer didn't know Jester at all.

❖

Although he had a psychological-sounding name, which I supposed he'd assumed about the same time he forged his medical license, Dr. Freudenberger didn't act the way I thought a psychiatrist should act, and he looked more like a Vegas blackjack dealer than a medical doctor. I despised him at first sight.

"Tell me again, Harry."

"Are you trying to help me or interrogate me, Freudenberger? I've told you three times what happened. If you're looking for discrepancies, then you're wasting the court's time."

"We're not in a courtroom. Now describe your conversation with Mrs. Lott again."

"That woman must be a witch or a fortune teller. She knew that Brad was dead." I gasped as realization struck me. "She knew. She's the murderer. Either that or she knew that Pastor Lott killed Brad and she was covering for her husband."

Dr. Freudenberger slapped my face hard. Was he allowed to hit me? He had to be a charlatan. "Stop jiggling. Both feet on the carpet. Now, Harry."

That's when I came out. Harry dwindled, unaware that his conscious self was closing down. He didn't know about me, but I knew everything about him. I'd been watching him fumble until I had no choice.

I checked my hand for blood but there was no need to quote Lady Macbeth. The damned spot was a figment. "I didn't want to stab Bradley. He made me do it. He was so crazy that I couldn't resist liking him, but I couldn't let him beat Harry to death. So I stopped him."

Dr. Freudenberger either didn't notice the shift or he'd been expecting it. "By driving a butcher knife into his abdominal aorta?"

"That's what I did." I giggled so hard that I fell out of the chair's soft embrace onto Dr. Freudenberger's carpet. "I'm alive. Brad is dead. I prefer things this way." I kept on laughing and couldn't stop.

Dr. Freudenberger gripped my shoulder. "Get up, Harry."

I shrugged off his hand. "I'm not Harry. I'm Killer, so watch yourself."

I remembered everything. Harry had been punched several times, and Bradley was still raving about Nazi authors. Harry started toward the bathroom, but Brad blocked him. That's when I took over. Harry was, after all, our meal ticket. He wrote the books that made the money that kept our concern going. He had to be protected, and besides, in protecting him, I was protecting us.

Brad threw another punch toward my eye, but he was slow. I ducked and hit him hard right over his heart. Our body was puny from sitting long at the desk, but there is strength in will. I meant for the punch to stop his heart, and it did delay him long enough for me to open the knife drawer.

"You fucking..." That was Brad's last word. His face crumpled in shock when I drove the knife into the center of his abdomen. I twisted the knife just to make sure that his aorta was well-severed. Brad's blood flowed up my arm. I left the knife in place as Brad collapsed.

While Brad was dying, I washed my hands and arms in the kitchen sink. Harry had gone to breakfast wearing a T-shirt and boxer shorts. I went into the shower wearing them and stripped them off under the spray. I washed and shampooed for ten minutes. Then I carried my discarded garments to the washing machine, dumped in our other dirty clothes, and started a load.

I dressed as if I'd gone for a hike: T-shirt, briefs, shorts, hiking shoes. If the cops had done their job, they would have learned that Harry wore boxers; whereas, I was more comfortable in briefs. Leave it to the detectives to ignore an important clue.

I exercised hard in the sun for twenty minutes, enough to work up a heavy sweat and then I crawled into the bushes to pick up the detritus of a wanderer in the woods. Back inside, I kicked off my shoes and tossed my filthy shorts down the hall. I opened two bottles of pinot noir and poured a glass. I looked over the scene I'd arranged and decided that it would have to do. I sat down on the couch and drank deep. Harry was going to get drunk, mindlessly drunk.

Then I was back, and Killer was gone.

"Harry," Dr. Freudenberger said, sitting me up. "You dissociated. You're afflicted with DID."

"What's that?"

"Dissociative Identity Disorder." He watched my face. "It used to be called Multiple Personality Disorder."

"What?"

"Caused by a childhood trauma. Later in life, often triggered by another trauma, the different identities begin to emerge."

"I didn't kill Brad," I said weakly. "Someone else did that."

Based upon Dr. Freudenberger's report, the prosecution reluctantly dropped all charges against me. Judge Bird accepted the findings without prejudice.

"Self-defense, as I promised," Lance Tumbril proclaimed as we left the courtroom. "Kindly note when my bill arrives, Harry, that I could have kept you off death row with an insanity plea. That was a last resort because it would have landed you in a place worse than death row."

Perhaps I should have been grateful to my attorney and to the court's psychiatrist, but being told that I had emerging multiple personalities, one a stone-cold killer, wasn't good news.

So I returned home. While I'd been incarcerated, my lawyer had arranged for a cleaning service. No trace of Brad's blood remained. Still, he was all over the place. His clothes hung in our closet. His personal items lay in our chests of drawers. Other remembrances were scattered on mantles, tables, and counter tops.

I gathered up everything of his I could find, including personal papers, and stowed them in trash bags. Then I dressed in khaki shorts, T-shirt, sports socks, and sneakers to take that hike I'd supposedly missed.

I followed the path, but the way that had led up to the church wasn't there. I walked on and there were no blackberry canes blocking my passage. I hiked warily, following the real and losing the imagined, until the way twisted back and I came home again.

"I am large," Walt Whitman wrote. "I contain multitudes."

I was many persons, multiple personalities. Perhaps I was a soldier and a coward, a demagogue and a revolutionary, a spiritualist and a scoffer. Yes, I was Harry the sensitive writer, and I was Killer, the defender of Harry. Would Harry still be alive without Killer? Probably not. Just as I'd been blooded in spirit when Hotspur attacked, I'd been bruised, concussed, and marked when Brad attacked.

In both cases, I'd devoured my attacker—symbolically, of course. Self-defense may be no sin, not to the legalistic mind, but what of vengeance? Through my father, I'd revenged myself upon Hotspur, and through Killer I'd evened the score with my lover, Bradley.

"Reverend Lott, whoever you are, pray that we be forgiven our trespasses."

And Jester laughed.

BECAUSE OF THE TIMES
EJ ROBINSON

Everything was prepared. May had scrubbed the ground floor of the house from corner to corner. Flowers filled the living room to eliminate, at last, the lingering odours of illness. The rugs were hoovered, the cushions plumped; every surface shone. In the kitchen the kettle was whistling to a boil on the hob beside plates of freshly cut sandwiches and triangles of folded paper napkins. Graham would have told her she deserved a sit down after such hard work. Not just yet, she would have said in return as she fished a clean rag out from under the sink. The pictures still needed dusting.

The photographs of May's life with Graham began in the front hall and advanced chronologically through the ground floor. Above the living room hearth hung their wedding portrait: two strawberry blondes standing amidst a flurry of rice thrown in a vanished world. They had been so young. On the nights when her complaining bones made sleep itself a dream, May would lie awake and think of those two blonde, rice-rained youngsters. If they had known back then how the world was going to change, would they have chosen differently?

A slam from upstairs made the lilies on the windowsill shiver. May lowered her rag and raised her eyes to the ceiling. Terrible, really. That her own son put her instincts on alert as though an intruder was in the house. May wouldn't change anything about her marriage to Graham. Except having Henry. She'd had many wishes for her son's life in his infancy. He had taken many years to arrive and been so wanted. But when he finally came,

Henry proved himself time and time again to be anything but a blessing. As the years passed, May's hopes for him winked out one by one, spent as ancient stars. The only wish she had left now was to give her husband the send-off he deserved. The mourners were due soon. May shuffled back into the kitchen and picked up a fresh rag.

One of the countless—and they really were countless—photos of his parents slithered to the floor when Henry kicked their wardrobe door shut. He tucked a tattered shoebox under one arm and crunched over the fallen frame on his way out, cracking the glass over his parents' faces. The night he returned home, Henry had worked his way through the contents of his father's liquor cabinet, then spent the granite-tinted hours of dawn puking over porcelain—shock, not booze, the cause of his twisting stomach.

It was impossible he'd been cut from his parent's will. He was their only child. The only explanation could be that when his father had been off his head on meds, his mother had made the old boy sign a new version of the will that excluded Henry. Knowing her mania for hanging onto every scrap of paperwork she ever handled, the original version had to be somewhere in their house. All he needed to do was find it. But after hours of hunting, Henry, weaving on his knees amongst decades of bank statements and mortgage payments, had to admit there was no other will. Upon his mother's death the house, the money, the shares, all of it would go straight into the pocket of May's only sibling, Esther. That freak. Their last and most public display of disappointment in him.

Now, on the afternoon of his father's funeral, he could hear his mother shuffling around downstairs, moving dust from corner to corner and boiling the kettle for the hundredth time in preparation for the guests. Everyone in town was coming because everyone in town had loved his father. Which was why the afternoon was going to be so satisfying. Henry had only one wish left: to give his father the send-off the treacherous miser deserved. The mourners were due soon. Henry tucked the shoebox—the afternoon's entertainment—under one arm, and felt in his pockets for a well-deserved cigarette.

❖

May stood at the door to greet the mourners. Everyone came to pay their respects: friends, family, neighbours from their street, the people of the town. As she welcomed them all, she was struck by how one spent one's youth on material acquisition: buying a house and filling it with comforts that seem important at the time, so vital. Later, near the end of it all, you discovered it wasn't the things you acquired that mattered, but those who fell into step with you along the way.

Those who shared your times. May found solace in the memories of Graham held by so many. Their recollections gave the empty space he'd left behind new shape as they gathered together beneath the wedding portrait of the youngsters they'd been, frozen in time with forever overhead.

When Graham offered himself as the solution to her problems, May had wept. Back then a girl like her did not have a wealth of choices on offer. She'd had two options, and her father made each of them clear: Graham and marriage, or shame and ostracism. Graham had known everything about her situation and wanted to marry her anyway. She'd said yes because the world seemed set in its ways and he was a lovely young man, no matter what they said around town. May had hoped Henry might find the salvation in his own marriage that she had found with Graham, albeit for different reasons. But Annalise had soon realised what she'd gotten herself into. It was only afterwards, listening to Henry rage down the phone, that May learned the lovely girl who was too good for her son had been pregnant when she'd taken the car and vanished into the night.

"You only have yourself to blame," she'd said. "No one forced you to act as you did."

"All right," he'd said, "but you didn't have to *tell* the bitch."

Marriage was a promise. The last thing May would do was watch her son philander and keep silent. That her actions had cost her the only grandchild she would probably ever know about was just something else she had to live with every day.

She looked around the crowded hallway. Graham would have been touched to see so many present today. She hoped her husband, free at last of pain, was looking down, and proud of her.

❖

Horns of smoke swirled from Henry's nostrils where he stood savouring his second cigarette beneath the fire alarm, the batteries of which nestled in his pocket. He leaned on the landing bannister and listened to the mourners crunch up the gravel drive. Cellophane crackled round bouquets; hushed voices murmured gentle greetings. The entire senior population of the town was descending on the house. With so many corpses doddering up, it looked as though a zombie apocalypse was underway. Henry realised his father attracted more company dead than Henry ever could alive.

His mother had asked him to invite his slag of an ex-wife to the funeral. Like everyone else who'd ever met him, Annalise adored Graham. His mother suggested she might want to say good-bye. Henry pointed out she hadn't been too worried about saying good-bye when she'd upped and vanished. His mother took the hint. Now, Henry rather wished Annalise was coming. He'd have loved to watch her jaw drop along with everyone else's. In one hour, everything that everyone admired about his father would go up in smoke. He stubbed out his cigarette and picked up the shoebox.

Henry was heading downstairs when every hair on his body rose to attention at the brisk click-clack of high heels approaching the front door.

Esther.

Henry sometimes wondered how May had turned out so dull when her early life had been so colourful: divorced parents when they still called such situations broken homes; step-siblings before the invention of the name. And then there was her younger brother, Edward. After years of dressing as a woman in secret, Edward changed his name to Esther in '69 and married a woman in '72. That same woman died after only three years with him, probably from confusion at being married to a heterosexual male transvestite who went by a female moniker.

Esther strode through the front door in a black gown and fur coat, pearls clacking around his neck. Henry dropped down onto the steps and began working a fresh cigarette from the pack in his jeans as he watched his mother fall into her brother's arms. The breeze from the open door stirred a flurry of paper scraps from the dish beside the phone that took flight and blew against Henry's shoes where they jittered, caught in the draft. Looking down at them, he saw phone numbers written in his mother's tremulous print, the same numbers in varying orders, scratched out and reassembled, half-finished nonsense. He scooped the scraps up in one fist and raised his head to find Esther's sable eyes fixed on him over May's shuddering shoulder. It took four attempts for Henry to light his cigarette.

Esther excused himself from May and strode around to the side of the stairs to look at Henry through the wooden bannisters. The scent of him made Henry's nostrils fizz with florals and bergamot.

"You suit this view," said Esther, trailing one night black nail back and forth along the bars between them. "You don't come home for seven years. Not when he's sick, not when he's dying. Then the day of the will reading, there you jolly well are. Coincidence?"

Henry swallowed. He offered the pack of cigarettes. Esther eased one free then held it out.

Henry flicked the lighter, heard the soft crackle as the cigarette tip glowed orange and the air between them thickened into fog as Esther exhaled haze.

"You're up to something," Esther said.

"What makes you say that?" said Henry.

"Sweetie, you look smug as a shagged lion with a full belly. You've either been left everything or you're up to something. And since I know you haven't been left everything, I can only conclude it's the latter."

"That sounds like too much thinking for you, Uncle Esther."

"Honey, who do you think you're talking to?"

"You know, I never was too sure how to answer that."

Esther's hand shot out and gripped Henry's bicep to yank him flush against the bannisters. Henry's eyes flicked to the front door, but the hallway was empty. May and the last arrivals had moved into the living room. Esther's grip tightened and Henry looked back at him, their faces centimetres apart.

"I'm warning you, sunshine," Esther breathed. "If you do anything to taint this day for your mother, you'll have me to contend with."

"What'll you do, Esther? Scare me to death by lifting your skirt?"

Esther put his mouth right up to Henry's ear. Henry could feel the tack of his lipstick. "And if you so much as breathe near Tessa's little girls..."

Henry clenched his teeth. One slip up—*one!*—and they marked you for life.

Esther gave Henry's arm one final pincer squeeze then released him and swished into the living room with a whisper of satin.

Henry dragged on his cigarette with quivering lips, and jaggedly exhaled. In the mirror hanging on the wall above the phone he could see the mourners mingling in the living room below that ridiculous photo of his parents having rice chucked over them. Esther be damned. It wasn't Henry that Esther would be watching. Henry got to his feet, and flicked the paper scraps of bungled numbers back amongst the others in the dish beside the phone. The star of the show was due in half an hour.

❖

May couldn't concentrate.

Henry had done the rounds with trays of teas and coffees and refreshed the food platters. He was now stationed by the living room window, puffing incessantly on those infernal cigarettes and watching the road outside. The intensity of his focus aroused May's suspicions. She looked around the room. Tessa and her girls were near the glass cabinet, talking with the Patel family. May had told Tessa they needn't attend today, that she would completely understand if they didn't. Tessa had insisted. May and Graham had looked after the girls when they were babies, it was only right they all came. Still, May thought, looking back at her son by the window. It was perhaps unwise to—

Annalise!

"What's that, darling?" said Esther.

May looked up at her brother and realised she'd spoken aloud. She gripped Esther's arm. "He mentioned he might have a surprise for me today. Henry, that is."

Esther raised an eyebrow. "Did he, now? And did he give any clues as to what this surprise of his might be?"

"Well, I don't want to get my hopes up, but I'd asked him to contact Annalise. For the funeral." The thought flourished in her mind like a springtime bud. "Perhaps Annalise is coming."

Esther held May's arm. "May. I love you. But when has Henry—"

"If Annalise comes she might bring the baby with her, Esther! Seeing that baby, on a day like today…"

May's heart rose like a star as she watched her son, a smile blooming on her lips, Esther's sighs passing unheard beside her. She saw Henry turn from the window to face the room. He took a pull on his cigarette, and smiled at her.

❖

Being on tea boy duty was the best way to avoid small talk with all the old fogeys, who between them must have bought out the town florist. Most people avoided looking at Henry. They took his offerings without thanks, and he moved on. Henry did the rounds so no one could say he hadn't helped, then positioned himself by the window. He had to be the one to spot the new arrival and get to the front door before anyone else, otherwise the whole afternoon would be spoilt.

Couldn't have that. His mother was huddled in a corner with Esther and Doreen from next door. Tessa was in a corner with her two girls, gassing with the Indians from the next road who also had children of primary school age, like Tessa's girls. Though the Patels had apparently left their offspring at home. Henry avoided looking at the children.

The back of his neck told him Esther was watching him. He turned and smiled at his mother and uncle, whose eyebrows rose. By Christ, if the corners of his mother's mouth didn't turn up a little. Poor woman had no idea what was coming. And to think, if they hadn't cut him from the will Henry would never have made the discovery. Well. This would teach them.

After the will reading, Henry's instinct was to hunt. If there were any other drafts of the will, he'd find them. He'd torn the house asunder, rifling beneath mattresses, scouring inside every drawer, raiding even the bathroom cabinets despite no document in history ever being hidden in a bathroom. He found nothing. No will. But he found something else.

Concealed at the back of Graham's side of the wardrobe, behind rows of sheathed suits and pressed shirts, underneath a pile of wooden shoe horns, he'd found it, crispy with yellow tape and trussed up with string. If he'd been looking for anything other than proof of his inheritance he wouldn't have looked twice at an ancient shoebox. Something somewhere was on his side.

Cross-legged on the floor of his parents' old bedroom, he'd pored over the contents of the box, his father's liquor bottles strewn on the carpet around him. Each letter and note he skimmed made him greedier for the next, his eyes leapt along the lines. It wasn't hard to put the puzzle pieces together, there was a lifetime's worth of correspondence to help him work it out; and not a single piece of it was from May.

There were declarations of love, of longing, letter upon letter to *My Distant Dearest; My Love; My Dear Friend.* Emotion seeped from every handwritten line, some letters were even tear blotched.

—forced to live our lives apart, yet I know—

—may be with another, but—

—think of me, even after all these years—

The letters were all signed, *Your Agatha.* Henry had found a treasure trove of treachery. His father, Graham the Great, had been conducting an affair for over six decades. Beneath the letters was a black and white studio portrait, with a white border and crimped edges framing the kind of face you didn't see anymore: cupid's bow lips, short waved hair; a woman from a dead time. Henry had laughed out loud. After all the years he'd spent being judged and compared to and disrespected by the man, *this* was what he'd been getting up to? And May. Poor, dull, conservative May, had spent her entire life looking after this man who every day had made a mockery of their marriage. The sad old cow.

It was when Henry found the mobile number taped inside the lid of the shoebox that his plan took form. This woman, Agatha whoever, probably didn't know the love of her life had croaked.

She had a right to be informed. She ought to have the chance to pay her last respects. Henry had not thought twice. He'd torn out the paper with the mobile number, and called it.

Now, sitting by the window in his mother's living-room, shoebox beside him, he trained his eye on the road for the first glimpse of his father's mistress. If May had just cracked her first smile at him in Christ knew how long, she wouldn't be smiling much longer.

The doorbell rang. Once. A stranger's ring. The hum of voices in the room died for a moment as everyone looked to the doorway at the sound of the bell. Henry leapt up and left the room in three strides. May watched her son go, and the hand that held her plate of cake began to tremor. She dabbed her lips and faced the door as muted conversations hummed again.

People could change. She'd dedicated her marriage to changing. And if she hadn't succeeded exactly, well, nobody was perfect. If Annalise walked through that door carrying her grandchild, nothing else mattered.

Henry bounded back into the room, beaming. May gripped Esther's arm.

"Mother?" Henry said, loud enough to make everyone look his way. "Mother, someone has come a long way to pay their last respects."

The fork on May's plate jittered. The back of her eyes began to burn. Her son reached into the hallway behind him, and with a flourish, drew the new arrival into the room. The only sound was Esther's intake of breath. May stared at the woman beside Henry, then at her son, her milky eyes round.

"Mother, this is Agatha."

Neither woman spoke. Henry glowed.

"If you're a little confused, Mum," he said, walking Agatha further into the room, "I was too at first. But it's quite simple. This is Agatha Simons."

May shook her head. "I don't understand."

"This, Mumsie, is a woman your saintly husband knew only too well."

"*Henry!*" Esther was on his feet.

"Graham?" May frowned. "No—"

"This is the woman Dad was conducting an affair with," said Henry, "for over *sixty years!*"

There was an audible gasp of collective breath, a soft thump: May's plate hitting the floor, the last of her cake bursting into constellations of crumbs on the carpet. Henry strode to the window to scoop up the shoebox and tear off the lid, shaking the contents in his mother's direction.

"He kept the evidence hidden in his wardrobe upstairs."

He held up a letter like an Olympic torch, then flung it at May's feet. Agatha flinched as Henry advanced on his mother.

"For all your talk of what a great man he was, how loyal, how I should have been more like him, all these years he was carrying on with this one here!"

He jerked his thumb at Agatha. He was in the grip of performance now. Everyone was watching. All the raised eyebrows, all the slack jaws, all the withered hands clapped to mouths were exactly as he'd imagined. Everything he'd ever wanted to say to his parents poured forth in an avalanche of derision. They had always been so quick to judge him. Now who was in the wrong?

Henry flung letter after letter at May, who raised trembling hands to fend him off, peering down at the debris as Henry shook the last treasures out of the box in front of her, triumph twisting his face. Esther wrapped his arms around May.

"I should have been more like him, eh?" Henry gestured to the paper coated carpet, "Well maybe he's where I got it from. That ever cross your mind? I had to get it from somewhere, right?"

Henry smirked in the midst of the horrified audience. Agatha hovered to one side like the unwanted spirit everyone pretended not to see. Henry looked from one old woman to the other, and it was then, in their continuing silence, that a chill of doubt entered his blood. There should be questions, fists beating ancient breasts, feminine hysteria. The woman her husband had cheated with was in front of her. Was his mother such a walkover she wasn't even going to be angry? Was she just going to stand there staring gormlessly at the pile of junk?

Henry gagged as Esther yanked him from the room by his collar.

"Get off me, you old queen!"

Esther tightened his grip and dragged Henry to the kitchen, flinging him away once they were inside.

"You have no idea what you're doing, you little good for nothing," Esther hissed.

Henry rubbed his neck. "He was a liar, Esther. All these years she's been holding him up as a beacon of honourable man, and he was carrying on behind her back."

Esther slammed the kitchen door. "Let me guess," he said. "You read a few letters and thought you knew the whole story, right?"

"The evidence is there in black and white."

"There's over half a century of history you know nothing about."

"The letters gave me a pretty good idea."

"How do you know those letters were to your father?"

"They were from a *wo*man!"

"Did any of them name Graham as the recipient? Any one of them. Did they?"

Henry snorted. Of course they'd had Graham's name on them, they were *to* Graham. "I know they did," he said.

But the harder he tried to recall them—*dearest friend; distant love*—Henry wasn't sure that he had seen Graham's name on the letters. He squinted at Esther, the air going out of his chest.

"They were to Dad," he said. "Weren't they?"

Esther sighed. "Henry. Get your things. Then get the hell out of this house."

❖

May would have known the date even if it hadn't been scribbled in the corner of the only picture of them together. April 19, 1954. They met, knowing it was for the last time, and so they had been careful to pay attention to every moment of that day on Brighton beach. The sparkle of the sun on the water; the pairing of their voices amongst hundreds of other voices, like they were any other couple; the friendly stranger with a camera whom Agatha begged to take their picture, this picture, on the floor before May now. Agatha offered him money and wrote down May's address for him to send the photograph to once it was developed. Perhaps he had seen it in them, there behind their eyes as they turned their backs on the impossible horizon: the terror of their impending loss.

The weeks following the taking of the photograph blurred in a torrent of torment, and in the midst of it all, May had married Graham, and time, as it always did, passed. Grief lost its sharp edges. It ceased to immobilise her for days on end, became easier to shoulder. And surrounding her, always, was love. Love from Graham, who'd always known, and love from Agatha, whose letters still smelt of her, each as tender as bruised skin. May looked down at the photograph of two girls who once had been, and now were gone. She breathed in and smelt salt, heard the crash of a Brighton tide and the forgotten vocals of Kitty Kallen's "Little Things Mean a Lot" that had floated on the breeze to them where they sat, their hands locked together out of sight beneath the sand, *a line a day when you're far away, little things mean a lot.*

A line a day and more, for 66 years. A lifetime's collection of love. May looked up.

Agatha didn't disappear when May blinked. She was there, a slim bouquet nestled in the crook of one elbow. Her hair had brightened to a gleaming white which made her eyes even bluer behind her spectacles. Her back, like May's own, curved forwards as though, after all this time, they were trying to lean closer to each where the other stood. The muted conversations of the crowded room had long died out. For May there was no crowd. There was only Agatha.

"I gather my son contacted you," said May.

"I gather you didn't ask him to," said Agatha.'

"No."

Agatha took a ragged breath. "A man phoned and told me about poor Graham. That if I loved him I'd show my face. I got the impression the fellow was drunk; it was after four in the morning. But he gave your address, and when I rang Doreen, she confirmed it was true, so I wanted to come." Agatha's hands were clasped just under her heart. "But perhaps I should go?" she asked.

May's lips quivered into a smile that faded as quickly as it came. "I think those ought to be in water," she said. Agatha held out the flowers. May took them.

"Graham was a wonderful man," said Agatha.

May looked at the detritus around her feet. "He was," she said. "How long has it been, Agatha?"

The corners of Agatha's mouth trembled. "Sixty-six years, seven months and—"

"—three days,' May finished, dabbing at her cheeks.

Agatha eased a tissue from her sleeve and touched it to the corners of May's eyes. "I kept all your letters," said May.

Agatha peered down at the pile. "Your filing needs work."

"Well, you know, I never did finish secretarial school. But you always said you can't re-read phone calls."

May couldn't look away from Agatha's face. It had changed, and yet it was the same. The same frame of waved hair, the same Cupid's bow mouth. Did more than half a century truly stand between them?

"Why didn't you tell me Graham had passed?" Agatha said.

"You're not listed," said May.

"My number never changed."

"I taped it to the inside lid of the box I kept your letters in, but, I went through them all. It vanished. I thought the tape was old, the note fell loose, perhaps got mixed in with the letters. But I never found it. I expect Henry. . ." May flapped one hand. "My memory isn't what it was. I didn't have it written down anywhere else. The hours I've spent, Aggie, annoying the people of the southeast trying different phone number combinations in the hope I'd reach you eventually."

Agatha nodded. "I drove here," she said.

"You drive? I never did learn," said May, turning to look out the window. As did the population of the room who all were gripped by the conversation.

"My car is just outside," Agatha said. "May. It's been ever such a long time."

"It has. Ever so long."

May stood, watched by all the people who loved her. Graham's absence from the reams of familiar faces seemed only temporary, as if he'd just popped out for some air. But Graham was gone. Graham. Who'd been a poor catch because no man who supported women working outside the home could possibly make a dependable husband. No man who saw nothing obscene in women of May's inclinations could be fit to raise children. No respectable girl's father would give him a second glance. Only, May's father had not had a respectable girl on his hands. Graham's proposal to May had given them both a lifetime of security and companionship, while Agatha had vanished into the new army of the National Health Service. The three of them had escaped the judgement of the times. The price for all of them had been different, but May had had Graham. Agatha had gone on loving May, alone. How many girls like her had so similarly suffered?

"My car is just outside, May," said Agatha.

May's marriage to Graham had done what it was intended to do, better than those two youngsters smiling in a hail of rice could have imagined back then. After her lifetime of sacrifice, why should May deny herself this final happiness? In the end, all anyone ever really had were those who joined them for the ride. Sometimes people fell off along the way. Sometimes they came back to you. The times had changed, and the world was a different place. May had lost the love of her life. Not everyone was lucky enough to have two. Everyone was watching her. Maybe it was time everyone knew.

May reached out, and took Agatha's offered hand.

Runner-Up

WHAT COVERS THE HOUSE IS A ROOF
MATTHEW HAYNES

When Small Man looks past the glare of spotlights, into the audience, he can see their white teeth gleaming, their smiles ear to ear. He's thinking about this song he's playing, this horrible slack key song called "Whee Ha Swing." These days he plays it before the tourists come to the stage with their sweaty dollar bills. They're full from Honolulu luau and drunk on Blue Hawaiians. They've heard it somewhere, maybe in a cab, or read about it in the *Hawaiian Airlines* magazine. They hear the first eight bars and aww and whistle. Small Man smiles, beads of perspiration catching in those lights, and throws his head back like he's into it, like he loves that swing. But he's not, and he doesn't.

He's thinking about how fat he's been all his life. "Ever since da bugga was born," his tutu would say. And she was there, so she would know. Small Man's mother gave birth at Tutu's one-bedroom house in Peahi, on Maui. She didn't have electricity, so the room was lit with half-spent white candles from the Baptist church, and several tall vertebrae of kukui nuts strung through with trussing twine and hung from the ceiling, their oil pushing a bitter, pungent smell into the air. After Tutu wiped the birth from his face and blew into his nostrils, he burst into low moans. Then she thrust him against his mother's bare chest and covered them both in an old family kapa cloth, its black and white geometric designs like a protection. "Da little bugga one baby Buddha," Tutu said, which was a sweet thing to say, because he was a baby, and even saying a baby is a little ugly can seem a little sweet. But that kind of sweetness doesn't translate into adulthood, and it's nothing less than nauseating at 30.

On Fridays after his last set, Small Man goes to Max's bath house on Hobron Street. In the dry sauna, there are boys who he knows will not notice him, or, when they do, his presence will drive them away. Mostly, he's given up on the expectation of any sex, any small talk, any sort of kindness. Now Small Man comes to sit in front of the full-length mirror and look on himself. His brown belly hides his penis and testicles. His Polynesian tattoos stretch and sag around his arms and chest. He doesn't eat on Fridays even though he knows it won't make any kind of difference that day. He thinks about being fat since he was just little and how, as he grew, the neighbor kids named him Small Man. He thinks about how that was never a bad thing, how it was also something sweet they did, like calling the transvestites on Hotel Street, "Honey Girls." Now, Small Man comes here to look on himself, get eye to eye, and affirm, *Despite all this, I am made to love.* This is what he remembers each lonely day.

At home, Small Man eyes the refrigerator. Many times he has thought about putting up pictures of ripped men looking hot on the beach or sad, fat men, but it seems too embarrassing. Instead, the back of a white business envelope held up by a small magnetic pineapple reads, "Whoa, boy!" And some nights that is enough to get him through to the morning, though those nights are filled with fever-dreams. But some nights it's not enough. Sometimes Small Man sees that envelope, taps it a few times with his pointer finger and says, "Fuck you, boy!" and turns it over to an empty cellophane window. Tonight is one of those nights.

He starts with a bag of broccoli and cauliflower, trying to fill his stomach. But it doesn't suffice and he's on to four King's rolls, Nutella, and a glass of 2% milk. For a minute he lets it settle, gives himself a beat to smile and pretend that he's not going to eat more. Then it's pizza rolls, because they take a little time to cook, another bit of time to rest and feel good, to feign moderation. Then there's the tub of cookie dough, which he knows will only make him restless. Still, he eats it, then retires to his sofa and the ever-deepening dip in the middle cushion. He's still hungry but he stops there because he's thinking that if he could just get through every Friday they might add up to something, and he falls asleep mumbling mantra 13 from the 21 Affirmations for Weight Loss: *I am choosing progress over perfection.* On Saturday morning he forgets and indulges his sadness with two burger patties and two mounds of rice, topped with three eggs and gravy with a short stack of pancakes.

After, he goes to his day job doing laundry at the Park Shore Waikiki. While he once managed the laundry room, all the walking became too much. While he was demoted, upper management has been kind and allows him to sit at the industrial washers and dryers transferring and folding sheets and towels. He stacks them neatly for the housekeepers to divide and stock and redress the rooms.

By mid-morning he is already thick with a smell, so he changes his shirt for the afternoon, which makes him feel sharp. At lunch, in the break room, he eats only a Greek yogurt, half a bagel, and a cup of fruit. The other employees smile and accept his facade, though he knows that they know that a 300 calorie lunch didn't get him to 450 pounds. When the day is done, coworkers invite him to barbecues or out for pupus and drinks, but he always declines. He returns home to his small apartment to eat like he's wanted all day. Then he moves to the sofa with his ukulele and plays until his fingers and forearms and shoulders tire.

He downloads Grindr and Scruff and sifts through the profiles on his phone. There are tight-bodied kanakas and scrawny Filipinos and sweet-eyed haoles. But there's no one there looking for love. He downloads OK Cupid and Plenty of Fish. He signs in and reviews his profile, which is relatively empty. He doesn't list his stats other than his age. He says he went to college. He says he likes the sea-beach and bubble tea and good conversation. He says he doesn't read much but listens to music like it's "going out of style." He's says he's looking for a man from 18-70 with any kind of body. He's never posted a photo, but he's thought about posting one of someone else—someone he's found in a Google search that looks just normal enough—and hopes that if they did meet up, that person would look past his lying, understand that he only did it because he just wanted a chance, that once they met him and got to know him they might not see his body, but see his love. Then he deletes all those apps and begins mantra 9: *I am surrounded and protected by healing white light.*

This is how Small Man's weeks move until Thursday when he practices ukulele all day, and the night comes and he climbs to the stage, and he plays and sings and perspires, but it doesn't matter, because the people clap and whistle and cheer because, he thinks, this is the only place a fat, Hawaiian man can be adored.

Friday morning, Small Man opens his eyes at 6:00 a.m. when the sun has risen. The ceiling fan spins fast enough that it rocks, and every ten-or-so seconds seems like it might rip into the white, popcorn ceiling. He speaks aloud Mantra 19: *Lots of new and exciting things are opening up in my life.* He visualizes those things. He sees himself not skinny, but thinner. He sees himself on stage at Blaisdell Arena, playing for thousands. Jack Johnson joins him on stage. He sees a Hawaiian man offstage, pumping his fist into the air, smiling, mouthing *I Love You.* Small Man repeats the mantra twenty times and it feels so good that he commits to another twenty, but before he can finish, the phone rings.

"Aloha," he says into the receiver, the cord bound in kinks, forcing him to roll to his side and crane his head to the night stand.

"Is your Auntie."

"Aloha, Auntie. Why you call so early?"

"Boy, is your mada." There is a small pause, which is enough time for Small Man to push himself to a sitting position. "She not well, Boy."

"What you mean?"

There is another pause and, suddenly, Small Man is standing with the base of the phone in his other hand moving to the wall, to the light switch.

"Henry's dog, da one at da corner, went bit her."

While his heart has gone into a rapid beat, it begins to settle. "Oh, go take her to the doctor then."

"No, Boy. She went got bit one week ago. She no get better."

"How you mean?" Small Man asks.

There is another pause, longer this time. There is the sound of his Auntie thinking, whether she is rubbing her chin or scratching her forehead.

"She mad, Boy," his Auntie says then continues to explain how after the bite, which wasn't too bad, they dressed the wound with mashed taro leaves to cleanse and draw out any poison then rubbed it down with kukui nut oil to soothe. After, her muscles cramped and a fever set in. "And now she drooling, Boy. Just like one mad dog."

"Auntie, take her to hospital," Small Man says, with a desperate pitch in his voice.

"Dr. Wanaka went stop by and said 'No can do anything but keep her comfortable.'" There was non-silence again. "She going da kine, Boy. You come home now." Then she hangs up.

Small Man thinks about the fridge and seeing what might be there to allay his anxiety. He knows there's deli ham and gouda cheese. He knows there's lau laus. He knows there's a Skinny Cow Mint Chip ice cream bar in the freezer. But he knows he can't. He mustn't. So he packs, though it's not so much packing as throwing random clothes into his plain black backpack. He doesn't think about which pair of shorts or how many underwear because his head is still in the fridge then back to his mom. But when he thinks of his mom and her dying, his head is back in the fridge. Within minutes he's toeing his slippers and grabbing his keys from the abalone shell on the small kitchen table, then he's passing the fridge.

"Come on, bruddah," he says to himself. "Come on," he says earnestly.

He opens the door, surveys, and sees the pint of low-fat buttermilk and he knows that it will calm him because he knows that it has only 100 calories per cup. He takes the carton and he's out the door.

Small Man stopped driving two years ago. The last car he had was a two-door Ford Fiesta, but he abandoned it when he got so heavy the car scrapped speed bumps and the kids would point and laugh, the steering wheel tight to his belly and chest. *What I must have looked like?* he thought. *Like I'd been there my whole life and the car just grew around me.* With a brief look from a woman pushing a stroller, a look that might have had nothing to do with him, might have been saying nothing more than anything about her own life, Small Man pulled over at Ala Wai Park and left the Fiesta, and when the notice came from impound, he didn't respond.

He waits for the bus because he stopped taking taxis soon after he abandoned his car. There were all sorts of crazies on the bus and that brought him a kind of comfort. Even if they judged him, he didn't care.

At the airport, in the security check line, he knows they're all looking at him. Their faces say: "Ke Akua, please do not let him be on my flight. And, if so, please do not let him be in my aisle. And, if so, just not next to me. Aloha." But the flight isn't full, and when the door closes he hoists himself from the aisle seat, where he is taking up half of the middle seat, nods to the woman at the window, and pushes his way to the back, where he can feel comfortable in his own row.

When the plane lifts off, his self-concern subsides and he is finally left without distraction to consider his mother. The last time he saw her was three years ago when his Tutu Mary passed, who was short and lean and a hard, troubled woman, which showed in the deep creases on her face. She was rarely rude, but when pushed was mean. She was skeptical and suspicious and kept her distance in conversation. And when the family was together, there was a tension that sat in the air above. Her children were cautious and overly courteous, ready to tend to any perceived need—though not desire, because they couldn't be sure what kind of desire that might be. She wasn't affectionate, even in her death, saying to her children, "just leave me here to go." And this, Small Man believes, is why his mother has always been so soft and giving, willing to bend in any direction, willing to offer any sort of comfort.

Because of that, Small Man feels terrible. He hasn't been home because he's gotten bigger, so much bigger than she will have imagined. To be stuck with himself is one thing, but to be revealed, made to really see himself through other eyes—the sense of it was unbearable. Still, here he is, making his slow disembarkment down the white, metal stairs, which strain under his weight, then across the tarmac, its absorbed heat pushing up and around him so that each step is like an ever-warming cocoon, and he can feel the sweat build and pour, and the anxiety explode until his legs are quaking, until he remembers Affirmation No. 2: *I choose to breathe in relaxation and breathe out stress.* And that gets him into the airport, past baggage claim, and out the shiny, sliding doors.

Home is 30 miles from the airport, on the other side of the island. He wants to walk because he's sworn off taxis, but he can't be certain that even a few miles won't kill him. Resistant, he stands in the queue.

"Aloha," says a tiny, aged, brown woman in front of him.

"Aloha," he says back, wiping his brow with the back of his hand. "So hot out hea, no?" she says.

Small Man thinks about how she has no idea. "Yes. So hot, auntie."

Then the woman beckons him down to her ear, and he bends, the perspiration dripping to the concrete. "No be shame. Hot cut hea for all us," she says and pats him on the hand.

Small Man smiles softly, hoping she will see how much he appreciates her kindness. But, really, he doesn't. He hates it. Because now he's thinking about how everyone is sorry for him.

"Ho! You fucka!" a thick, bass voice catches his attention. "Small Man, that you?"

When Small Man turns his head, he sees a police car at the curb. A shaka is extended out the driver's window. Small Man shakas back, trying to place the man's tough, dark face, his eyes hidden behind reflective sunglasses.

Small Man doesn't respond, but changes his kind smile to a generic grin.

"Hui," the policeman calls out, and Small Man moves to the car window. The policeman takes off his glasses. "Shit, bruddah. Dat *is* you!"

Small Man can see it's Paulie Boy, one of the neighborhood kids from his hometown.

"Ho," Small Man says, "you one cop?"

"Long time now, brah."

"Shoots," Small Man says. "Das alright." And they both pause in that for a moment, unsure of what to say next.

"What you standing over there foa?" Paulie asks, pointing to the queue.

Because Small Man has a grip of memories about Paulie that all end with Paulie being generally stupid, he has to catch himself before saying anything rude. "Getting one cab."

"Where you go foa?"

"Home," Small Man says.

"Get in, brah. I go take you," Paulie says.

Without hesitation, and because he thinks how any judgement that Paulie could bring at him would mean nothing, Small Man starts for the passenger door, rounding the car's front end. Paulie revs the engine as he passes, and Small Man startles for a second. He hears Paulie laughing and saying in a high-pitched voice, "Sucka."

Initially, Small Man is concerned because the ride started with Paulie asking so many questions about living in Honolulu and singing at the bar and if there were any lovers. The first questions were easy enough to field because they required yes or no answers, but it was the last question that Small Man stutters on until he finally says, "Not really," which makes him feel worse because he thinks he should have just said "no" or "look at me" or nothing at all. Small Man stares out the windshield, watching the white, shoulder stripe continue. Then Paulie is on to talking about his own life, of which Small Man pays attention only briefly enough to hear that Paulie's girl left him in a bad way, until he realizes that it doesn't matter if he is listening or not, that simply nodding his head will be enough.

Small Man remembers how hard and nice Paulie Boy had been as a child. He was the first to call Small Man *fatty* and the first to defend him when others did the same. He once told Small Man that, because he was so fat, he would never get a date to the County Friendship Dance, then abandoned his own to watch music videos through the night, not once complaining even when they could hear the music spilling past the walls of the dance hall, even when it died out and there were beach parties to be had. Outside of those memories and a few more generic, now nebulous, scenes there was nothing more to their friendship, if that is even how it should be named.

"You wanna suck my dick?" Paulie asks, pulling to a stop at Small Man's home, the long, dirt driveway climbing up and over a poky hill.

Paulie slowly leans toward him, pauses, then laughs and gives him a double-punch in the arm. "Fucking got you, brah. Fucking got you." Then Small Man's laughing, too, and the ringing subsides. "Brah, you no paying attention."

"Sorry," Small Man says looking down, trying to find any kind of words to string together that would explain it all, because he thinks he might want to tell it all to someone, that it might change something, though he can't imagine what.

"Why you home foa?" Paulie asks.

Though it's only seconds, it's as if time has stopped, where—maybe—any consideration could be made.

"My ma no good, brah. She da kine," Small Man says, looking out the front window then, without really meaning to, at Paulie.

Paulie's face is tight, his jaw clenched. "Mm," Paulie says then purses his lips, keeping his stare straight ahead.

The mood is adrift so Small Man opens the car door and thanks Paulie for the ride to which Paulie nods and says, "Brah, you gotta fix that fence. This place look junk."

"For reals," Small Man says.

Standing there, watching the dust explode behind Paulie's car as it peels and fishtails, Small Man feels a comfort—the kind that comes from being a part of something that feels like acceptance, or having never been separate, the kind he hasn't felt in a very long time.

At the top of the hill, he rests on the broad stump of a mango tree. He surveys the small house. Nothing much has changed since his last visit, though he can see how two siding boards have rotted and the blue paint has faded. When he widens his gaze, he sees the unkempt lawn. The Bermuda grass is tall and thick and gray. At the fence line, five feet from the outer wall, the lilikoi has gone wild, the bright yellow fruit spreading itself along the ground to a young carambola tree, choking out the starry fruit, reaching for the sun. Past their simple home, the land is crowded. Old houses have been razed and replaced by winter cottages and sprawling boutique ranches. The country he knew as a child was slowly becoming another kind of country, a gleaming kind of country.

"Der da boy," his Auntie bellows from the front door.

"Looking good, Auntie," Small Man says, hoisting himself from the stump.

"Oh, stop, you," Auntie says pulling at the collar of her hibiscus mu'u mu'u. "So fresh."

When Small Man hugs she trembles and that scares him, but the hug itself feels so good. He thinks it's been those three years since he's felt real touch, not simply the shaking of a hand or the kiss on a cheek, so he holds into the hug a bit longer.

"Where's ma?" he asks. Auntie pulls her head from his shoulder and motions to the house, keeping her gaze to the ground.

Inside, the curtains are drawn, which makes the must that much thicker.

"No light?" Small Man asks.

"She no like."

"Can open the windows, though," Small Man says and Auntie moves from his side to pull the slats in the living room then onto the kitchen.

Nothing has changed; every same old object in its place. The nappy, green couch. The Korean War mug that belonged to his father—though he was never in the war, never once saw any battle, but drank himself to death just the same—on the doily, on the sandalwood coffee table, its scent long gone. The most uncomfortable koa wood chair, still with no cushion. On the hutch, the dark, varnished ipu his mother used to keep time while she sang mele next to the pink, feathered ili ili hula gourds. On the wall, the four white frames of her three brothers and one sister, all, except for Auntie, gone now in one way or another, surrounding a gold-painted frame of Tutu. He'd never been sure if it was there as a symbol of his mother's love, or a reminder of his grandmother's sternness—her chestnut hair wrapped atop her head, her dour face, her pursed lips, her glassy eyes peering through thin, rimless spectacles. Past the small room, a hallway. To the left, a bathroom, still no shower. To the right, the bedroom door closed—the ticking of a fan pushing through.

"She in der," Auntie says, pointing like beyond is something otherworldly. "Swallow one time real hard, Boy." Though he wants to show some strength and cast her advice aside, he does as told then turns the knob.

There's the yellowed, oscillating fan. There's the peeling white chest of drawers. There's the square white matching nightstand. There's the rusted metal folding chair. Then there's the bed where his mother lies in a rose-tinted nightgown, moisture pasting the fabric to her boney body. Her breathing is truncated. Her head twitches in time. Her eyes are closed.

Small Man takes in a large breath, and it's not even must, it's like inhaling the sweltering drip and stink of a deep rain forest. It's hard to be faced with such a scene, so Small Man turns to leave.

"Well, ain't you a sight for sore eyes," his mother says.

"Hi, mama," he replies, pivoting back.

"We're fixing to luau," she says, and he doesn't know how to respond because they are clearly not.

"Come sit," she says, pointing to the chair. Small Man eases himself onto the metal. "You been gone so long," she says.

"Been busy," he says. "You know how it get."

"Oh, don't I know it," she says and begins a long series of dry swallows.

"You want water?" he asks and quickly rises.

"No, no. The water make me sick." She puts her first two fingers in her mouth and sucks. Her nails are long and have grown dark. When she removes them, a thick strand of salvia follows.

She turns her head to eye him. "Looking so healthy, my boy. Look so," she pauses and raises both hands in the air, her fingers balling into fists, "ikaika."

Then he's up and out the door, his heavy foot falls reverberating through the living room until he's back in the yard, to the stump, the tears coming. He thinks, *It's one thing to feel weak; it's much harder to be told you're strong when you're not.* Then he's thinking about his 16th birthday luau and the buffet that was prepared and how he ate two proper plates at the long church table on the front lawn, under the mango tree, and how it made him so nervous, all the people from the village and the school kids that he was sure weren't his friends, all their talking and playing and singing, and how he grabbed the bowl of macaroni salad and walked away, eating it with his bare right hand, all the way down the dirt road until he reached the small village cemetery, and perched himself on a headstone at first, the shame of disrespect coming over him even at 16 so that he sat on the ground alongside a patch of gardenia, and finished off the salad, catching the last of it all with his first two fingers circling round the rim—two fingers, just like his mother moments ago. *And this is how's it been for a long time now*, he thinks—all the anxiety and the terrible things pushing him to eat.

"Honey," Auntie says and gathers up his one big hand into her two tiny ones, so tiny they look like old child hands.

Dr. Wanaka tells him that because she is older, and because she waited, all they can do is comfort her suffering with drugs, probably morphine; she will sweat and drool and seizure and hallucinate, maybe fear water, maybe light, maybe become agitated, maybe paranoid, and, eventually, the swelling of her brain will lead to a coma, and that it, most likely, will happen within a matter of days, maybe just one. All of this, Small Man hears with a kind of strange calm, the kind that happens when life is sudden.

That first day, at home, Small Man and Auntie prepare the bedroom with leis of sweet smelling pikaki. They draw kukui nuts on long nails, fastened to the ends of scrap 2x4's—a low, gentle, light. Auntie burns dried hala palm husk, and the room clouds into a brindled haze. They take turns watching her fade in and out of consciousness.

Ku'u, their neighbor to the south, comes with laulaus and chicken long rice. She stands on the porch in her pink mu'u mu'u and slippers, her grey hair in a bun. She knocks and waits and Small Man greets her and he takes the food to the kitchen while she stays on the porch—certain not to enter, keeping her respect—

and when he returns, she takes him by the forearms and says, "You a good one," and pats him on the face and slowly makes her way down the path to the road.

By early evening the news has spread, and in quick succession Dano and Cirella bring pork, fish, and beer. Jasmine brings fried chicken and haupia and iced tea. Kanani brings vodka and orange juice. Then it's T.J. and Leina'ala and the Agbayanis and some others that Small Man does not know. Auntie tells each of them to stay and they do, forming a circle of folding lawn chairs. None of them asks to see his mother, and Small Man isn't sure it's respect. He's thinking it might be the kind of distance that means *who wants to see a woman dying? Who wants to be reminded of their own mortality, of how bad it can be or get?* And he wants to blame them, as if, in his absence, they didn't take care, or enough care.

Soon they are all drinking and talking story about his mother. There are stories he's heard before: of her youthful beauty, of how her hula was graced by the gods.

Then Cirella says, "Boy, how she love your fadda."

Then Kanani says in a vodka glaze, "Da bruddah could drink," her eyebrows raised, a dark kind of story in her tone. She laughs, but no one else does, because that kind of dark might fill the night and find its way into the house.

So, Dano begins a story about Small Man's father, who, after being laid off from the pineapple plantation, which was to be shut down and moved out of country for cheap labor, became furious, starting his drunk early in the morning, and made his way to the plantation offices—a gleaming, white sprawling kind of building—and pulled down his pants and shit right there in front of the main doors, right on the foundation placard, and when the bosses came to the windows to look, he yelled over and over, "You like? You like?" And Dano says it in a funny way, which lightens the evening back again and eases Kanani's comment.

Then there is song and more drink deep into the evening, until eyes are glassy and words become mumbles and there is only the crackle of a fire.

Then Kanani raises her 8th glass and says, looking at Small Man as best she can, "You know what your ma did?"

Dano interrupts, saying, "Come now, K," worried she'll tell something terrible.

"Boy," Kanani says, "your ma made da life okay." Then pauses. "We all get given what we get given, and she made da life okay." There is silence. "You understand?"

When he searches his memories, though they are scattered and threadbare, he knows his mother has turned what kind of life they had into something good and acceptable. But, in some ways the stories don't matter. They are just moments in a woman's life, times which Small Man cannot recall or before he was born. *They will not fill the void,* he thinks.

When Small Man looks around, the party nods solemnly. And, as if it were a convocation, they begin to fold their chairs and leave with parting hugs and kisses. Then Auntie retires too, and Small Man is left alone.

The second day Small Man sits on the porch, staring out into the thick of the trees, imagining what it will all be like when she is gone, hoping that maybe she will never go, that by keeping watch it might spark something unseen, yet unknown to him, and bring her back. And while he is in prayer, his hands clasped over his lap, he hears the sound of a car approaching, the loud beats of rap getting louder and stopping at the fence line.

Small Man watches as Paulie Boy makes his way to the porch, carrying a white, plastic grocery bag in one hand, a six pack of Twisted Tea in the other. He isn't boisterous; he walks with a kind of reverence.

"No good inside?" Paulie asks.

"Just need some air," Small Man says.

Paulie cracks two teas and pulls a bottle of peach schnapps from the grocery bag. Small Man giggles.

"No laugh, brah," Paulie says. "This the real kine shit. Get you where you need to go." Paulie uncaps the bottle and takes a long pull and passes it to Small Man.

Small Man can't tell if he wants to drink or not. Not drunk, he can see and feel everything carefully, systematically. There are no surprises. At the same time, he thinks how nice it would be to let all the control go. He pauses.

"Come, brah," Paulie says.

Small Man grabs the bottle. "You going give me diabetes."

"You not already get?" Paulie asks. "All us kanakas get."

Small Man thinks how it is good to not feel careful or have people act careful around him.

"She going maké?" Paulie asks, and it's the kind of question that, when put frankly, makes Small Man's throat tighten, makes his stomach curl, creates a blinding flash.

"The doctor says she going. Maybe in a few days, maybe," Small Man says.

Paulie clenches his jaw again and pulls the bottle of schnapps from Small Man and takes a long gulp. "Sorry don't cut it," he says. "Still, I sorry, brah. Your ma was so nice to me even when I was a fucka."

"Dat da truth," Small Man says and Paulie laughs, sniffling then wiping his nose. Small Man doesn't look.

"What you going do? Stay hea or go back?"

"Don't know."

"You got one good life in da city?"

Small Man wants to say that he is happy, that he has all the friends, that he is in love, that he is full.

"Nah. It's junk," Small Man says. "One day to da next."

Paulie Boy nods his head and puts his arm around Small Man's shoulder, bringing Small Man's head tight to his neck, but Small Man pulls away taking the bottle back and drinking.

"What, no can be affection cause you gay?" Paulie asks.

"Just, no can," Small Man says, and he's trying not to think about how he is built to love but maybe not to have affection.

"How you then?" Small Man asks, and that's enough to get Paulie Boy talking about his girl again and all the troubles.

"Always got the girl troubles," Paulie Boy says then continues on about his life on Maui, and then they leave talking about love and a dying mother. They talk about comic books and music and movies, and if they'll ever go to the mainland and why, until they've finished the six-pack and half the bottle of peach schnapps.

"You want me stay?" Paulie Boy asks.

"No, brah. You go. Next time," Small Man says.

"Shoots then. You call me. We go find you some hot meat."

Small Man Laughs.

Paulie moves down the path then looks back and says, "Big Boy. Remember, you beautiful."

Small Man gives a shaka.

In the following days, Dr. Wanaka occasionally stops by to administer the morphine shots. A few neighbors bring pork and fish and cake, sometimes just leaving dishes at the doorstep. There are times when Small Man eats it all, and there are times when he sits in the metal chair searching his memory for an affirmation that might fit, but nothing comes. And then there is just waiting, which can be the cruelest of things.

On the sixth day, her breathing is shallower and her skin wets, and Small Man thinks it's impossible that she has any fluid left in her but blood, and maybe not even that. Auntie stays in the living room, kneeling on the hardwood floor, shredding and weaving ti leaves into strands, a kanawai to ward off the evil spirits who prey upon the vulnerable. And that night, through the ticking fan he can hear the wind pick up, whistling along the shutter slats. Then the rain begins, first in time with the ticking then quickly rising above until there is only a roar off the tin roof. When Small Man looks to his mother, her eyes are open, blinking rapidly. Then she's holding her arms over her face and screaming, and it's the only sound he can hear over the rain.

"Sista," Auntie yells, coming to Small Man's side, pressing herself tight under his arm.

"Help me," his mother says, "No can, the rain."

Auntie is saying back to her that there is no rain inside the house, that they are protected, but she keeps on and Auntie keeps on back, occasionally trying to pin her sister's arms to show her there is nothing but the sound. And while they scream back and forth, Auntie becoming maniacal in her argument, swept up in the momentum, Small Man hurries to the front door where an umbrella hangs from a two-penny nail. He pulls Auntie away so hard she stumbles to the wall then runs out of the room. He opens the umbrella right above his mother's head, and says, "Ma. It's okay." He's meeting her eye to eye, staring into her now, repeating "it's okay, it's okay," until it becomes a drone.

Slowly, her twitching subsides. Her face, once a contorted, purple mash, unfolds. Her eyes lagger until she is not blinking at all, until she looks away and stares at the ceiling. Her chest isn't moving, and he worries she's passed. Then the rain eases, and, once again, he can hear the fan and, past that, the low mumblings of Auntie in the living room. And just as Small Man thinks it's happened, that the time has come with all its sadness and relief, she clasps her hands together, resting them on her chin—not as a prayer, but as a blessing—smiles, tears mixing with perspiration, and says, "Boy, you my roof."

With that, Small Man knows he's been given the only affirmation he'll ever need, that he could stand there for days, for weeks, past the shaking and sweating, his body consuming all his fat, his muscles becoming stone, until his skin sags in great folds, until his toe nails have grown into the floor.

TOM OF BOALT HALL
GAR MCVEY-RUSSELL

1988 marks my 50th law school class reunion, an appropriate time, I feel, to discuss my experiences attending UC Berkeley's Boalt Hall in the mid 1930s. To do so properly, I also have to include the story of Tom Kelly.

Very few have seen this letter Tom sent me in 1937. But in order to tell the whole story, I must include his words.

My Dearest,

Hopefully, by the time you read this, I will have already departed for my journey. I'm not one for long goodbyes, hence this letter. I hope in time you'll understand. But before I go, I wanted to leave you a full account of my time at Berkeley in which you played so essential a part. It's the very least I can do. I owe you a debt I could never fully repay.

So, that first day, September 2, 1935. Why was I late? I had left my little room at the Downtown Berkeley Y in plenty of time. I arrived on campus from the west and was stunned by its beauty. The Eucalyptus Grove! The stately Life Sciences Building! The Campanile rising majestically in the distance! As much as I loved rustic UCLA, I felt that at Berkeley I had truly arrived. There I came upon The Statue. You know which one I mean. I had never seen two muscled men, footballers no less, so beautifully rendered or in so tender and intimate a pose. I always loved the dominance of the standing player, his foot on the thigh of the kneeling player. Yet at the same time, he's touching the kneeler's back and gazing on him so tenderly as the kneeler wraps the dominant's calf with a bandage. I stared at it for an eternity that morning. I felt so proud to be associated with a campus that displayed such art.

I strutted up the path to Boalt and entered the building all puffed up, tail feathers higher than a peacock's, and then, well, you know what happened next.

"Ah! How good of you to join us at last, Mr. Kelly," Professor Wicker announced.

Standing just inside the backdoor was a handsome, tall, ginger-haired young man, clean-shaven and nattily dressed in a tan suit, white shirt, and a striped tan tie with matching handkerchief in his breast pocket. Tufts of his hair swept carefree over his ears. A dandy who arrived late to make an entrance.

The professor, who had a deep voice and slow, authoritative diction, began humbling the new guy with Socratic questioning.

"You are aware, Mr. Kelly, that class commenced some three minutes ago, are you not?"

"Yes, Professor Wicker."

"And, of course, you already have received, via the largesse of the faculty, a one-week deferment to allow you time to get situated in Berkeley, did you not, Mr. Kelly?"

"Yes, sir, I did."

A posh dilettante who wants to play lawyer but couldn't even bother arriving to law school on time. Better and better, I smirked.

"And yet, despite this luxurious time allotment, you arrive at my lecture three minutes late. Explain, Mr. Kelly."

"I…"

I was lost, deflated. Not 30 seconds into my career as a law student and already I had failed miserably. I looked around the room in hopes of finding something, anything, that I could hold on to, just a modicum of sympathy. And then I saw you. Those deep brown eyes, that velvety dark-brown skin, that gorgeous face. And you looked so fine in that blue suit. I had found my salvation, and he was looking back at me.

In my head, I went into a ridiculous rage—Why is posh boy staring at *me,* the only Negro in the room? We got nothing in common. Is he looking at me for sympathy? Guess what? I got none to give—but such was my way at the time. I used indignation to smother my real question: why am I transfixed by his penetrating grey eyes? I often locked away questions that mattered into a mental vault fortified by indignation or anger or some other inappropriate emotion.

Eventually, the man turned to address the professor again.

"I thought class met in Boalt Hall, Professor. I do apologize."

"Ah! So, you went to the classrooms in Boalt first, did you, Mr. Kelly?"

"Yes, sir."

The class snickered, exchanged knowing looks. None of the four classrooms in the ornately built but highly diminutive Boalt Hall could contain so many students.

"And you discovered," the professor continued, "via the class announcement cards outside the doors that you had made a mistake, correct?"

"That's correct, sir."

"So how did you come to learn where this class actually meets, Mr. Kelly?"

"I went to the library, sir, and one of the librarians told me where to go."

"Resourceful. Our law library is always a fount of information, one I encourage all students to use frequently. But not during lecture."

The professor paused. Snickering continued.

"Are you aware of how many students are in this room, Mr. Kelly?"

"I believe the entering class size is 150, sir."

"151, Mr. Kelly," the professor corrected. "Do you know the size of the second-year class?"

"I do not, sir."

"We have 74 students in our second-year class. This time last year, their class size was 141. Therefore, the putative class of 1937 already has lost via attrition nearly half of its members." The professor paused again. No one snickered. "So it has been for every class at the School of Jurisprudence. And so it shall be for this one, the putative class of 1938. Only those who have proven themselves up to the rigors of a legal education shall return for a second year. Then, and only then, will you have earned the privilege to sit for class inside the Boalt Memorial Hall of Law. For now, Mr. Kelly, you are here in Wheeler Hall with the undergraduates, a rank beginner in law just as they are rank beginners in their fields of study."

"Yes, sir."

"You may take a seat, Mr. Kelly."

"Thank you, sir."

Empty desks surrounded me like a moat. After a week, no one had ventured to sit next to the sole Negro. My old buddy Dorothy Legend would have, of course. And her friendliness might have warmed others up to me. But I thought it best if we kept our friendship under wraps while at school. She was one of only seven women in our class, and thus had her own cross to bear. I don't want to add to your burden, I told her. She sighed and told me that I wasn't a poison petunia. Dorothy had no problem flouting convention. We met in freshman Chemistry lab when she marched directly to me, introduced herself, and suggested that we buddy up for the day's experiment. I froze, my Louisiana-born father's admonition filling my head: "Stay away from the white girls! They got a lot of trees up there on that campus and rope ain't hard to find." She had smooth, fair skin, deep-set eyes under low eyebrows, pretty nose and lips, and neatly cropped, dark brown hair. She wore a long-sleeved blue dress, but also had on these big, clunky sneakers that could pass for army boots. I laughed at the sneakers. That was what broke the ice.

Mr. Dandy breached the moat and sat right next to me with a bright smile on his face and an extended hand.

"Tom Kelly," he whispered.

Astonished, I weakly took his hand.

"Philip Hines," I whispered back.

Philip is my middle name and was my identity at that time, stuffy, uptight, outwardly passionless. "Philip" brings to mind a persnickety bank clerk who fusses over the placement of a paperclip on a finished report rather than the quality of the report's content.

I glanced across the room at Dorothy after Tom sat next to me. She was staring at me, as I knew she would, her head tilted, her mouth in the neatest little smile. I knew what was coming. At our next get-together at her apartment, just a few blocks north of campus, she will lubricate me with wine and then mercilessly badger me with "Do you like him?" until I cry uncle or, more likely, throw a pillow at her. For years she played matchmaker with me, much to my amused annoyance. I explained to her over and over that I already had my life planned out. Go to law school. Become an attorney. Join the NAACP legal team. End lynching, segregation, Jim Crow, and all the nightmares black folks faced. A boyfriend was not part of the plan. "Everyone's gotta fuck sometime," Dorothy often retorted.

In truth, my self-denial led to a miserable life.

"Would you explain to us, Mr. Burr, the three basic elements of contract law?"

Edgar Burr stood, a man of short stature, dressed in a dated black suit. He had a rounded face, short-cropped hair, small ears, a virtually lipless mouth, and dull eyes behind round, wire-rimmed glasses. His assumed urbanity could not hide his good old boy core.

I had already seen his true nature a week earlier. While changing textbooks at my locker in the basement of Boalt, Edgar stood at his locker glaring at me, his face tight as a ball. Then he slammed his locker and I jumped. With the evilest smirk I'd ever seen, he said, "Do I scare you, coon boy?" as he walked out the room.

In truth, no one seemed to like the man much. In every class, he went out of his way to ingratiate himself with the professor, always raising his hand, always answering in long sentences peppered with needless $10 words.

"Fine, Mr. Burr," Professor Wicker said, interrupting one of Edgar's tangents. "Now discuss for us the third basic element."

Edgar stood still, his stubby fingers clasped, his thumbs fidgeting. The steady drone of his voice ceased.

"Can you not recall the third basic element, Mr. Burr?" the professor asked. After a slight pause, Edgar, looking down, admitted that he could not.

"Can someone give Mr. Burr some assistance? Yes, Mr. Kelly?" Tom stood.

"A consideration is required, sir, to make the contract enforceable."

"And what exactly is a consideration, Mr. Kelly?"

The Dandy turned into a crack scholar and went to town. Bargain theory. Adequacy of Values. The Pre-existing Duty Rule. Formality. For each concept, he cited case after case of precedence, by name, year, and jurisdiction. He spoke with authority, not from aged wisdom like the professor, but from his effusive passion for the subject, and his delight in sharing that passion with us.

Dorothy raised both eyebrows while nodding her head. I sat in awe, my resistance to his charms weakening. By contrast, Edgar's face turned beet red, his mouth pinched.

Professor Wicker finally ran out of questions. "Well, I think we have thoroughly covered the subject. Thank you, Mr. Kelly."

Class ended. I stood and gave Tom a solid handshake. "That was masterful," I said.

"Thank you!" His smile was as warm as the touch of his hand.

"So, what's up with Mr. Burr?" he asked.

I rolled my eyes, said I'd explain outside. Tom asked me to wait for him, then walked toward the front row where Edgar sat. Various hands slapped him on the back accompanied by words of congratulation. Then Professor Wicker walked up to him, regarding him with arms folded.

"A beginner, Mr. Kelly, but perhaps not so rank after all. Well done."

"Thank you, sir."

The professor walked away.

Tom stood in front of Edgar, smiled, stretched out his hand. Edgar rose stiffly, clearly perplexed by the friendly greeting and intimidated by Tom's height. Instead of responding, he brusquely pushed passed Tom and departed the classroom hurriedly.

Tom and I had a good laugh about him as we exited.

❖

The basement of Boalt Hall was a men-only space, a holdover from when various restrictions governed the lives of the students in the tiny law building. Who could study where, who had access to tobacco, and so forth. By the 30s, only the basement gender restriction remained. The school had set aside a Ladies' Cloakroom that doubled as a study hall in a small anteroom off the law library on the second floor. By contrast, the spacious basement had the air of a private men's club, with clubrooms, a locker room for storing books and clothes, and a restroom with a shower stall.

OK, it wasn't just the statue that delayed me to Wicker's class. When I first entered Boalt, I jogged down to the basement to stow books in my locker and saw a guy walking around naked, except for a skimpy towel around his waist. Who knew we had a shower in the men's room? Such amenities for law students! My eyes followed him into the shower. Only my eyes! I did not go in with him. But I stood there daydreaming. And eventually, as you know, the shower became my domain for the whole first year.

One evening at the end of spring term, I went to the basement with the intention of retrieving books from my locker for a planned all-nighter at home. But first I really had to go pee. I flew through the locker room, into the restroom, and straight to a urinal just to the left of the doorless entryway. The release felt so good. I had sat in the library and held it for too long.

Truth be told, the release I experienced actually came from holding my cock in that space at that time of year. At the end of term with finals looming, overstressed guys emitted pheromones that called to each other for sexual release. I knew this because I once experienced it in the third floor men's room in Doe Library as an undergrad. At that time, it scared me, and I avoided the restrooms at night during midterms and finals from then on. I never allowed myself to sate that energy, which flowed through me as naturally as Strawberry Creek flows through campus. That evening, I brooked no denial. I turned my head to the right and stared at the shower. I heard its water running.

I saw *two* pairs of feet under the curtain, slightly staggered by their stances and facing each other. The man whose feet were turned away from me lowered himself to a squatting position. His ass crack appeared just below the curtain. He's giving head, I marveled, as I kept staring.

A face appeared between the folds of the curtain. "Tom!" I muttered.

Steamy mist curled around his flattened red hair. Our eyes fixed on each other, until Tom slowly withdrew back into the mist and curtain.

When I saw you standing there in profile, my love, your beautiful cock at full attention, I swear my own cock added inches. How much I wanted to touch you, feel your cock against mine, put my lips to it and suck its essence, as the shower waters anointed both our hot bodies.

I heard someone walk into the locker room. I clumsily shoved my hardened cock into my pants, flushed the urinal, and loudly coughed. The squatter giving Tom head ran out of the shower and into the adjacent toilet stall. Tom remained unseen in the mist. I went to a sink opposite the toilet stalls and rinsed my hands. Afterward, I leaned my head through the entryway into the locker room. Whoever it had been did not linger. I turned to face the shower again in time to see Tom step out with a towel wrapped around his waist. He walked up to me, placed his hand on my back, brought his lips very close to the side of my face; I held my breath, thinking this can't be happening.

"Thank you," Tom whispered.

Then he walked into the locker room, opened his locker, and dropped his towel. For a few glorious moments, his ass appeared, round and firm with whiffs of red hair on each cheek. It flexed as he shifted his weight while slipping on his underpants. Tom finished dressing quickly, then turned to me again.

"Are you heading home?" he asked, an obvious invitation to walk out of the building together.

"I have to get something in the library before it closes," I said, a complete lie. Tom smiled and bid me a good night then departed. The squatter emerged from the toilet stall, still wet but fully dressed. He also departed, but not without giving me a warm smile, a silent thanks for running interference.

I drifted into the last toilet stall, the one farthest from the little shower. A tear trailed on my cheek.

That tall, red-headed dandy brought fiery passion into my otherwise rote existence. Don't just study life away! Tom chided. Come on! The year had been a feast. Ibsen in Wheeler Auditorium for lunch. Frankenstein at the movies for supper. Britten at midnight on Dorothy's record player for a nightcap.

And my mind undressed Tom each time we got together, my eyes following every contour of his clothing, the bulging muscles, the lump in his crotch, the crease at his ass crack. Never before had I fallen so hard for someone. And now this, naked from head to toe, a more magnificent body I could not have imagined. It was more than I could stand.

I pumped good and hard sitting in that stall. At climax, I wanted to let out a blood-curling scream, but kept the sound within while my mouth gaped wide open. My ears rang, my mind and body drained. As the ringing abated, my panting eased and my heart slowed. Come dripped from my hands to my legs and into the toilet bowl. Feebly, I took some tissue and wiped my hands. For a long while I sat, undisturbed, unnoticed, alone. Then I closed my eyes, cupped my hands over my face and sobbed as I had never sobbed before.

I do hope that future classes perform some kind of ritual to mark surviving that first brutal year at Boalt. I know that people credit me and my whimsies as one of the reasons they survived. For this I am grateful. Please let them know. And tell Professor Wicker, too, how grateful I am that he was such a good sport, and great professor. I'm going to miss him.

To celebrate becoming second-year law students, Tom organized a special matriculation ceremony for our class. His popularity and passion for fun induced 69 out of 78 students to participate. Dorothy and I naturally took part.

On the first day of classes, our group gathered at 7:30 a.m. outside Room 124 Wheeler, our former home in exile. We wore bathrobes because black graduation robes were hard to come by in August. At 7:45, a procession clad in multicolored bathrobes moved single file out of Wheeler and across the street to the north side of Boalt Hall. We stood in front of the building in respectful silence to honor the 48% of the class who had not survived the cut. After the Campanile struck eight, Tom strode up the shallow steps and faced the crowd, the engraved BOALT HALL OF LAW sign looming over his head.

"Having proven ourselves up to the rigors of a legal education," he shouted, mimicking Wicker's voice and words, "I declare that the class of '38 has now earned the privilege to sit for class within the Boalt Memorial Hall of Law!"

We went crazy, creating a din that echoed between Boalt and neighboring California Hall behind us. Folks in both buildings and on the sidewalk looked at us as if we were mad, sweetening the moment. As the event ended, our former Contracts instructor himself appeared and walked up to Tom, arms crossed.

"Your idea, I take it?" he asked.

"Yes, Professor Wicker," Tom uttered, sheepishly. "I made sure that we ended in time to get to our 8:15 classes, sir."

A wry smirk appeared on Wicker's face. "Well played, Mr. Kelly. Welcome back."

I saw Edgar Burr standing inside the door, glowering, before turning sharply and walking away.

One could call Edgar the anti-Tom, someone perpetually dour, who lived in the past. For Edgar, modernity went no further than the age of hand cranked Victrolas and ragtime. All laws enacted past 1900 were suspect; I believed he wanted to reestablish slavery. No one knew much about Edgar's background, except that he came from Bakersfield, his father was a farmer, and that he had six siblings. People assumed he was deeply religious, but no one knew what church he attended or if he went at all. Tom thought he lacked passion for anything, including religion.

Edgar mostly associated with a small clique of similarly humorless people who held equally antiquated views. They should form a misery society together, Tom joked, a poor man's Diogenes Club where they could glower in each other's presence to their mutual dissatisfaction.

❖

What can I say about that Friday, my love? What can I say?

Slim Jenkins' Place on 7th Street in West Oakland was one of the few clubs in the East Bay that catered to a mixed-race crowd. I knew Dorothy and Tom would love it. But I hadn't expected the hero's welcome we received.

"He goes to Boalt Hall of Law up at Cal! So be real nice to Mr. Hines and his friends, now!"

I guess I should have realized, since two-thirds of the staff either knew me since childhood or went to my family's church. So "real nice" translated into extra barbecue, extra drinks, and the best table in the house. To top it off, the headliner that night was Duke Ellington and his Famous Orchestra, Harlem's greatest ambassadors visiting the Harlem of the West.

Cutting the rug with you and D was the best. And I loved how we could Lindy Hop together, even holding hands, and everyone thinking it was just college kids acting goofy. I think we stole the show, my love.

It wasn't much of a secret that I brought them to my neighborhood with the ultimate goal of asking Tom to come home with me. But despite that, and the gin and tonics, I still lacked the nerve to ask him over as the evening ended. But Dorothy, bless her, had a plan of her own.

"I'm going to my parents' place in Kensington, so I'm taking a cab," she said, yawning. "The club already called one for me. In fact, here it is."

She pecked us on the cheeks, French style. In my ear, she whispered, "Good luck, stud!"

In a flash, she was gone. Tom Kelly and I stood alone at 7th and Wood, just blocks from my place.

"Wanna walk me home?" I nearly whispered.

"Of course!" he said brightly.

I lived on Chase Street between Wood and Willow. When I started at Cal, my father suggested that I move to campus for privacy and a sense of independence. That option proved too expensive.

Mrs. Holloway, a senior member of our church, stepped forward and offered to rent the basement apartment in her Victorian to me.

"It's meant so much to me to stay living here while going to Cal," I told Tom.

"That's so beautiful the community has your back," Tom said.

It was a small studio. I augmented the pony wall separating the sleeping and living areas with sheer curtains. The bathroom was off the kitchen. Its ceiling was low enough that Tom had to consciously negotiate it. He did so while giggling. I invited him to sit on the bed, since I didn't have a couch or loveseat, just two chairs and a kitchen table that doubled as my desk. I put on a Bessie Smith record, bringing down the mood from hot swing to sultry blues and heated water in a pot for tea.

Tom slipped off his wing tips, removed his tie and beige suit jacket. "I like the boutonniere," I said.

"I like your pinstripe suit."

"Thanks."

The banter was sweet and short lived. Our lips locked as soon as I sat on the bed next to him. We had no reason for playing footsies with each other, having done so our entire first year at Boalt.

Tea never happened, though I turned off the pot before it burned. Disheveled sheets and the smell of come bore witness to our love making. We lay next to each other in the dark, bathed by the music of shared breaths and silence. I had never felt such bliss in my life.

"You sure your landlady couldn't hear us?" Tom asked.

"Naw," I laughed. "She's hard of hearing. Anyway, she plays the religious station until she falls asleep. The radio's probably still going, playing static."

Tom chuckled. "What does the J stand for in your name?"

"Oh, it's 'Jay.' J-A-Y. That's my first name."

"Mind if I call you Jay? It's less formal than Philip."

The very thought tickled me. Tom divorced me from the persnickety banker. "Of course you can."

We were silent for a long while, until I finally asked, "What are you thinking?"

"You hear my gears grinding?"

"Maybe."

"Just thinking about D. She's pretty amazing."

"She's one of a kind. Her parents are Quakers."

"Ah! Should have guessed."

"You know her father's a doctor at UC Medical in San Francisco." I felt Tom nodding. "He did part of his internship at a Negro hospital in Mississippi or Alabama. I forget which. He wanted to practice medicine for the most needy."

"Nice," Tom whispered.

"Her mother studied piano at a conservatory in New York in the 1890s. Get this, Antonin Dvořak taught there."

"No!"

"Yeah! D's mother studied with freaking Dvořak! Anyway, it was a very liberal school that encouraged girls and black folks to enroll. So, at the school her mother accompanied this black singer, a tenor named Harold Richard. They became lifelong friends. Dorothy grew up knowing him, and his boyfriend Winston. She calls them her uncles."

"Wow! Have you met them?"

"No. They moved to Paris when D was 10. Harold couldn't get any work. But she says they're doing fine. Van Vechten took a portrait of them. It's beautiful. They're beautiful." I started sniffling. Tom held me closer. "Dorothy's the first person to see me, really see me and acknowledge me. And when we met, I was scared. I couldn't handle it. She treated me like a human being from the start and I just couldn't handle it!" I wept a little, soothed by Tom's embrace and his voice.

"Don't cry, baby, don't cry."

That was the first time he called me "baby." I snuggled closer to him.

Tom sighed. "I wish I had done more for D. She's so special. I failed her."

Edgar made Law Review, along with Tom and Dorothy. The first thing out of Edgar's mouth at their first meeting was the rule about women in the basement, where the Law Review office was located. A rule is a rule, Edgar insisted, so she can't go down there. Dorothy was not the first woman to receive an appointment to Law

Review by the faculty. On previous occasions some sort of deal had been worked out. But those occasions lacked Edgar Burr. Dorothy didn't dwell on it at the club, but she did remark about Edgar, "He probably wants to repeal the fucking 19th Amendment, too!"

I could tell from your silence that you knew why I didn't go to the faculty to fight for a co-ed basement. I was thinking selfishly. You and D showed me too much kindness.

Rather than argue for a rule change, Tom spearheaded a compromise. He suggested that the group continue to hold board meetings in one of the classrooms after hours. And that Dorothy could work in Professor Barbara Armstrong's office, since she was scheduled to be on leave half the year anyway. Professor Armstrong was the only woman on the faculty and the architect of Social Security. We idolized her. She agreed to the arrangement. That way, Dorothy didn't have to do Law Review work in the dinky Ladies' Cloakroom.

"She appreciated what you did," I said.

"But she's still being treated like a second-class citizen. I feel awful about it. I should have done more." He shifted, put his left hand under his head. "Before I went to UCLA, I went to Lost Springs, this two-year college for men near Lone Pine, east of Mount Whitney."

"Never heard of it."

"Yeah, most haven't. It's totally isolated. In addition to the usual classes, we had to do ranching and farming. Fixing things, herding cattle, all that stuff. Imagine me at 19 with a bunch of guys getting sweaty every day. Shit, I couldn't even jack off in private half the time. When I got to UCLA, it was like the floodgates opened up. That's where the cruising started."

We sat in silence for a while, touching each other in strokes and caresses on the thighs and chest.

"I could have been on Law Review, but for one grade," I muttered.

"How's that?"

"Professor Fritz told me that I deserved an A in Property, but that he couldn't give it to me, because I would possibly end up on

Law Review and that as a Negro, I couldn't handle the burden. He said he was doing me a favor by giving me a B."

"Fuck him!" Tom exclaimed. "Does D know?"

"No."

Tom took my head, kissed it, then held it close.

❖

Tom's plan was a simple one. Put my extra credit paper from Property in the Law Review as a student note, thereby avenging the shitty grade and making Fritz look a fool. At that time, the faculty ran Law Review with the aid of a student board and it mostly printed faculty articles. Each issue usually only published one or two student notes, a short treatise on a topical item.

Tom faced immediate and predictable opposition from Edgar. A night of fierce debate ended in a stalemate. The student board more or less concluded to discuss it again later for the next issue, not the one currently in production. Tom disregarded that decision and took my paper to the faculty lead of Law Review. The professor loved it and insisted that it be included.

This put Tom firmly in Edgar's crosshairs. He loathed everything about the man, his sense of dress, his bon vivant airs, his dandy behavior, his flaunting of rules, but promoting me was a bridge too far. This made Tom a nigger lover.

How he found out about the cruising scene in the restroom no one really knew. But Tom had a theory.

Likely one of Edgar's cronies, a member of the Ersatz Diogenes Club, cruised there. Who knows, my love, maybe the guy I played with the night you were in the restroom ratted me out to Edgar. At least you didn't get called out. I'm grateful for that.

An anonymous note appeared in the Dean's office, warning about a pervert attending Boalt Hall and threatening to expose the school publicly if he wasn't removed. The note called out Tom by name. Sodomy—broadly defined as anything but marital coitus—was illegal in California and homosexuality fell afoul of the moral character section of the California state bar in the 1930s. Thus, an "avowed homosexual" could never become an attorney. The Dean met with Tom, read him the note, then asked him to withdraw.

It would have looked bad to expel their best student, so he asked me to voluntarily resign, to avoid any 'controversy.' Alternatively, he told me I could name names. That was my choice: take the fall or be a rat. Tom Kelly is no rat, I said to him. That's when he twisted the knife. 'Go and become a haberdasher, then, a job better suited to your talents.' Translation: Go and be the little faggot you are. A little faggot with scissors, a mincing walk, a lisping voice, and lurid eyes for every male crotch who came into the store seeking a suit. That's what he called me, his best fucking law student. I only kept from crying to deny him the satisfaction of seeing how much he broke me.

No proper words, much less treatments, existed at that time for clinical depression, though Tom knew he suffered from it, calling it his malignant malaise. He mockingly wrote about going to Cowell Hospital, the campus student infirmary, and what little good it would have done.

They'd have told me that I'm just sad and it will pass or have given me either a mixture of noxious drugs or a lobotomy. Or, if they'd found out I'm a queer, they'd have given me electroshock therapy. God knows I'm no saint. But I deserve better than that. I deserve to be treated like a human being.

Tom wrote that his father used to beat him regularly, sometimes with closed fists. He ran away from home when he was 15 and lived on LA's Skid Row. He thought his life would end there, but a wealthy Hollywood mogul offered to take him in, for a price. Penniless and near starvation, Tom submitted. The man covered Tom's suits and education in exchange for sexual favors. (Tom never said who it was.) He also helped Tom get into Lost Springs, where he learned to punch cattle and solve differential equations. By the time he started at Boalt, he was already a thousand times the man Edgar would ever be.

Watch out for Edgar, my love. I was wrong about him lacking passion. He has mastered the darkest passion: he is a natural sadist. Watch out not just for this Edgar, but for all of the Edgars. They are everywhere. We created beauty for ourselves, you, me, and D. We celebrated and fortified each other. But we threaten the Edgars of the world and they are hellbent on our destruction. Watch out for his lot for the rest of your life. They want to destroy you, every part of you, including the fact that you ever existed. They see that as their purpose in life.

Remember, my love, you are better, stronger, smarter, warmer, and gentler than any them. And the gentle can fight the hardest when threatened. I know you will go far.

I love you, Jay Philip Hines.

Yours forever,

Tom

They found Tom's body soon after the jump off the Golden Gate Bridge, his final journey. An old seaman saw him moments before hitting the water, so they had an idea of where to look before the sea could reclaim his body. He went in like an Olympic diver, the seaman described. Tom jumped May 31, 1937, four days after the bridge opened.

I listened to Mozart's Requiem that summer, repeatedly. To this day, I can't hear the *Lacrimosa* without choking up.

Society teaches blacks that passion is a sin. Do not display passion or suffer the consequences. I played by that rulebook, until Tom's love and life and my grief over losing him transformed me. I returned to Boalt no longer the silent Negro in the back of the room. I freely expressed my passion for civil rights and freedom for all, gaining much respect. I had never realized how my earlier rigidity had limited me. I also changed my name to Jay. Philip was dead.

Dorothy and others organized peer discussion groups for those in grief over Tom. I led a very special group. We gathered secretly at The Football Players, the statue that had greeted and mesmerized Tom on his first day. Then we snuck off to a wooded area far from Boalt and talked about Tom, being homosexual, the state of our lives, things we had never discussed with anyone, including ourselves. I may well have led the first rap group for homosexual men at Cal. How proud Tom would have been.

I also spent my third year making life as miserable as possible for Edgar Douglas Burr. I led a successful drive to repeal the gender exclusion rule for the basement. I made Law Review myself, finally. And I faced off with Edgar in a moot court competition. We argued Plessy vs. Ferguson, the infamous 1896 Supreme Court decision that legalized segregation. I argued against it, authoritatively and passionately citing facts that buried Edgar's arguments, and won. Getting whipped by a Negro broke him more than I realized at first. Two days after the competition, Edgar attacked me on an obscure corner of campus during one of my walks. It was savage. I somehow got myself to Cowell Hospital where they treated and documented my wounds and reported the attack to the police. I stayed at D's parents' house in Kensington that night rather than at Cowell. Her father looked after me.

The next morning, D and I went to Boalt and sat outside the Dean's office, refusing to leave until he saw us. Others heard about our sit-in and joined us. By the time the Dean arrived, 60 of us refused to leave until he brought Edgar to justice. Cowed by our numbers and haunted by the criticism he received from the faculty for his handling of Tom (Professor Wicker reportedly called Tom's dismissal a criminal breach of due process), the Dean capitulated. Confronted by the school and the police, institutions he no doubt thought would protect him from "coon boy," rule-bound Edgar confessed to the beating and the Dean expelled him, just a month shy of graduating.

❖

I'm on campus for the first time in 50 years. Dorothy plans to meet me here. I'm retired from the NAACP and she's Senior Judge Dorothy Legend Harper on the First Circuit Court of Appeals in Boston, semi-retired, taking cases as she pleases. We're both 75. Before our official reunion starts at the Law School's current building at Bancroft and College, we plan to sneak off to the old building, now called Durant Hall. The East Asian Library sits where the Law Library used to be. They still have the old wooden desks. We plan to bring a flask of Tom's favorite Irish whiskey and drink it over the desk he used; I had written his name on the inside of the desk drawer: TOM KELLY '38 WAS HERE. Maybe a drop of whiskey will land on him, so that he can have a sip as well.

I love Tom Kelly. And I miss him to this day.

—Berkeley, 1988

Miss Boots of Gramercy Park
John Kane

It was winter before James noticed the changes. His routine had long been unvarying: work, then the gym, home to watch a DVR taped episode of celebrity cook Ina Garten as The Barefoot Contessa, some Thai take out for dinner, a container of Haagen-Dazs, half a joint, a Titan porno tape on the computer, and, finally, sleep. The gym was the first to go, which was fine with him. The exercise only delayed the ritual devouring of the Pad Thai or the Pan Nang Curry, the real purpose of the evening, along with the ice cream and the porn. Then, later that fall, he let his subscription to Vanity Fair lapse during the same month he decided to skip the annual Coen Brothers film. James had begun to lose his edge.

Part of leaving the gym was his increasing weight. When he turned 50 last year, he told himself he could now eat whatever he wanted. But whatever he wanted turned out to be an endless variety of Thai noodles. Some nights he dreamed of them, like spools of Christmas ribbons, unwinding endlessly down his throat. What the hell, they tasted great with the all the different sauces and gravies that the old man who ran the Thai take out shop poured over them.

As he trudged up the stairs to his third floor walk-up with his take out, he sometimes saw the Korean window dresser who lived above him rushing out for a taxi to a Brazilian dinner, a rap concert, an Indian pop up taco truck, something, anything that called up the promise of Manhattan to the young. James guessed he was anywhere between 21 and 30—was it racist to say you had trouble guessing the age of a Korean?—and noted that he never seemed to wear the same thing twice. A gray argyle sweater would be paired with cream linen pants, a Chanel scarf would be called into play as a headband, a Navajo belt would be pulled tight over a pair of denim overalls.

James knocked on the door of the second-floor apartment; the building, between First and Second Avenue on 21st Street, was so old and narrow that it allowed only one apartment per floor. A petite woman in her 80s opened the door. Her silver-gray hair was parted in the middle and she was wearing a lavender silk kimono. Mona Kula was part Polynesian and her looks had led her to appear in the choruses of several mid-century examples of Broadway musical exotica: *Kismet*, *Shangri-La*, a musical version of *Lost Horizons* that closed as soon as it opened, and endless revivals of *The King and I*, which had helped her earn her Equity pension.

"Spicy green beans with cellophane noodles," James said as he handed her a bag.

"He didn't have any eggplant?"

"Not until tomorrow."

"Come in and have some wine," commanded Mona. "You look exhausted." There was something motherly in Mona's manner with James, but motherly in the sense of Mama Rose in *Gypsy*, not Mother Goose. She handed him a glass of the cheap Merlot she kept on hand as he settled down on the sofa. He looked at all the old show posters that lined the living room wall.

"Was Yul Brynner well hung?" asked James. Mona had appeared as Tuptim in the Broadway revival of the show with him in the 70s.

"You'll have to ask the late Mrs. Brynner," laughed Mona as she took a seat next to him. "I was never accorded the honor."

"But you told me you slept with some of your co-stars."

"Until I got married," she shrugged. A picture of Mona's late husband, Sandy, hung next to a poster for a summer stock tour of *Deathtrap* in which Mona had played the psychic. "I slept with Fernando Lamas when we did *The King and I* at Westbury Music Festival. Those Hollywood guys. Big comers. Quick leavers."

James secretly loved hearing Mona's backstage stories of the theatre since they were as close as he had ever managed to get to it. Moving to New York almost three decades ago, he had taken acting and singing lessons which led nowhere, unless you considered teaching English to middle school students in the Bronx something, which James did not.

"You're putting on weight," said Mona.

James shrugged. "I stopped going to the gym."

"Why?"

"What's the point?" Suddenly James felt claws on his neck and the brush of fur across the back of his head as Mona's cat jumped past him and onto the floor.

"Miss Boots!" scolded Mona. "Momma told you not to do that." The aggressive tabby, gray and white striped, curled herself around Mona's leg and purred. "Behave yourself Miss Boots of Gramercy Park," she scolded. Mona believed her cat deserved a fancy address, even though the dilapidated walk-up she and James lived in was more than two blocks from the fabled New York landmark.

Miss Boots bounded away to the other side of the room where she began to wrestle with a pencil. Bic pens were scattered throughout the floor of the apartment.

"She has this thing for cylinders," explained Mona. "One day I came home and my medicine cabinet was open. She was rolling around the bathroom floor playing with my thermometer."

"I guess it's worth it if you love her," said James.

"You should get a pet," offered Mona. "A cat or a dog. Or even a fish. If you got a dog you could lose some of that weight by walking him every day."

"Why don't I just keep eating and I can turn myself into a bear," replied James. "I'll become my own pet."

Mona took a sip of the wine. "You're watching too much of that Ina Garten cooking show. She's fattening you up."

"I worship that woman," said James, putting down his wine and spreading his hands apart as if to create a stage. "She's one of those women who's totally in control of her own world and she has her own personal style. Like Diana Vreeland or Lauren Bacall."

Mona snorted. "Diana Vreeland and Bacall were skinny. Ina Garten is such a tub I'm surprised her hips don't get stuck on the counter as she moves around the kitchen."

James smiled for the first time all day. "She's making her own pot roast recipe tonight. With a sauce of cognac and rosemary."

❖

Later that month James went back to his parents' house in Muncie, Indiana for Christmas. He slept in the same room and bed he had slept in four decades ago. The small, battered dresser he had used still had some of his old Timberland sweaters in it, the ones he had hidden his copies of *Honcho* and *Mandate* under. It was here that he had masturbated to thoughts of Richard Gere and dreamed of living in New York City.

He and his older sister, Ellen, took their father to a new Christmas comedy starring Mark Wahlberg as a depressed superhero who discovers he is related to Santa Claus. After this singularly joyless experience, they went to Tony's Spaghetti House, where their parents had taken them as children, for dinner.

"That was a load of crap," said Ben Deavers as he sat down in the booth with his children.

"Not every movie can be *It's A Wonderful Life*, Dad," said Ellen, handing him a menu.

"I'd have rather gone ice fishing," replied Ben.

"Dad, I just don't think I can take those temperatures anymore," said James.

"What's the matter?" said his father. "Has New York made a sissy out of you?"

"I thought we'd just have a fun night out," interjected Ellen.

"I'll have the spaghetti and meat balls," Ben said as he handed the menu to the waiter, a nervous looking high school student who had just arrived at the table.

Later, after two glasses each of chianti, James and Ellen grew giddy recalling old classmates. "Remember she had that Farrah Fawcett hairdo at graduation but then it rained and she wound up looking like a swamp rat?"

"Ellen, you're the worst."

"Well, it's true." Ben sat back in the booth and checked the news on his phone.

"Jimmy Deavers?" A man in a blue blazer had come over to stand next to the table.

"Yes?"

"Warren Carlyle," he said stretching out his hand. "We were in Chemistry together. I said to my wife over there, that's Jimmy Deavers."

"Hello Warren."

"You're back for the holidays?"

"Pretty much. Staying at home."

"How are you, Mr. Deavers?" Warren said to Ben. "I was sorry to hear about your wife."

"Thank you, Warren," replied Ben. "That was some time ago. I'm fine."

Warren turned back to James. "There's no place like Muncie at Christmas. Though I guess New York, with that big tree. That's where you live, right? New York?" James nodded. "We keep wanting to go there but the kids always vote for Disney World."

Warren shook James' hand and then his father's. He pushed a card into Ben's hand. "If you ever need a new roof, please call me. Mr. Deavers. Carlyle Roofing has the most competitive rates in the state." Ben tucked the card in his jacket pocket. "Well, folks, it's been good talking with you. Merry Christmas."

"Seems like he's got a good business," said Ben. "He's made something of himself." James looked over at Ellen and rolled his eyes. "Well," he continued, "if you'll just move, I'll go out and get the car while you two settle up."

"Sure, dad," said Ellen, letting her father out of the booth. At 78 he still walked with the ramrod straight posture of the Air Force captain he had once been.

"He hates me," said James as Ben walked out the door of the restaurant.

"You don't know that," protested Ellen.

"He's made something of himself," said James, mimicking his father. "Come on, Ellen."

"He's just always had a hard time being comfortable around you."

"Yeah? Well, he's had his whole fucking life."

"How many more years of teaching till you get your pension?" asked Ellen.

"Ten," replied James as he took the last slice of pizza.

"And then?"

"Well, I'm sure as hell not moving back here."

Ellen laughed. "Why not? We'll get you a new roof and all." She smiled at her brother as he scraped the final shards of mozzarella off the plate. His round face and tentative grin took her back to a playmate she had known years ago. It had been so long since she'd seen that person. "I love you Jimi-Bear," she said.

Dragging his suitcase up the staircase of his building two days later, James paused and saw a padlock on Mona's door.

"It was the police," said a voice from behind him. He turned to see the Korean window dresser.

"What happened?"

"She died. The day before Christmas. The police padlocked the place after they took the body away. I think it's a city law. Until they can locate the next of kin."

James leaned again his suitcase for support. A wave of nausea passed through him. "There's no next of kin. How did she die?"

"It was a stroke," said the window dresser. "I heard a huge crash around ten o'clock at night. So I came down and knocked on the door. I knocked and I knocked, but there was no answer. Just the cat who kept meowing. I was creeped out, so I called the police and they broke down the door and found her."

"Jesus," said James, shaking his head. They fell into a short silence.

"I'm Willy," the window dresser said.

"James." They shook hands.

"Come up to my apartment. I have something for you."

The something turned out to be Miss Boots, who was curled up on Willie's futon furiously licking her paws. "I took her in because the police were going to put her in a shelter," he explained. "But I can't keep her. I'm a stylist for a photographer and sometimes I go out of town for as long as a week. So, I'm hoping you'll take her."

James paused. "I've never had a cat."

"If I give her to the shelter, she's got two weeks, and then they put her down," replied Willie.

"I don't know what to say."

Willie lit up a half-smoked joint, inhaled deeply, and offered it to James. "Want some?"

"Like that's going to help me make up my mind?"

Willie took another long drag. "Couldn't hurt." James took the joint and inhaled. As the smoke filled his lungs, he looked over at Miss Boots, busy cleaning herself, and thought that she had no idea that she could be dead in a couple of weeks. Or not.

"Listen," said Willie as he got up and put on a purple beret. "A friend of mine is performing at a bar tonight. Why don't you go with me and you can think about it."

"Your friend's a singer?" asked James taking one more hit.

"He's a drag artist," said Willie. "His act is called Paralyzed Cher."

They wound up at Therapy, a popular Hell's Kitchen bar, at one in the morning, packed with millennials and James, who didn't want to tell Willie he hadn't been to a gay bar in years. Paralyzed Cher turned out to be an act in which Willie's friend sat in a wheel chair and gesticulated wildly while doing karaoke to "Half Breed," "Dark Lady," and "Gypsies, Tramps, and Thieves." Funny like a crutch thought James, but the crowd seemed to love it.

"Can I get you another?" asked a young waiter who had come to his table. He was wearing a thong and there was glitter on his ass. Willie was off with some friends on the other side of the bar.

James looked at his vodka tonic and thought about how hung over he wanted to be tomorrow morning. "I probably shouldn't."

"Work tomorrow?" The lights from the disco ball played over the boy's face, seeming to change it from innocent to teasing in a flicker.

"No," replied James. "I'm a teacher. I have off until next week. But I hate having headaches."

"I love teachers," said the boy. "I was going to be one until I decided to become an actor. What do you teach?"

"English."

"My favorite language. Let me buy you a drink."

"I don't know if I should…"

The boy gave him an impish smile and took out his phone. "I'm Brice and I'm buying you a drink. What's your name and number?"

Later, in the Lyft home, James replayed the scene in his mind in order to make sure it had actually happened. A half-naked waiter in his early twenties had openly flirted with him and asked for his phone number. His perfectly round, glitter sprayed butt cheeks had been eye level with James while he had been doing so. As Ina Garten would say, "What's not to like?"

He opened the door to his apartment to be greeted by an anxious Miss Boots who threaded her way through his legs. Jesus, he thought, I don't have any cat food. Foraging through the refrigerator, he came upon some cold cuts, ripped them up, and put them on a plate. Miss Boots dove for them with the fervor of Hannibal crossing the Alps. He stripped off his clothes, brushed his teeth, and got into bed while she was still eating.

Lying there, still thinking of his good fortune in meeting Brice, the kind of thing that hadn't happened to him in ages, James suddenly felt a large weight crash onto his chest. Miss Boots. She curled up there, ready to go to sleep. "You're not serious about this, are you?" said James. But apparently, she was. After a minute or so, he reached up and pulled her off and to his side. She tried to squirm away, but he held her in place and petted her. "You're fine baby. Just not on my chest." Eventually she relaxed and curled into a ball under his arm. Her sandpaper tongue darted out and licked his flesh. After years alone, James was sleeping with someone.

Almost three hours later, at four thirty in the morning, his phone rang. He sat up groggily and picked it up off the night stand. "Hello?"

"Hey, it's me. Brice."

"Brice?"

"Yeah, the waiter you met tonight. Wanna fuck?"

Still shaking off sleep, James was transported back to a time over 20 years ago when his youth and his looks dictated that there would be an endless stream of tomorrows. "It's awfully late."

"I know, but I just got off work. Come on, let's do it." He couldn't calculate when he had last heard words like this.

"Okay." He gave Brice his address and rose from bed.

What followed was both familiar and deeply satisfying. Cries of "Oh Daddy" and "Harder" as well as post-coital chatter on Brice's part about Sondheim, Beyoncé, and his hopes for a career as an actor. Finally, at seven a.m., with dawn breaking, they both fell asleep, only to wake again at nine and decide to go out for coffee and bagels.

By this point James had come to realize that Brice had been talking for close to a full hour, yet had said nothing of any importance. Just as well. So he let him keep running his own personal talk show. "What is your ultimate goal in life?" Brice asked him.

"I don't know," replied James. "I kind of stopped thinking about that. What's yours?"

Brice took a short drag on his Marlboro Light. "I want to live on the moon."

After getting him a cab, James went to Target and bought a litter pan, litter, a feeding tray, twenty cans of Fancy Feast, and a box of straws for the cat to play with. He carted it all home, telling himself that the exercise was good for him. Miss Boots looked on as he set up her new home. He emptied a can of Fancy Feast into the tray, but she didn't seem interested. Later that night he offered her some of his Thai noodles, but that was another no sale. Worried that she was not eating, James walked two blocks through the bitter January night and bought a rotisserie chicken at Papa Joe's, which he had passed every day since it had opened four years ago.

Coming home, he carved slices of the flame broiled poultry off the bird, chopped them into little pieces, and put them in Miss Boots' bowl. She devoured them greedily as he looked on with a smile. Then he dumped his Thai food, which had grown cold, in the garbage, and sat down and had some chicken and the salad that came with it. "Okay," he said to the cat who watched him eat, "we agree on something." Later, when he watched his nightly recording of Ina Garten, Miss Boots jumped up and sat in his lap.

❖

Four days later James was back in school for the start of the second semester. Looking out at the largely black and Asian faces that made up his first period 8th grade English class, he wondered, as he often did on the number 2 train to the Bronx, if any of them ever thought of him when they left the classroom. He knew that he never did, and sometimes he even felt guilty about it. When he had been young in Muncie, sensing he was different, he had only wanted to grow up and come to New York City and be with adults who went to bars and theatres and dinner parties. Somehow it had worked out that he made it to New York, only to be trapped in a series of rooms with children.

James usually had lunch with Tom Spiers, a younger 7th grade English teacher who had worn a bow tie for the first day of school. "Your first period was my last, last year," said Tom.

"Anyone I should watch out for?"

"They're pretty much all little beasts," said Tom as he opened his juice carton. "Wouldn't know a book if they tripped over it. But be careful of Gloria Sanchez. She tried to set another girl's hair on fire last Halloween."

"You're kidding."

"With a barbeque lighter no less. She was dressed up as Cinderella and using it as a wand. These fucking kids. And Hollis Diggens is another real prize. I was disciplining him, and we were on the first floor, so he just opened the window and jumped out. Ran away. Of course, Chang did nothing. She never does. He'll be making license plates in Dannemora in five years, guaranteed."

"What we go through for a paycheck, huh?" said James.

"Tell me about it," replied Tom. "Did you get the tray lunch?" He indicated the school cafeteria lunch he had ordered. "Mystery meat and enigma vegetables."

When first period came around the next day James gave an in-class essay assignment of "My Favorite Christmas Gift."

Experience had taught him that if he gave it as homework, mcre than half the class would never do it. That night, after sharing some more Papa Joe's chicken with Miss Boots, he began grading the essays. They were the usual collection of tributes to video games and princess dresses, complete with poor grammar and non-existent paragraphs. One essay stood out from the pack, however. It was from Hollis Diggens, and read, in full:

My Grandady says hes a preacher. But hes allways getting arrested for sellin crack. I thought they said black people dont crack. Waz up wi dat? They say black people cant have guns cuz they shoot white people. Waz with the white people who have guns and shoot everyone? Thats fucked. My girlfrien tole me she woodnt give me none unless I boote her some clothes. so I boote her some socks. Why she go an get pissed at me? and what about airplane peanuts? can they fly? Waz up wi dat?

James came to the last line and chuckled; the simple act of having been entertained prevented him from failing Hollis for not having written the essay as it had been assigned. He would have to talk to him tomorrow.

He pushed the papers aside and took a few hits on an cld joint. Miss Boots sniffed the air in disapproval, wagging her tail and moving to the other side of the room where she where began to chew on a straw. "Sure you don't want a hit?" asked James with a smile, holding the joint out to her. She buried her head beneath her paws. He stubbed out the joint, walked over to the refrigerator and began to eat some coffee ice cream straight from the container. The joys of living alone. Satisfied, he went back to his desk, found the Titan porno site, and entered his password. He began to search for a video he hadn't tired of, something that still held a sense of mystery or lust for him. He wound up with a short of two men sitting on wooden boxes in jock straps, rubbing themselves as they looked at each other. He unzipped his jeans and began to rub himself in unison with them. Heat was beginning to emanate from both sides of the screen. Then James felt a tug on his pants leg and looked down to see Miss Boots clawing on it. In one swift motion she jumped into his lap, rubbing herself against him while she purred as loudly as a furnace sending up heat in winter. Onscreen the two men had progressed to kissing and pulling down each other's jockstraps. James faced a choice: the lady or the tiger. He reached out and switched off the computer as Miss Boots curled into a ball in his lap. No way the lady could not win tonight.

The next day he asked Hollis to remain after class to speak with him. The boy, tall and wiry with short cropped hair and dressed in an Atlanta Braves jersey, regarded him with deep suspicion.

"I wanted to talk to you about your essay," said James.

"Are you gonna give me a pass to Social Studies?" responded Hollis. "Cause Miss Toabe is a real bitch about being late."

"Don't worry about Miss Toabe," replied James, handing Hollis his essay and pulling up a chair for him to sit next to him. "I want to ask you what you meant by turning this in as an essay."

"It's just a thing," said Hollis, looking quickly at James, then looking away.

"A thing? What kind of thing? I asked you to write me about what you got for Christmas."

Hollis took the paper and crumpled it up. "I knew you wouldn't like it."

"I didn't say that, Hollis. I just want to know why you wrote it."

"You're gonna fail me, right?" Hollis stood up. "I gotta go."

"Sit down. I'll write you a late pass for Miss Toabe," said James. "I just want to know why you wrote it."

"I thought it was funny," he replied, shifting in his seat.

"Some of it is. But it's not written in proper English."

"It's the way people talk," Hollis protested.

"Maybe. But I can't accept it in an essay."

"So you're failing me." Hollis stood up as the second period bell rang. "Miss Toabe is gonna dump on me."

"I told you I'd write you a pass," said James, who had his second period free. "Now I can't accept an essay with this much bad grammar in it. I don't care about the jokes. I care about the grammar. You have some good things in here. You're writing phonetically, which is the way people talk. That would work on stage. And you use words well. Like the way you use crack as a drug, and as a reference to aging."

Hollis looked mystified. "That's a pun," explained James.

"Uh huh."

"Look it up and write the definition of a pun on the paper. That's part of your assignment."

"What else I gotta do?" asked Hollis.

"Take this home. Rewrite it in proper English. Then resubmit both papers to me, and I'll give you a grade."

"For real?"

"Let me ask you, Hollis," said James. "What is your ultimate goal in life?"

"I wanna be Dave Chappelle."

"Good answer. Now here's your pass to Miss Toabe's class."

The following month Ellen called James, who had only been to Paris in his late twenties, to tell him that she and her husband were taking a Viking Cruise down the Yangtze River and then going to see the Great Wall of China. A two-month vacation. James mustered up some enthusiasm to cover up whatever envy he felt for a sibling who had married well and told her to send postcards.

"What's with you, Jimi-Bear?" asked Ellen.

"Well, I got a cat."

"A cat? You were never a cat person."

"I am now. She's here sleeping while I fix dinner. The apartment's pretty much hers already."

Ellen laughed, happy to hear her brother in a good mood for once. "What's her name?"

"Miss Boots. I inherited her from my upstairs neighbor when she died from a stroke."

"We're all getting up there, that's what Earl said to me about going to China. That's what I wanted to talk to you about. How do you feel about looking in on Dad?"

"You mean flying out there?"

"Oh no, just giving him a call now and then while we're gone."

"Ellen, he and I haven't talked on the phone in years. He's got neighbors who know him better than I do."

"I hear you," she said with a sigh.

"Aren't you the one who said that not every movie is *It's A Wonderful Life*?"

"You're right. Love you, Jimi-Bear."

James tried texting Brice that night—after all it had been a month—and got back a text that read "Kool to hear from u. M auditioning. Sorry." Well, what could you expect if you were trying to hook up with the next Brad Pitt? Not having bought new clothes in several years, James went into his closet and dragged out some of the sweaters and pants he had not worn recently. There were a couple of nice Polo sweaters and some khaki pants he had always favored. But tight. That was the only possible way to describe how they felt when he squeezed himself into them. Miss Boots had no such problem, finding a nice home for the night on a red Polo cardigan that James had thrown onto the bed.

Walking home on the first day of daylight savings time, savoring the extra hour of sunlight and carrying a bag full of vegetables and a bouquet of yellow freesias for Miss Boots, James saw Willie waiting on the doorstep of the building. He was wearing a large tan overcoat and a panama hat. A straw suitcase was beside him.

"This is so Audrey Hepburn/George Peppard, our meeting like this," Willie said to James.

"How so?" James rested his groceries on the steps.

"*Breakfast at Tiffany's!*" he exclaimed. "They're always meeting in front of their building as one or the other of them is running out somewhere. Don't tell me you've never seen it. I'll kill myself."

"I've seen it," said James with a chuckle. "But I think it happened in a better neighborhood than this."

"Imagination, honey. Without it, you're dead. You're looking good."

"I started going back to the gym," James replied. "Just a little each week. Where are you going all dressed up?"

"To Puerto Vallarta for a week. We're doing a shoot for Estee Lauder. Skinny girls playing dead on Mexican beaches in peach lipstick."

"Sounds fun," said James, thinking that everyone was travelling except him.

"Could you do me a favor?" asked Willie as his town car pulled up to the curb. "Could you check on my plants and piss on them once or twice while I'm gone?"

"You bet."

"You're an angel," he said, ducking into the car. "And by the way, a copy of *Breakfast at Tiffany's* is sitting on top of my DVD player. You should watch it with Miss Boots. It's the ultimate cat movie."

James watched the movie after dinner that night, seeing something about Holly Golightly he had not noticed before as a young man. Despite being played by the luminous Audrey Hepburn, Holly kept people at a distance. She rejected Buddy Ebsen who came from her past, and she seemed never to notice how George Peppard was falling in love with her throughout the film. She even called her cat "a poor no name slob" and dumped him out of the cab during a rainstorm. Of course, that made for the ending that reduced everyone to tears, but there was no disguising the fact that Holly was a frightened soul. "Not like you, Miss Boots," said James putting his face up against hers and feeling her cold wet nose on his cheek.

Miss Boots didn't sleep with him that night, but James paid it no mind. Like Cat, as Holly called her pet in the movie, Miss Boots was independent and couldn't be pinned down to a routine. But when James woke up the next morning at 6:15 he found her lying in the bathroom in a pool of vomit, struggling to breathe, the hair around her face and neck sticky and matted. "Jesus Christ," he exclaimed, "what the fuck?" He grabbed a bath towel and picked Miss Boots up, carefully drying her off. She felt weak, almost floppy. "Don't worry, baby," he said. "I'm gonna take care of you."

The animal hospital on 14th Street made him wait an interminable forty-five minutes before they admitted Miss Boots, although an orderly did come out and make sure she was still breathing. James called school and told them he would not be in. Finally at eight o'clock he brought Miss Boots in to the medical area and placed her on an examination table where a young Indian veterinarian, Dr. Mushar, examined her.

Miss Boots lay on the table panting, as if she had suffered some great and dire exertion. Dr. Mushar moved his hands up and down her, feeling around ribs, checking her organs, opening her mouth to see what might be revealed there. Then he turned to his assistant. "Let's start hydrating her." The girl nodded and began the procedure. "Come into my office Mr. Deavers."

"Miss Boots is in a state of septic shock," said Dr. Mushar after they sat down. "To tell you why and what it means, I will have to keep her here for some time."

"How long?"

"Overnight. We have to run some tests on her, check her blood, her vital signs. Her condition may be temporary, it may be more."

"More, like what?" asked James as he felt his body turn cold and had the sensation of his blood draining down to the bottom of his legs.

"We don't know anything yet, Mr. Deavers."

"It could be cancer, right?" He thought he could take some of the fear away just be saying it out loud.

"That's not likely. If it's anything treacherous, it's most likely to be feline leukemia. But we don't know that yet."

"And that's fatal?"

Dr. Mushar nodded. "But we don't that yet."

"When will we…"

The doctor held up his hand. "Not until tomorrow afternoon when I have the test results in. Mr. Deaver, are you going to work today?" James shook his head. "Then call up a friend. Go to a movie. Or a museum. There's nothing we can do until then. Call me tomorrow around three o'clock."

James wandered through the city aimlessly, crossing 14th street, walking up the High Line, eating a hot dog in Bryant Park and then walking around 34th Street, where he sensed the ghosts of B. Altman's and Gimbel's as he walked past the grand survivor,

Macy's. He wound up sitting outside Gramercy Park, watching the wealthy people who had keys to the Park walk their dogs on its well-manicured paths. He could not decide if he was Ishmael or Travis Bickel. He only knew that he was never Holly Golightly or Miranda Priestly. The dreams that had brought him to this city had faded over the years. And now everybody was travelling. Why couldn't he even have a fucking cat?

The next day he was signing in at the main office when Vice Principal Helena Chang approached him. If she gives me shit, I'm going to tear her head off he thought, knowing that he would never do that.

"Mr. Deavers?" inquired Ms. Chang who favored black nail polish. "I believe you have Hollis Diggens in your first period?"

"Yes, I do," replied James. He was pleasantly surprised and was about to launch into a small tribute to Hollis's potential.

"Then I need you to sign this." She thrust a form at James which was entitled "Expulsion/ Replacement." "Just initial on the first period line, please."

"Something happened?" said James.

"Indeed," said Ms. Chang. "Now if you'll just initial."

"Well, I'd like to know what happened. I found Hollis to be a very promising student."

"Hollis Diggens has been declared a dangerous and disruptive influence to the faculty and students of our school. He has been expelled as of yesterday and is being transferred to another school."

"But why?" insisted James. "That was not my experience with him. I think I'm entitled to know."

Ms. Chang lowered her voice. "Hollis Diggens made death threats."

James made a pained face, knowing how school bureaucracies worked. "Real ones?"

"He threatened to throw Miss Toabe out the second story window when he was late for class. There is no more discussion about this, Mr. Deavers."

James initialed the form. "Do you know how I can get in touch with him at his home?"

"You should be careful about something like that, Mr. Deavers," warned Ms. Chang. "It may well be against school policy."

"I was supporting him in a project he was working on. Something to better himself."

Ms, Chang paused. "You'll have to see me after classes about that, Mr. Deavers."

For the rest of the day, James welcomed the disruptions—a fire drill—loud speaker announcements, "Will all students with headaches please report to the nurse for testing"—and random rudeness, a black girl told a Korean girl she had "no tits" and the Korean girl told her to "please die"—that comprise a regular school day because they took his mind off the phone call he knew had to make. At lunch Tom Spiers said, "Did you hear they finally got rid of Hollis Diggens?" and James simply said "Shut up," pleased by how angry the comment had made him.

Once the final bell rang, James went back to his desk and dialed the animal hospital. He was so nervous he had to do it three times to get the number right. After being on hold for two minutes, he was connected to Dr. Mushar. "It's Mr. Deavers, Doctor," he said.

"Mr. Deavers," said the Doctor. "The news is good."

James' body went limp with relief. "Tell me."

"Your cat does not have feline leukemia. She does however have toxic fluids in her liver which have caused her septic shock. She is hydrating and recovering nicely. You can visit her tonight and I think we can probably release her to you tomorrow evening."

The words rushed by James in a blur. All he knew was that Miss Boots was safe. That was all that mattered.

"Let me ask you, Mr. Deavers," continued the Dr., "have you been feeding your cat anything strange?"

"Strange? Like what? I try to give her fresh chicken most of the time."

"Does she ever eat plastic? Because we have found traces of that in the toxicity reports."

The straws. The fucking straws! He would throw them out tonight and buy Miss Boots a year's supply of pencils. James thanked the Dr. and ended the call.

He put his head in his hands and began to sob. His body shook as he sat at the desk he had sat at for twelve years, correcting papers and quieting students. In a setting he associated with numbing routine and mild depression, he was having a moment of transcendent joy. He dried his face and blew his nose. If only there were someone to share his luck with. But everyone was travelling. Even stupid Brice was probably on the moon. Why was he always alone at moments like this?

He picked up the phone and dialed. A man's voice answered and said, "Hello?"

"Hi Dad," said James.

Jingle-Jingle-Pop
Miah Jeffra

Champagne would have understood, I don't need no one telling me. She didn't take nothing personal, and she wouldn't want me getting all crybaby and shit in front of the girls.

Someone had to be mama bad for those pansy-ass chochas. And Champagne knew, knew that I was getting close, and to lose a day, lose an hour, would have been a setback. A *setback*. I was getting so close. Not just the money, but the whole thing, you know? What the head does. It's like what Donald Trump say in that show, you got to keep the *eye on the prize*. Champagne knew that, though she was a dumb bitch. That's what got her dead. She stopped looking the johnnie boys up and down, getting the real deal off them, and wound up popping her ass in any car that rolled by. Ooh, the money, it did that thing, you know.

She was probably dying in that mother fucker's hands, knowing she bleeding all over, but her eyes went way outside the car window into that place where the promise was, probably smiling away at how soft the life beyond was going to be.

It's good I didn't go, for reals. By the time the girls got back from the funeral, I turned a whole day's worth of tricks. Sunday wasn't usually a good day, the johns at church with their familias, but with all the girls gone, I got the whole spread. Easy bread.

Champagne probably say it a better use of my time. I can almost hear her, give me a hi-five, "a T gotta do what she gotta do."

I see them at Benito's, the tiny taco shack in the warehouse parking lot at the corner of Las Palmas. The warehouse used to be a porno slinger, but now it some fancy artist studios. Benito's once be jamming, all those fat porno guys slopping it up, flirting with us, working their job and loving it, but those artists with their skinny ass jeans and beards walk sideways around the damned place, oh, they eat organic or some shit. Hey though, the shack got shit for food, and that's embarrassing for any Mexican joint in L.A., but it was open all night and became the spot. The taquitos were greasy enough to slice through the cum in our mouths. Champagne and me used to come by between tricks and she would play this game. She shimmy up on the stool and lay her head on the counter like she be busted, it was so funny, and say "Where'd you be right now if not here?" and we'd take our turns saying the Bahamas or Paris or one of them hotels on the Sunset Strip, or some shit.

The girls were done up in black, all respectful and funeral like, but there was no hiding who they were—pencil skirts stuffed in the hips, stilettos, low slung blouses to the titty-nipple, fake eyelashes with crystals on the tips. Fantasia had a bird in her hair, black as her skin, with white eyes staring out, a whole damn bird. Now, what bitch can do that? They were muy glamoroso, popped up on the cracked red plastic stools, crossing their legs like it helping any, three of them in a row, looking like Elvira just blew up all over Hollywood. So the fuck what? Straight bitches are jealous we do it full out every day. They wish.

Cheilah, Fantasia and Mimi, and no Champagne. Something about them sitting on those stools without her made it feel real. I pretended to fix an eyelash, cuz I'm not crying in front of nobody, honey.

"It was nice, real pretty, all the flowers." Mimi, always trying to play like some elegant bitch, her hands all folded on her lap. She had to, being the age she be.

Cheilah touched the white lily in her platinum wig, too big for her face, big enough for her eyes. "I took one for my hair. That ain't against the religion or nothing, right?"

"Like you worried *that* gonna throw you in the fire, girl?"

"Ain't that right, honey."

"You should have been there, Lalo," Cheilah said, and I just looked at her.

"If I die, my best friend better be there," Mimi said, cleaning under her jeweled nails.

Fucking Lee Press-On shit, but they look good in that cheap way.

Fantasia laughed all husky and warm. "Girl know she couldn't wait that long to have a jimmy up her mangina. Ain't that right, Lalo? How else all that shit gonna stay up in there? Them dookie-lips singing some big-time opera and shit."

"Your heart probably fall right out that bitch if you didn't keep it all plugged up," Mimi said, her eyes not even leaving those janky-ass nails.

I just looked at Mimi with all the eat shit that I could, because I was saving my tongue for now, and we'd see about who be talking when I'm up out of this place, and she still dropping to her knees while I'm buying earrings on the QVC.

"Oh, hell, Mimi, like you all tight?" Fantasia said.

Cheilah rolled her eyes. "Serious, though, Lalo. It was nice. You should have been there."

I just said, "You know the motherfucker that did Champagne like that was a Carlos."

We all nodded, and Mm-hmm, and Uh-huh, and You know that's right, girl.

I looked out, past the girls, at the block—the parking lots, the boxy warehouses, the concrete, the trash in the gutters, the trash cans, the concrete. The L.A. sun just kind of sat there, no breeze, just dry, still, dead heat. All the stanky sweat from plastic backseats and fat-ass johnny boys. It was gonna be real tough on the Boulevard without Champagne. She was my girl, my family out here, no matter how dumb she be.

Cheilah found her on Lexington, behind the Circus Club. Cheilah was inside a john's car across the street, her face pressed against the window. She saw the whole damned thing, watched Champagne get pushed out of the car, and the motherfucker speed off.

"She just fell out, her arms and legs all like *this*, you know? Like a doll."

She'd been beaten to death. No knives, no wrenches, she hadn't even been raped. It was all fist on that sweet face. Only some crazy Down Low motherfucker would kill with a fist. A Carlos. Champagne wouldn't stick it in him, I'm sure of it, and that's what got her waxed. She would never use her jimmy, refused to, never wanted to be reminded it was there, and that's all a Carlos wanted. Jesus, nothing worse than a DL pansy chocha.

"I saw the car, though. We need to go to the police."

"And do what, Cheilah?" I asked her, tossing my hair—my real hair—back, looking high and mighty, the only one with any sense at all. Like the po-po ever give a shit.

We called 911 and didn't give our name. I told Fantasia she could move into the efficiency with me, which was an honor, taking my girl's place like that. Fair enough.

Fantasia made me laugh, tried to keep things light, even though she be the dylan of the bunch, with her big teeth and linebacker shoulders. Girl so ugly it make me like her.

Besides, I didn't want to pay for the efficiency by myself, not this late in the game. But when I got back to the pad, I couldn't throw none of Champagne's shit away. Every time I tried to touch her clothes, or makeup, or that chipped Wonder Woman coffee mug she loved so goddamned much, I'd get that pit in the gut that's all empty-like but heavy at the same time, and hear her laughing like she at the other end of a tunnel. You think I'd be done with the crying, but I couldn't help it. "You dumb bitch, you dumb bitch," I said to nothing but the tore-up shag carpet.

Me and Champagne go way back, both 16 when we started tricking out on the Boulevard. We were sweet meat, so good that the girls didn't mess with us, so long as we didn't steal their regulars. We upped the real estate. This was all back when the Yukon Diner was still open down the Boulevard, and we'd dress up after the worknight over, or after we dancing at the club, like four in the a.m., and parade ourselves through the place, before we feel all beat down by the Boulevard. All those drunk WeHo faggots and their hags be woot-wooting telling us how fabulous we looked, the girls with their look of pure envy—half-lids and too-wide smiles—as we worked it in our strappies and fringe, God

Damn we were something, and the juice still swishing in our asses.
Such fools, honey. Such fools.

We'd do the twirl in the Yukon, go back to the efficiency,
and count our money. We both saving for tits back then, because
we knew we both better than the Boulevard, wanted to get them
together, but we spent our fair share chasing the dragon, too, cuz
sometimes you needed a little numbing for the Boulevard. She
more than me, though. I wanted nice tits. And honey, when we
got them, we were unstoppable, the sexiest motherfucking Ts in
the mix. Ah, the feeling of walking down the street, feeling them
jiggle to my shimmy, it was one of the first moments I felt *right*,
you know what I'm saying? Like some kind of snap in the crackle-
pop. I loved when the johnnie boys would first open up my shirt
and see the woman on me. I would imagine when I no longer had
to trick, would imagine my real man opening up my shirt like that,
with love on his mind. Ooh, that feel right.

You bought these, baby, I'd say to the johnnie boys, and crush
their face in between.

I'm not gonna say that getting my ass hiked was a calling. It
was the only thing that I could find easy, and believe me honey, I
looked. No one wanted a pre-op T working their cash register, and
that paid shit next to the Boulevard on a good day. Besides, even
if some straight job hired me, they wouldn't let me wear what I
liked, and that's a problem. No one tell me what I can't put on this
body, and it's a fine-ass body. I lost mi familia for this shit, so I
ain't covering up these titties just to give some rotted fat-ass his
midnight donuts. I earned these motherfuckers, and they're not the
jacked up shit a bunch of these bitches settle for in some pendejo's
dirty bathroom at half-price. I went to a clinic in Beverly Hills for
these, straight up. White walls, clean waiting room, good magazine
selection. Nice doctor, friendly eyes, sat me down proper for a
consultation. And I did it right, nothing too big. And no doubt I
got the best ones on the Boulevard. But I'm more than my tits. I
got legs that make you wanna give up chicken your whole life, and
a thick ass, so strong I can tuck my jimmy way back between my
cheeks and hold it while I walk. And if they wanna see it, I lean
way back and make it pop right out like a jack-in-the-box. Some of

the boys really like that, and I'll do it for the dough. Wind me up, johnnie boy, *jingle-jingle-pop!*

The bus stops were the best places to go, the ones on the Boulevard between Orange and Las Palmas Streets, until the po-po started giving a shit and scaring the good johns away, trying to ass-lick the mayor, make the rents go up. I miss those boys. They would roll up in their Toyota Tercels and Honda Civics, very reliable cars, fiddle with their wedding bands as we talked rate. They would look at you with appreciation, make you forget you just a cheap-ass T. They never argued the price, so willing to give tips. Yes, honey, everybody wants a steady man.

Nowadays, the clientele's not the same. It's not so simple and easy, no Murphys, no sweet-talkers. The Honda Civics come less and less, now they got Grindr and shit. Now, it's johnnies not so afraid of the fuzz, but plenty afraid of what they are, so it's a whole different ballgame. They so fucked up they don't know they afraid, smelling like Tecate and all kinds of desperation, honey. We call them all Carlos. They be these pendejos all with wives and little niños running around in the yard, fixing cars and working construction jobs, muscles and big belt buckles and cowboy hats, but really they little faggots on the DL that want a big fucking jimmy up their ass. No shit. Champagne hated Carlos. They all skip work and go to this bar called Tempo, a fucking dump of a spot in a strip mall, down the street at Western, next to the Korean nail shop. You should see this place. You walk in, Tejano music blaring, and all the Carlos just standing there, all alone with their mustaches, pounding beer after beer. They get all worked up, glaring like animals on the hunt, but none of 'em say or do a damned thing to each other. Silent. They just keep drinking their beer until they get crazy fucked up and horny, and then they drive down the street, to us.

Shit gets more *unpleasant* with them, for sure, some rough fucking or a slap in the face here and there. Fantasia swear she hear them crying sometimes, but you never know seeing how hopped up she be on whatever she get her hands on. Cheilah said once that a Carlos was reciting the Hail Mary while she slipping him her jimmy, bent right over his back seat, and then he turned and slapped her right at the Amen. And that just wasn't my deal, oh no, but no Carlos ever did nothing crazy like what happened to Champagne. We just all knew they had it in them.

I started to T when I was 15, sneaking makeup and walking up and down Pacific Boulevard, pretending I was all Veronica Castro, the most glam bitch on mami's telenovelas. So many cars showed their appreciation, and I was born to walk in heels. I swung my leg cross the other just enough to let the booty roll, and the horns would be honking. Child, that was the shit right then, feeling so tall and ready for it all. I would walk until just before dinnertime, slip through my bedroom window and tug off my sister's dress, wipe the makeup off, go back to being the boy I knew I really wasn't. I think Esperanza knew what I was doing but never said anything. She had to, sharing a room and all. I wasn't exactly a ghost, and the more I did it the more I owned it, started getting a little cocky feeling so good about myself, staying a little later and a little later. Of course I was going to get caught, and maybe I wanted to, a little bit.

I went out on Pacific Avenue during Carnaval Primavera, and that was the end. It was risky, because my mami, sister, tia and that pendejo Alex my mother was talking about marrying were all out watching the parade. But so many people, I just couldn't help but get all dressed up, and I thought it would be easy to get lost in the crowd. I took one of Espie's dresses, the fuschia one with the empire waist and sequined top that she wore at some dance thing she did. It felt just right draping on my hips, showing that little scoop where my ass hit my waist, just made for a man to rest his big hand. My legs were already getting long then, and even though my shoulders were not so thin anymore, I knew how to pull them back to look smaller. With some Wet n' Wild on the lips and some of my mother's blue eyeshadow, I stepped out into the zoo of smiling people, looking fine. People looked at me, some woot-wooted, like I was part of the parade, and, honey, I floated, that was for sure. I moved the way I was supposed to—the swish and bootie—not that boxy, shoulders-down shuffle bullshit I had to fake so I wouldn't get my ass kicked. Huntington Park High School was no place for a woman like me. All the days of hiding beneath those dumb-ass baggy jeans and white t-shirts slipped away when the sun reflected off the sequins into my eyes, strutting down a sidewalk. As a boy, I was a sad looking thing, skinny and like I be sick. As a woman, I was Phoenix, I was Nefertiti, I was motherfuckin Xena. I was transformed.

But my mami recognized me. I didn't even have time to turn away before she be standing, out of the crowd, right in front of me. She saw her own black eyes looking back at her, and she was about to smile like mothers do, you know, but then saw the eyeshadow, the dress, the wilting hibiscus in my hair. "Eduardo?" she asked, her mouth looking like she was ready to suck the whole world in. God Damn I hated that name. Her forgotten plate of chicharrones slowly slipped onto the sidewalk, and I wanted to bend down and pick them up for her. I wanted to say please, mami. But she so shocked and I so shocked we couldn't see all the love we had right then. I ran the two blocks home in my sister's heels, and knew change was coming quick. The whole way home I saw my mami's face at that moment she recognized me—usually she see me with all the light in the world—sunk down and old, and that hit my gut like a bullet. Honey, what you can understand, running fast as hell in four-inch heels.

Everyone was yelling something. My mother, my tia, Alex screaming at them, this is your fault, you don't discipline him, you baby him, he needs a man in his life, and my mami yelling at him that he had no right to hit me, and me screaming, fuck you, pendejo, you're not my father, and I'm sorry, mami, and Espie hiding in our room, her dark hair shaking around her face, packing some of my things in a duffel bag because she knew how it all be going to end. He hit me so hard in the face that I fell down as quick as the blood came, but I still spit out you no man, you chocha, you fucking chocha. My mother started beating on his back, you can't hit my son, my baby, you get out of here.

You call me a pussy? What the fuck are you, maricon? You want to know what it's like to be a woman? Do you? Let me show you, you fucking maricon. Let me fucking show you. And he grabbed my mother by the back of the throat, slammed her face against the fake wood paneling, lifted up her skirt, and fucked her. See there, maricon? I was screaming on the floor, blood all in my mouth, red angry and red blood, and I watched as he jerked himself in her, each time her arms flailing out to nothing but the air, a low scream like it coming from her gut, like it knew this was a death. And I watched, and I didn't move. I laid there through the whole thing and didn't move. I couldn't move, and that's the thing. I didn't get up and beat that fucking pendejo, rip him off my mami. I just cried like a fucking spineless pansy-ass, my mami's cheek rubbed in her own spit, me whispering sorry mami, sorry mami, so low I bet she didn't hear it. I laid there after he was finished, after he fumbled with his pants, after he yelled through tears, see maricon, see maricon, after he left the room, after my mami slid down the wall onto the floor, her mouth still wide open but no sound coming out anymore, staring straight at me but not seeing me, both our faces laid sideways on the dirty, worn carpet.

I ran to Hollywood right away. There was no living at home after that, and it had nothing to do with me dressing all quincenera. I wasn't a man, and clothes had shit to do with that. I knew I could never look my mami in the eye after that, couldn't see that hurt in her ever again. And knowing that took me away from mi familia, from all of it. And Hollywood was as far away as I could get from Huntington Park. That's what had to be done.

At first it was sucking guys off for a place to stay, some Craigslist hookups. I hung out at this day shelter in Hollywood called My Friend's Place, where some dipshit rich fat white girl in grad school would try to have me "write down my feelings." Shit, write down that I didn't want to be a boy anymore, that I never wanted to be a boy, but I wasn't a girl, either, and mi familia was all I knew but I couldn't be with them? Who want to read that? It was stupid and made me feel like shit. It didn't take much time for me to find the Boulevard.

But me and Champagne, we were done with it, the hiking, the smell of cum and spit all over us and the long showers that never took it off. We'd been doing it for years, and it was time to go out before we be grannies like Mimi or Fantasia. And shit was going south, anyway, not like it be a vacay before. But it was the pinch and Mariya's OD that finally did it. We'd all been pinched before, but this time it was like a conspiracy or some shit. The fuzz came with this big-ass paddy wagon and just scooped us *all* up, I mean really hunted us down, like rats. You should have seen the back of that van, fingernails and glitter and running mascara all over the goddamned place. And when we got there, we were too many to book. I had already wiped the lipstick off, but they didn't even throw us in, just gave us a warning, took our money, made us walk all the way back, from downtown. That was some humiliating shit, all day in the SoCal sun, burning right through my dirty-ass clothes. No one walks in L.A., and none of us gonna ride the janky-ass bus. None of us. You seen the people on that thing? Hell. The po-po knew what they were doing, and that did it for me, let me tell you.

And then Mariya, the next day, and I knew it was a sign. After she OD'ed on Judas—her tongue all bit up and her eyeballs looking like they pulled out with a spoon—me and Champagne came home that night and threw all that shit away. Flush-a-lug. I knew we were chasing that shit just as much as Mariya, and I didn't want to go down that road. At first, I used to do it for kicks, but then it was something to do, keep things feeling far away when we hiking. But, hell no. Not no more. After we flushed it down, Champagne cut up some blow and promised to get serious. She was going to save the money for real now. The snip would happen. We were going to get off the Boulevard. Suck it up, do our business straight, no matter how much we hated it, get the snip, and get off the Boulevard.

"We'll do it together, just like last time," and shimmied her titties.

I watched her tilt her head back and nodding like it was the last yes there'd ever be, rubbing her nose and laughing a little in between "yes, yes." I could have been saying her wig on fire and she'd be the same way, nodding and laughing.

"Yeah, honey, that's what we'll do," I said.

She started crying, like real hard and shit, her mascara running crazy down her cheeks in big black lines.

"What is it, honey?" I asked.

She sucked the snot back in and said to me like it was the most truthful thing she ever say to any fool, "I never wanted to be no Tutie, Lalo."

Her face was a mess, something you'd kick out of the car, let me tell you. But, there she was, and you could see the light in her even when she be fucked up as all hell. It was something like pure gold in that girl, and not that fake shit. She had the kind that shines like it coming from within, even in the dark. I reached out and wiped her face, and she rested her head in my hand.

"None of us did, honey. It's all we had." And boy, I meant that more than I thought, and it made me miss a life I hadn't even lived yet, so much.

So, I went back to the clinic where I got my titties done. His name be Dr. Alter. That the funniest goddamned thing to me, but he's good, so he be the first I thought to do the snip. Honey, 25,000 dollars just to do the deed, and then all the other bread to make that shit look real. I was like oh, Hell. It time to get serious, been fucking around long enough. I came into the efficiency that afternoon with a grin that could eat shit, and some wine and cheese—real fancy. "No more of this half-life, Champagne." I poured us a glass and we clinked and sipped it with our pinkies out. I gave her the 411 for the plan, how we'd save, how we'd get the snip within the year. One year, Champagne, we can do it. I swear the smile on that girl was enough to make you promise the world. And I told Champagne that I was for real and, honey, her eyes light up like a Christmas tree. We put our foreheads together the way we do, our fake eyelashes almost touching. We must a looked like a pair of pussy-lickers, but we didn't care.

We talked about it every night after that. We'd sit at Benito's, with our taquitos, while the other girls gone chasing the dragon.

"Real pussies?" she'd ask, like I ain't tell her a hundred times already.

"Yup, honey, one real chocha for each of us."

"They can even fuck us *in* it?"

"And it would feel good, honey. All real-like."

"Could they catch the Bug from me in my new pussy?"

"No," I lied, cuz I didn't have the heart. I had asked, cuz I knew about Champagne, but Dr. Alter said they couldn't do the snip if someone had the Bug, too hard on their bodies, low T-cell count, or some shit. I wanted to tell Champagne, but all I could do when she laid her head on my lap and waited for me to dish the story again was trace the shape of my mami's name along her arm with my fingers. No one ever talked about the Bug, but I knew most of the girls had it, cuz they were dumb bitches. I just wish Champagne hadn't been such a dumb bitch, too.

"We'll come back from the snip and start life over, just like that. Take a jimmy off, and bring a Jimmy home," I'd say, and she'd giggle into my lap. "Fall in love, get married, make dinner for our men, let them watch sports on the weekend while we go shopping. Familia."

"Nordstrom's," she would always say.

"Yes, honey, and Macy's and Saks," I'd say, and finish filing her nails.

I didn't give a shit where we go, but Champagne wanted New York City. All right, I said. It didn't make any difference to me, as long as he nice and had a nice family. As long as it wasn't on the roachy-ass Boulevard, the smell of hot piss in the afternoon. Sometimes, I'd see our dream so much I'd even forget that Champagne wasn't coming with me. But damn, how you gonna tell a girl her dream done, just like that? What she live for, then?

And Champagne was a dumb bitch. She spent way too much money on all her shit, and even though she went off Judas a la cañona, she still bought blow and Oxies. I knew she wanted the snip, and I believed she meant it, but she wasn't gonna save, not fast enough, anyway, and I definitely wasn't going to wait for her ass, I couldn't, not anymore. I know how that work, seen most of these girls never get out. And I knew she couldn't get the snip, anyway. That's why I didn't feel as bad skimming off her money stash. I'd just take the top twenty off the pile every other night, that's all. That might not seem like a lot, but that shit add up, and she never noticed, not once. Champagne was too fucked up, and I knew she couldn't see the future as clear as I did. She thought of us as some Thelma and Louise bullshit, *we'll do it together, we'll do it together*, in that baby-doll voice she had. But I didn't want to drive off no goddamned cliff. I wanted to back the hell up, punch that motherfucker into fifth gear, and roll right through to something new. I wanted to get the hell out of L.A. and meet me a nice boy who would buy me some pollo adobo at a nice restaurant and then cuddle on the couch and watch old movies together. And, after we all settled in, doing the domestic thing, that's when I'd finally go back to HP and see mi familia.

Thanksgiving. I'd get a nice dress, all nice-girl like, with flowers on it and nice sensible sandles, no heels. I'd learn to cook and bring pibil in a casserole dish. My man would kiss my mami's hand, laugh at tia's jokes, and they'd know I'd done good for myself. I'd ask Espie about college. I know she going cuz I Google her name sometimes when I use the internets at the public library. I know she study at Cal State and her major is Psychology and she in some club on campus that feed the homeless.

God Damn, I couldn't wait. I also couldn't think about how it broke my heart that Champagne wouldn't be going with me. I'd just tell myself that if you think anyone is *really* with you, you a fool, plain and simple. I was going to Dr. Alter. Champagne would understand.

About a month after Champagne gone, I had my first appointment for the snip. I had 25,000. I'd been working it, more than ever, saving everything, counting it every other night. I even got a bank account, just in case Fantasia had sticky fingers. And I was saving. I quit drinking, quit the pills, wouldn't even take them when the johnnies asked me to. I would just slip them on my tongue and spit them out when they got all into it. I needed to keep my eye on the prize. Take the money, and take the money. Snip snip, and then the new life. Take the money, milk and honey. And I did it. I did it, Champagne. Mami, I did it.

I wore the sundress that covered my knees and took a cab to Beverly Hills. The office was in a high-rise, the marble walls so clean you could check your makeup. I felt like I was auditioning for one of the Hollywood movies, my mouth all dry and everything else sweaty. Dr. Alter met me in the waiting room and held his hand out like a gentleman, led me to his office.

"This is a very invasive surgery, Ms. Arana," he said.

"Call me, Lalo, Doctor. And you don't have to worry about that. I been eating good, and I stop taking pills and drinking, and all that."

"That's good, Lalo. But your tests show you are HIV Positive. Did you know this? In fact, your T-cells are well below 200." He leaned towards me, the skin between his eyebrows all bunched up. "Lalo, we need to get you checked out and put on medication immediately. You need to take care of yourself."

He look like a different man now, not a doctor but just any man, could have been a johnnie, and I was in any office. The pictures on the wall were travel posters, to Bermuda, to Paris, to The Great Wall of China, all looking fake as hell, like they were paintings, not real places. There was a clock on the wall above his head. The plants were real, one in every corner. The carpet looked like it was vacuumed right before I walked in. My hands were folded in my lap, but I couldn't feel them. I couldn't feel nothing, and something about the room got longer, like more clean carpet laid out, and I was being pulled far back from Dr. Alter. I looked down to see if I could move my hands, and they were little fists, between my legs. "I always wrap when I fuck. Every time. I'm safe."

"That's not the only way to contract the virus, Lalo. Who knows what it was. But, in your...line of work, and lifestyle, the risk is very high."

"You mean, I get the Bug from sucking dick or something? I never heard that."

"We need to get you care right away. It's important."

I could barely ask, and I guess I knew, but needed to hear it. "No snip? Ever?"

"Your T-cell count is very low."

I walked all the way back to the efficiency. I walked along the Sunset Strip, all the rich white bitches shopping or brunching or some shit, down to Santa Monica Boulevard, the muscle queens wearing their tank tops and puffing their chest out, lattes and patio tables. And I wanted to laugh at them, how fucking stupid they looked, but I knew they had more life than me, and always would, even in their dumb-ass way. And they probably laughing at me, anyhow. How could I think I was the one tranny bitch to get up cut of the Boulevard, think I was that special? That I'd have a man, have a life that looked like some straight bitch's, that I'd see mi familia again. I realized there ain't no story I heard ever end like that.

And I thought I'd been so careful, had done it as right as I could. That's the shit of it, ain't it?

Back at the efficiency I took off my dress and looked in the mirror. My titties, my long shiny hair, my flat stomach, my jimmy. My jimmy. I grabbed a trash bag and started shoving shit in there, I mean a real housecleaning. Dumped the ashtray, picked all the wrappers off the floor, even dirty stockings and clothes. If this was it, what my life was, I'd better make it clean as I could, right? At least a clean little space, clean and clear, a nice clean, fucking, tiny space. I brought the bag to Champagne's old table and swept my arm right across it—makeup, hairbands, the Wonder Woman coffee cup—all into the bag. I sat on the floor to catch my breath.

I went to the bank and took it all out, all the money I had saved for the snip. I got one of those big envelopes and put it all inside. I addressed it to Huntington Park, and wrote a note: "I was saving this money for a real life, Mami. Go out and buy yourself one." I stop just before I closed it up, took out the note, and added quick: "I'm sorry." I looked at the words, and it felt they were staring back at me, so I quickly crossed them out. I threw the note into the envelope, into the chute, and into the dark, before I could change my mind.

When I got back, I dressed up in a purple mini-skirt, my red bustier, pulled my hair up with a hairband. I looked in the mirror. The tears started coming, and I slapped my own self in the face. "What you crying for, you pansy-ass bitch? You chocha. Like you got the right." They wanted to keep coming. I leaned forward, real close to the mirror, my nose almost touching. "Fuck you," I said, stared hard into my eyes for a long time, until them tears pushed all the way back, and then went out the door, to work.

About a month later, me and Cheilah be working both sides of the back alley off the Boulevard, and an old brown El Dorado with a white replacement door drove all slow, like they do, up to me. He was in his 30's, looked like he was in good shape, and I thought maybe this one could be a little nice, for a change. When I saw his eyes, though, I could tell he was drunk as hell, and I knew he was a Carlos. Oh, well. I didn't give a fuck anymore. I'd just popped four Vicodin, so it was all smooth go for me anyway. I was leaning into the car window. Hey, I said. Hey, he said, and unlocked the passenger door. I said something like "not even gonna compliment a girl on her outfit?" or some funny shit, and before I opened the door I heard Cheilah yelling my name all sharp and shit, she forgetting to raise it high, like we do, and hell if that shit ain't deep as fuck, like Barry White and some shit. The hairs on my neck came right up, cuz before I even walked across the alley and she told me, I knew what she was going to say. This was a Carlos for sure, because he was *the* Carlos. And wouldn't you fucking know, but he looked a little like my mami's old boy, Alex.

"What should we do?" Cheilah asked. "About...?"

"I don't know, can't they fingerprint him, or do that CSI stuff on him?" Her face was real big, looking into my eyes the way she was, like she was a big moon and I was the planet she spun around. She was such a pretty girl, she really was, but it was cuz she made those eyes so round and open, and she meant them. How could she be on the Boulevard with a sweet face like that? Like Champagne. I wanted to cup that face in my hand and kiss it. And then slap the shit out of it.

I dropped my own face, instead, away from her sight. I let the hair fall all around it.

"No, honey, they wouldn't do nothing."

"Then, what we gonna do?" She was wringing her hands then. I looked back at the car. Champagne died in that car.

"What we gonna do, Lalo?"

A fucking El Dorado. That just be the shit of it, no, to not just die in a Carlos' car, but in that piece of shit. That piece of shit.

"Lalo, what we gonna do?"

I grabbed her wrists hard—even surprised myself—but I was shaking, like the question was some kind of attack on me. I looked her in the eyes like a tiger, and I wanted to hug her and tell her why, but what that gonna do if you haven't figured it out for yourself? I wasn't gonna kill her dream cuz mine done. I wasn't gonna bullshit her, either.

"What we gonna *do*? We gonna go to *work*, honey."

I dropped her arms and turned back towards the El Dorado.

"Lalo!" Now, this was said with all the high pitch, and then some. My name was shrieked at me, like a dog caught pissing on the floor, or a child about to put her finger in a light socket. Cheilah was fire red, balling her fists, tears coming down her face. "No."

It took everything I got, and I even breathed in some before I said it, cuz I knew it killed me, too. "It's what we do, honey," and kept myself together, like a statue. One stone cold bitch, because that what it take.

And she spit on me. Chucked one up right at my face. Got me clean on the cheek and eyelid. "Puta," she said, "you fucking puta," and walked away.

I watched her stomp around the corner, wiped the spit away. It's fine if she want to be like that. I knew why. She was young, still thought there was something else after this, an after this, at all. She'll learn, that being all high and mighty and all Kumbaya don't mean shit. Her friends will die, she'll get the Bug. Shit, her dreams dead by the time she first walk the Boulevard, and there ain't nothing more. At least I'd get her ready for the rest of it.

Carlos was too fucked to know what was going on with me and Cheilah. Inside the car, I saw that he had already taken his jacket off. I rubbed him through his jeans to get him started and asked him what he wanted to do. He didn't say nothing, buried his face, kissed me on the neck.

"Oh, honey, that's good," I said, and I wanted to stick my nails in his skull. "What you want Lalo to do for you?"

He hiked my skirt up real fast and started stroking me. "Is that what you want, honey?" I asked, and he whimpered, then reached into the back seat and grabbed a condom, tore open the package, and slid it down my jimmy. I said, "Sure, honey."

See, Champagne said no to Carlos, and that's why she dead. I looked down at my jimmy. And honey, that's why he dead. "Sure, honey."

He was young for a Carlos, and kind of had a sweet face. I tried to imagine him angry, enough to hurt Champagne the way he did. He probably was a nice motherfucker before his dreams taken away, too. Isn't that what it all is, why we all get so nasty? My teeth grit a lot more, now, I tell you that.

I did him from behind, how he wanted it. Still only whimpering, he held onto the dashboard, pushing himself back at me. As I got faster, his voice got higher. "You like me fucking you, baby?" I asked him, but he was gone, gone far away, into that place we all go when we dead. He didn't hear me, didn't see the streetlight glaring into the window, and didn't feel the temperature do that drop it does when the night wears on in L.A. I bet he was flying, way past his whole life, honey, somewhere beyond the cigarette-burned insides of his El Dorado, past the wife that was waiting for him back home, past the city limits, if there were any. Maybe he was even flying past Champagne's busted up body, her tittie popped out of the halter top, arms bent into the concrete like she was dancing to her favorite song, her bruises the color of an L.A. sunset when it hasn't rained for months.

I kept at it, and looked outside the car window, too, could see a little bit of Benito's behind the warehouse, the counter where we'd play the game. Champagne ask, leaning against the counter all sweet, "Where'd you be right now if not here? Tell me, Lalo."

I sighed, like one do. Oh, Champagne. I'd be doing something besides fucking this whimpering Carlos in the back of a jank-ass car, the smell of his shit and sweat on my hands, on my tongue, and Champagne's face staring back at me from that little corner of Benito's. *We'll do it together. We'll do it together.* Her face in my hands, her laughing at some funny shit I said, her looking at me sometimes like I was the last bitch in the world who told the truth. Those times when we were woot-wooted in the Yukon Diner because we believed we were that fucking hot, when we danced at the club to get the Boulevard out of our heads, eating our Del Taco and picturing the men we'd meet when we done got the snip, thinking this all was the means to some end, and not the end from the beginning.

And her busted up dead body in the concrete, her mouth wide open but no sound coming out anymore, staring straight at me but not seeing me.

I moved my hand from Carlos' cock to my own, but I kept pumping. I wrapped my fingers around me, and rolled the rubber off, but I kept pumping, and dropped it to the floor. Carlos kept whimpering. And I kept pumping and thought about the handsome boy who was never going to carry me up the stairs, that I would never curl up with on a couch, who'd never meet mi familia. Mi familia. And when I came inside Carlos, I bit my lip, didn't make a sound, but made sure that I was all the way up in there. I filled him up, filled him up with everything I was and everything I was never gonna be, motherfucker, and kept going after that, just to make sure. I leaned down to his ear, and said real softly through my gritted teeth, so he didn't know I be crying, "You want to know what it's like to be a woman? Do you? Do you, Carlos?" and I kept going after that, because what else is there.

LIFE AND THE THEATER
MICHAEL H. WARD

At 7:45 a.m. on the first day of the fall semester, Pat Kelly paused in the center aisle of the theater at the University of Omaha, noticing the utter stillness in the space, which was lit only by the red emergency lights above the exit doors. Feeling a little shiver up the small of his back, he briefly imagined the presence of the myriad actors and characters that had inhabited the wide stage. The ceiling rose two stories, and there was an elaborate technical booth high up in the rear of the auditorium, which could be accessed either from a long ladder on the first floor or from the hallway on the second. He made his way down the aisle and turned left, climbed a short set of stairs and then pushed through a heavy pair of black curtains to a tiny anteroom with two doors. The one on the left led outside to a parking lot, the one straight ahead contained a silver nameplate that said, in large black lettering, Norman Lewis, Ph.D., Director. Pat inserted the key that had been given to him by the Office of Student Affairs and opened the door.

The office was remarkably small, maybe ten by twelve feet, and was saved from generating claustrophobia in its occupants by the presence of two long windows, one facing east into the parking lot, the other south toward Elmwood Park. The sunlight was so bright, the room felt like a theater set. The office held a standard-sized metal desk, with drawers on one end and a filing cabinet on the other. A small, narrow desk in the shape of an L abutted the larger one, with a typewriter at the end. Bookcases of various sizes filled every other possible space. There were piles of papers, books, files, and scripts of plays on every surface and on the floor. This would be Pat's work-study placement for the next four months, assisting Dr. Lewis for two hours each weekday morning, for which he would receive a reduction in his tuition.

Pat was still standing in the doorway when he felt a hand grasp his shoulder and a deep voice said, "You must be my new secretary. My God, you're tall!"

Pat yelped, jerking forward and scattering a pile of books on the desk in front of him.

Dr. Lewis barked a laugh and, squeezing past Pat, sat down on the rolling chair on the other side of the desk. He looked his new assistant up and down. Pat had seen the professor in the halls during his freshman year and knew he was short, but with Pat at six feet, three inches, the doctor looked almost Lilliputian. He wore his silver hair a little longer than was fashionable in the Midwest and had on a charcoal suit with a white shirt and red-and-blue striped tie.

"I asked for a male this year. The girl last year was terribly fat, and her monthlies were fierce. We had to have the windows open most of the time and she complained endlessly. I hope you aren't a complainer."

"No sir," said Pat, wondering what "monthlies" were. Clearly not magazines.

"Well, sit down then and stop looming over me. Can you type?"

"Yes sir," he said, not adding that his typing was neither fast nor particularly accurate.

"Well, you'll have to do my correspondence and order play scripts and the like. I'm usually not here before 9:00, especially when I'm directing, but this first week of the new semester we have a lot of paperwork to deal with." He looked around the space and added, "You can neaten up when you first get in. But don't touch the papers on my desk. I know exactly where everything is. Neola, your predecessor, constantly fussed with my papers. It infuriated me."

"Yes sir."

"Please!" He drew the vowel out theatrically. "No more sirs. You may call me Professor."

❖

It took Pat weeks to relax even marginally when Dr. Lewis was in the office. His moods ranged from pleasant to critical to indifferent. After a time Pat suspected that the professor's state of mind might be affected by alcohol, which, in such close quarters, Pat could often smell on his breath. Occasionally, and for no apparent reason, Dr. Lewis would engage Pat in conversation, calling him his proper name, Padraic, and asking about his family and his hopes for the future. Dr. Lewis seemed intrigued by what he called "the working Irish," as if there were another group called "the non-working Irish." Pat was grateful that his family belonged in the former group. Other times the doctor talked about his life with his wife, Tanya, who was the chair of the speech and drama department at the tony Beekman Day School for Girls. Then he might go for days hardly speaking, while Pat tapped away on the typewriter, transcribing letters and order forms from the doctor's fussy cursive.

On Mondays and Wednesdays, promptly at 9:50 a.m., they would rise together and walk through the theater to the main hallway of the building and march briskly to Room 105, for the Oral Interpretation of Literature class. The first time they made this trip, Pat was instructed to walk several paces behind his boss, who said Pat's presence at his side made him look "diminutive."

Pat intended to major in drama, even though his oral interpretations in the classroom mostly garnered criticism. He got through only the first stanza of his reading of T. S. Eliot's "The Love Song of J. Alfred Prufrock" before Dr. Lewis said, "Stop! Stop! This sounds like a dirge. Da da da da da, da da da da da. Start over and read with feeling. Take your time. Breathe." Pat started once more, trying hard to feel the words. Mercifully, he was not interrupted again, but the doctor drew a laugh from the class when he said, "Well, now I know first person what the line 'like a patient etherized upon a table' means." Pat took comfort in the fact that Dr. Lewis was equally critical of nearly everyone else in the class, with the possible exception of Fred Gaeta, a senior athlete and drama major whose smarmy earnestness made Pat nauseous.

The fall play that year was Tennessee Williams' *The Glass Menagerie*. Pat secretly hoped that he would be cast as Jim O'Connor, the Gentleman Caller, but his hopes were dashed when Dr. Lewis announced that he needed Pat to be the Assistant Director. They were sitting in the office creating a master schedule for rehearsals when he saw the disappointment on Pat's face.

"Padraic! Surely you weren't planning to try out for the part of Tom Wingfield. You're only a sophomore, and you have no college acting experience."

"No, not Tom Wingfield. The Gentleman Caller. I thought maybe…"

"Dear boy, maybe next semester. I'm thinking of doing *Guys and Dolls* in the spring, and there are several parts you could do handsomely. But producing Williams is exhausting, both for director and cast." He looked at Pat speculatively. "You know of course that he's gay."

"Who?" Pat asked.

Dr. Lewis made a face. "Williams! But we'll talk more about that later. For this production I'll need you at my side. We have important work to do."

Pat took note of his use of "we" and felt somewhat mollified. On the downside, it meant many more hours together, evenings as well as the morning office hours, but being an Assistant Director sounded important. And, as a bonus, he would get an additional class credit hour.

On the second Monday evening of October, a group of about 25 students showed up in the auditorium for a general information meeting about the production. Some were theater majors hoping for parts, others wanted to work lights and sound or create scenery or do props. The professor and Pat sat in folding chairs at the edge of the stage, with the students scattered throughout the first few rows of seats. Pat felt drama in the moment, the beginning of something new and exciting in his life. Dr. Lewis began by sharing his experience of living in Manhattan as a young man after World War II, completing his classes for his PhD in theater at NYU while studying at the Herbert Berghof Studio. He had even sung in the chorus of two off-Broadway shows. In those years he'd seen multiple productions of Tennessee Williams' plays. He gave a stirring talk about Williams' place in the American theater, sharing that *The Glass Menagerie* was his personal favorite, "the intimacy of only four characters, the power of the relationships. So much is said, and so much not said." Pat was deeply touched by his words.

The students were quiet for a moment, then Frankie Hunt raised her hand. She was a senior, a theater major, and had had the female lead in nearly every play since she'd come to the university as a freshman. In high school, Frankie had been a star pupil and protégé of Mrs. Lewis. Pat had a hopeless but enduring crush on Frankie. Twenty-one years old, she seemed vastly more sophisticated than the other students. She had poise and self-assurance, plus the dark good looks of a 1940s movie star. She was headed for New York City after graduation in June.

"Dr. Lewis, when will we be reading for you?" Frankie asked.

"Since there are only four roles, I think we'll read for all of them tomorrow night. Be sure to take a script home with you. And a schedule! We'll be rehearsing four nights a week through the fifth week, then doing run-throughs and dress rehearsal the sixth. Opening night is Thursday, November 21, four shows that week, four the next." He looked at Pat sitting beside him and smiled benevolently. "For those of you who don't know him, this is Padraic Kelly, my student staff person this semester, and he'll also be the Assistant Director for this production." Pat felt mildly embarrassed but smiled, unexpectedly making eye contact with Frankie Hunt. He hoped he wasn't blushing.

As Pat had imagined, Frankie was cast as Amanda Wingfield and Fred Gaeta as her son, Tom. A small, thin girl named Tricia Larsen was cast as Laura, and George Hardy as the Gentleman Caller. They were both sophomores and very excited to be part of the ensemble. Fred had done lead roles in several plays but had never had so many lines or been on stage so much of the time. He and Frankie immediately began running lines, but he clung to his script, glancing down frequently for reassurance. Soon Frankie was not using a script at all, though she continued to hold it. Pat suspected she was trying to be supportive of Fred.

Halfway through rehearsals, all scenes had been blocked. The stage manager had assembled enough furniture to represent the Wingfield apartment adequately. The pressure was on the actors.

Dr. Lewis had been remarkably patient up to this point, giving notes at the end of each scene, talking directly to the actors about motivation and affect. While Frankie was clearly superior to everyone else in the cast, Dr. Lewis still gave her direction. Pat thought he was less friendly to her, or maybe less kind, than he was to Fred and the others, almost as if he appreciated her talent but didn't actually like her. Fred was having trouble with his monologues, but Dr. Lewis was invariably nurturing, speaking calmly to him, encouraging him to access Tom's barely repressed frustration and rage. That is, until Fred, in what was supposed to be a dramatic moment, walked rather than stormed across the stage, turned to face his mother, and flubbed his lines for the third time in a row. Dr. Lewis, sitting in the front row of the auditorium, rose up and threw his clipboard across the stage, where it slid under the Wingfield's dining room table.

"FRED! MY GOD, FRED! Have you ever acted in a play before? This is unbearable! We have two more weeks of rehearsal and you still need the FUCKING SCRIPT!" And he stormed up the aisle of the theater, the heavy door to the hallway clanging shut behind him.

The cast looked stunned, Fred shamefaced and refusing to make eye contact with anyone. Frankie walked across the stage, took his script and hers, and flung them under the table to join Dr. Lewis's clipboard. Slipping an arm around Fred's waist, she looked out at Pat, still sitting frozen in the front row, and said, "I think rehearsal is over for tonight. Right, Pat?" He nodded as Frankie steered Fred out the side door of the theater.

Pat tossed and turned all night, wondering what he had let himself in for when he took this job. He dreaded going into work the next day, imagining all sorts of abuse from the professor. But when Dr. Lewis came into the office, he was carrying two paper cups of coffee.

"You take cream, don't you, Padraic?"

"Yes, thank you." This was a first.

Dr. Lewis settled into his chair and rifled through the mail. Finally he looked up. And smiled, a real smile, maybe the first sincere smile Pat had ever seen on his face. "What did you think of my performance last night?"

Without filtering, Pat said, "You scared me to death!" And they both laughed.

"There's a point in every production in which I have to assert my authority and model how to express feeling, how to steal the scene, as it were. Fred is a moderately good actor and will be better when he's older, but he's still frightened to let go. I demonstrated letting go."

Pat sipped his coffee, pleased that Dr. Lewis had been unexpectedly thoughtful, and said, "Professor, may I ask you a question?"

"Of course, Padraic."

"You said when you talked to the cast that Williams leaves much unsaid. What did you mean?"

"There has been a lot of gossip in the theater world about Williams' male characters, often single, often alone. Some have suggested that Tom Wingfield was secretly gay and going to bars at night, not to the movies. But when the play was first performed in the 40s, and even today, that subject can't really be talked about openly in the press."

Pat nodded, uncertain what else to say.

At rehearsal the following Monday, nothing was said about the director's outburst, and Fred seemed to find his way into the role of Tom Wingfield a little more fully each day. He and Frankie were spending every spare minute running lines, and by the end of that week, both without scripts, Fred rarely needed even to be prompted.

❖

Much to Pat's surprise and delight, Frankie had taken a liking to him. His role as Assistant Director wasn't much different from his job as office assistant, but he was happy that the cast and crew treated him respectfully, and he offered help as best he could. Pat didn't have a car and took the bus home from the university if no one was going his direction. One night Frankie drove by as he waited at the bus stop, and from then on, she always checked with him to see if he needed a ride. He felt like her kid brother, but she treated him as an equal, and they spent hours talking about life and the theater, and about Dr. and Mrs. Lewis. Frankie said they were complicated, that they presented themselves as a loving couple, but she had reason to suspect that they were both closeted homosexuals. At Frankie's high school, there had been persistent rumors about Mrs. Lewis and the French teacher, Angelique Raymond. Frankie believed that the doctor had had sex with at least one of his male students the previous year. She also thought they were both alcoholics.

"Has he ever come on to you?" she asked. They had stopped at the Longhorn Diner for something to eat on the way to Pat's house.

"Oh God, no, I don't think he would."

"Why not?"

Pat didn't know what to say. He felt out of his depth. Teachers were to be respected and to stay at arm's length. "The idea creeps me out. But I do smell alcohol on his breath most mornings, especially since we started rehearsals."

"Pat, I think he's got a crush on you. I'm not saying this to flatter you. I just notice how possessive he is of you, and how he looks at you. Are you gay?"

Pat nearly choked on his coffee. "No. Maybe. I don't think so," he sputtered. He thought of Lenny, the one man he'd been sexual with a few months before. It had been one of the happiest nights of his life, but the subsequent guilt and shame, and the fear of being found out, had pushed him back into celibacy.

"I hope I haven't embarrassed you," Frankie said. "There's nothing to be embarrassed about. My older brother is gay. He's moved to San Francisco and has a boyfriend."

Pat thought she was the most sophisticated person he'd ever met.

Opening night, November 21, with the cast and crew assembled on stage, Dr. Lewis raised his hand for silence. As the young people settled down, he cupped his hand to his ear, and at once everyone became acutely aware of the sounds on the other side of the curtain, several hundred people talking and laughing as they settled into their seats. Pat wondered if Dr. Lewis was himself nervous. Dress rehearsal had gone off the rails twice the night before.

"People," he said, "I can only ask you to do your best. I know some of you are nervous, but a little stage fright can sharpen your performance. Stay focused and listen for your cues, especially in Act II." He made eye contact with each of the cast members. "You are not your usual selves tonight. You're working class people in St. Louis during the Great Depression. Before the curtain rises, let's give thanks to Tennessee Williams for this great play, and remember his words: 'I don't want realism. I want magic!' Let's make magic tonight." And he turned and left the stage, leaving Pat to find a Kleenex for Fred, who had tears running down his face.

Pat followed the professor, entering the office in time to see him taking a bottle of Jack Daniels out of the filing cabinet. He smiled at Pat and said, "Do you want a swig?"

"I don't think so. I'm nervous enough as it is," Pat said, feeling like they were comrades in this moment, six hard weeks of work coming alive outside the room as the curtain came up. Grinning, Dr. Lewis toasted Pat with the bottle.

They moved noiselessly from the office, downstairs and through the green room, ending up in the rear of the theater, where Dr. Lewis jotted notes on the cast's performances. During the intermission they slipped outside and smoked a cigarette, then returned to their posts for most of the second act. When the curtain came down, there was a long moment of silence, then the sound of thunderous applause. "Well, Padraic," the professor said, "I believe we have another hit on our hands." The applause continued through the entrances of Tricia Larsen and George Hardy, became even louder when Fred came onstage, and rose to a roar and standing ovation when Frankie came out, looking fresh and radiant. "God damn her," Dr. Lewis said grudgingly. "She does it every time."

Later, at the after party, cast and crew shared what liquor they had been able to secure, and Fred, who was the host, had bought chips and dip and some blocks of cheese, as well as two cases of beer. Spirits were very high, crew members acknowledging misplaced props, cast members talking over each other about near disasters with dialogue. Fred toasted Frankie for quick thinking when he dropped several lines in a scene with his mother on the fire escape and she effortlessly covered for him.

Frankie had brought a pint of Scotch, which she offered to share with Pat. Unused to drinking hard liquor, and completely exhausted from the press of the recent weeks, he soon felt tipsy. Fred put an Ella Fitzgerald album on the record player and danced with Tricia while another couple made out on the couch. Pat had been sitting in a wing chair, Frankie on his lap with her head on his shoulder, and he felt dizzy from the alcohol and their proximity to each other. He was vaguely aware that he was aroused. Frankie finally sat up and stretched, kissed him on the cheek, and said, "We'd better get going. I'll never get you home if I fall asleep here, and I know your mother worries about you." Pat had told Frankie that his mother always referred to her as "the older woman," which they both found hilarious. When Frankie dropped him off at home, Pat impulsively leaned over and kissed her on the mouth, then bolted into the house. It was after 1:00 and he tried to be as quiet as he could, but his mother called to him in a loud whisper from his parents' bedroom, "Are you ok? Did it go well?"

"Tomorrow, Mom. Tomorrow." After he used the bathroom, he slipped into his bedroom and passed out on top of the covers, head spinning but filled with bliss.

Pat had no classes on Friday morning and had instructed his mother to let him sleep, but he was jolted awake by her shaking him and saying frantically, "Wake up, Padraic, wake up!" She only called him by his proper name when she was upset and he wondered what he'd done, but she immediately went back to the living room. He stumbled out to join her and found her literally wringing her hands.

"They don't know if he'll live," she said, her voice shaking.

"Who?" Pat asked.

"The President. The President was shot in Texas." Pat tried to make sense of it. *Who would shoot the president? Doesn't he have bodyguards?* Then the announcement came, voiced by Walter Cronkite:

"From Dallas, Texas, the flash apparently official, President Kennedy died at 1 p.m. Central Standard Time, some 38 minutes ago."

❖

In a decision that left the students dumbfounded, Dr. Lewis instructed Pat to call the actors and crew and tell them the show would be performed as scheduled at 8:00 p.m. that evening.

"Are you sure, Professor?" Pat was pleading. "I've talked to all four actors and everyone's a mess."

"Padraic, this is indeed a tragedy. Worldwide. But we have a responsibility to our audience. We have 300 seats sold for tonight and many people will welcome the chance to escape this trauma for a few hours." When Pat remained silent, the director continued. "Last year we performed *Death of a Salesman* during the Bay of Pigs invasion! Especially in crisis, people need relief."

Pat was glad he was on the phone and Dr. Lewis couldn't see the scornful look on his face. *Right, and we won't have to deal with rebooking tickets or adding an extra performance.* He felt outraged, but simply replied, "Yes sir. I'll make the calls." Then Pat watched the coverage on television with his mother for an hour, both of them crying. His mother's framed photograph of JFK sat on the dining room sideboard on one side of a vase, a picture of the Blessed Virgin on the other. Pat's mother had taken the candle from in front of Mary and put it, lighted, in front of the president.

❖

The run of the play, eight performances over two weekends, ended on Sunday, December 1, with a matinee performance.

The days between opening night and the closing had been filled with confusion and grief. The cast had been diligent in their performances, and while most of the students remained angry about having to perform on the day of the assassination, and to a very small audience, many theatergoers thanked Dr. Lewis for providing a play of great beauty at such a troubled moment. He intoned, "It is a tragic play in a tragic situation."

Pat, who was still grieving, found it odd that, during their office hours in this period of national mourning, the professor was downright cheerful. He and Mrs. Lewis were moving into a new house at the beginning of December, and he asked Pat if he could "borrow his brawn" to help move the items that they didn't trust with the movers. "I'll pay you five dollars an hour," he said, "and Tanya will make us lunch." After the move, there would be only one more week of classes and then final exams. Dr. Lewis had already asked Pat to stay on in his office job for the second semester, and Pat had said he would if his class schedule permitted.

All the students, Pat included, were cramming for exams and trying feverishly to finish term papers that had been ignored during the run of the play. Pat and Frankie had seen each other sporadically, but she was very busy working on her senior thesis and rehearsing a monologue for her final project in acting class.

During this same week Dr. Lewis praised Pat's recitation in class of Dylan Thomas' "Fern Hill," though he apparently couldn't resist making a small joke about an Irishman demonstrating admiration for a Welshman. When Pat told Frankie over coffee what had happened, she rolled her eyes and said, "Stay alert. Everything he does has a hidden agenda." Pat recalled her warning the next morning when the professor entered the office whistling and, squeezing past Pat in his chair, ran his fingers through Pat's thick coppery hair and said, "Padraic, someday I want to run barefoot through this hair of yours."

Pat was speechless.

❖

The day of the move was sunny and cold, and at 7:00 a.m., Pat was dressed and waiting to be picked up in front of his parents' house. The professor and his wife had already had the movers take the furniture and bulky items over the day before, but he wanted their clothes and artwork to be moved in his car. This task would entail most of the day, given the size of the job, and Pat was to drive the Lewis' Ford Country Squire station wagon, a "workhorse," according to the professor. Pat would pack the car, drive to the new house to unload, and return to the old house for another load. Meanwhile the Lewises would unpack and arrange the furniture and artwork in the new house.

Pat was excited and a bit nervous. He'd never spent time with Dr. Lewis outside the University, nor had he met Mrs. Lewis. They were often pictured in the *Omaha World Herald*, attending social or charitable events, always looking glamorous in black. Pat had answered phone calls to Dr. Lewis from his wife in the office, and her deep and somewhat theatrical voice had intrigued him. He hoped for an enjoyable day, and for some much needed extra cash.

In due time the professor arrived, the station wagon already partially packed with boxes, and reached across the front seat to unlock the door. Pat slid into the passenger seat and they exchanged good mornings. Dr. Lewis looked tired and said, "It was a long night. Tanya's mother was taken ill in Kansas City, and she had to drive down to see if she needs to be hospitalized." He punched in the cigarette lighter and offered Pat a filtered Winston, which Pat accepted, and they lit up.

"I'm sorry," Pat said, and the professor waved his hand dismissively.

"She's a hypochondriac. It's probably nothing."

Pat said, "I'm sorry I won't meet your wife. Who else will be helping today?"

Professor Lewis smiled. "Just us chickens," he said, squeezing Pat's knee.

Pat felt a sudden lurch in his stomach.

Soon they arrived at the old house, a small but lovely Tudor with a two-car garage. The scene looked chaotic, framed artwork stacked against the walls, small sculptures and *objects d'art* waiting to be wrapped and packed in the boxes scattered across the floor.

The professor was suddenly brusque, giving directions and detailing how he wanted the car packed and how to manage the several closets full of clothes without items getting dirty or damaged. Pat listened carefully, nodding agreement and beginning, ever so carefully, to wrap the smaller objects in packing paper and place them in cartons. They filled the back end of the station wagon and headed west, encountering little traffic on a Saturday morning. The new house, which sat on a well-landscaped lot, was a contemporary design, with many large windows and a cathedral ceiling in the living room. Pat backed the car carefully into the driveway. Before they unpacked the car, Dr. Lewis took Pat by the arm and walked him through the house, clearly very proud of what he called their "new digs." Pat felt awkward in the grand rooms, one after another, all of them painted a soft white. Then he and the professor unpacked the station wagon quietly and efficiently, and Pat was soon driving back by himself for the next of many trips to and from the new house.

After the fourth trip it was midmorning and the professor called for a break. The smell of whiskey was strong on his breath. Pat had been working hard for almost three hours and was sweating, despite the cold outside, so he shrugged off his coat and sat down on a kitchen chair. Dr. Lewis handed him a cup of coffee, "the way you like it," having already added cream, and a large blueberry muffin. The professor drank his coffee black. Pat assumed it was spiked.

"It's so pleasant to see you under these circumstances, Padraic. You've been my rock in the office this semester. You're so responsible! I hope your parents are proud of you, the first one in your generation to go to college." Pat knew this was meant to be a compliment but it felt condescending.

"My father has been taking classes at the University for years, Dr. Lewis. But he's quirky. He only takes classes in subjects he's interested in. So he'll probably never receive a degree."

"I think we can dispense with you calling me 'Dr. Lewis' for today. It makes me feel old. Call me Norman. But never Norm!" and he laughed as if he'd said something funny.

Pat stood up and stretched. He was wearing an old blue tee shirt and khaki work pants and sneakers. He realized too late that Dr. Lewis was admiring his body.

"Make me a bicep, Pat. C'mon."

Flushing, Pat moved backwards toward the door to the garage. "I need to get moving if we're going to finish the job today." He grabbed his jacket, slipped into the garage and was gone.

In the car he turned the radio up. KOIL was playing the weekly top ten, and Pat tried singing along to the Drifters' "Up on the Roof" but snapped the radio off half way through. Feeling agitated, he surveyed what was left at the old house and thought he might be able to make it in two more trips, three at the most. He packed rapidly, in his haste dropping a small crystal bowl, which shattered. He swept up the pieces, placing them in a paper bag on the floor in the front seat of the station wagon, planning to tell the doctor when he got back to the house.

But by then Professor Lewis was beginning to slur his words. He was sitting on the sofa in the living room, stacks of boxes and artwork still unpacked, looking at a picture album. He leapt up when Pat came in and took two shot glasses out of a cupboard.

"Let's have a toast, Pat. A toast to us."

"I don't drink hard liquor, Doctor. It makes me sick to my stomach. And I'm driving."

"Call me Norman, darling. You promised," he said. "And don't be stupid." He handed Pat a brimming shot glass, clicked his glass to Pat's, and drank it down. With a grimace, Pat swallowed his as well. It burned unpleasantly in his stomach. When the doctor turned to look for another bottle, Pat fled the house and drove away. He parked outside the old house, paralyzed with anxiety. Despite the accumulation of heavy-handed clues, he couldn't believe that Dr. Lewis would actually try to force him to have sex. The idea was revolting. *Run barefoot through my hair, indeed!* But he was trapped: the professor was his classroom teacher, his boss, and the person who would be directing his major in drama. He could think of no one to ask for help. Even if he called Frankie, what could she do? He had to finish this job and then get the doctor to drive him home. He packed the car until it was jammed, leaving behind only small things that the Lewises could easily move on their own. He drove slowly and carefully to the new house, fearful of being arrested for drunk driving, and hurriedly unloaded the car into the garage.

Pat startled when he turned to see Norman standing in the open kitchen door wearing a bathrobe, with a shot of whiskey in each hand. As much as he wanted to run, all his training in passivity came into play. *Never resist authority. Don't talk back to your betters. Finish what you start.* No one had ever said to him, "If you're terrified, run for your life!" Shoulders sagging in defeat, he downed one shot of whiskey, then the other, and Norman, smiling, led him into the bedroom. Eyes closed, he could feel his shoes being taken off, then his khakis unbuckled and removed. Feebly, he let go of the waistband of his Jockey shorts, while Norman cooed, "such a beautiful body, and what a nice piece of meat you have there." Pat silently began to pray to the Blessed Mother, who had always, even when Pat began to question his faith in God, been the go-to person when he was afraid. He said the Hail Mary over and over as he felt Norman rubbing the inside of his thighs and grasping his testicles. Bile backed up into his throat, but he didn't choke. "Holy Mary, Mother of God, pray for us sinners, now and at the hour of our death, Amen." And then he passed out cold.

When Pat came to, it was dark in the bedroom. He was wearing only his tee shirt and socks, and he was freezing. Sitting up, he put his hands on both sides of his aching head and tried to get oriented. The only light he could see was on in the bathroom, so he managed to get in there and relieve his bladder. Dr. Lewis called from the living room, "Are you finally awake, Padraic?" Pat cringed when he heard his voice. He looked around for his clothes and got dressed, then went out into the living room, where the professor was again sitting on his sofa, this time dressed in slacks and a shirt, looking at the same photo album he'd had out earlier.

He said, "Come sit here, dear boy. I've made some more coffee. It's nearly five o'clock and your mother will be expecting you for dinner." Pat was startled to realize that nearly two hours had passed. Then he felt a moment of panic.

"What did you do to me?" he asked, his voice rising.

"What do you mean, 'to you'?" You seemed to enjoy it, what little that happened."

Pat asked again, "What did you do to me?"

The professor seemed not at all drunk now, and he teetered between amusement and cruelty. "Sadly, you were too drunk to do much of anything, including getting hard. I'm disappointed not to have seen the goods in action. I finally had to give up and make some coffee. I've already showered, but I think you'd better take yours at home."

Pat's head was throbbing, and he didn't know if he believed him or not. Then Dr. Lewis put the album on Pat's lap and pointed to a photo of himself and another young man in uniform.

"I want you to see me in younger days. This is my friend, Sam Reardon. He was my buddy in the Army. Look at us! We were still in our twenties!" Pat said nothing. "This was before I was married, of course, and when I came home from France, I wanted only to finish graduate school and make some kind of life for myself. Sam wanted more, but I couldn't imagine how we could have a life together. You know." He hesitated and cleared his throat. Eyes damp, he said, "Sometimes I wonder...about the road not taken." He looked up at Pat, who remained silent, refusing to make eye contact. Dr. Lewis closed the book with a snap and said, "OK, I guess we're done here. Can you put on your shoes?" His voice had grown nasty. Pat put on his sneakers and coat, and in complete silence, Dr. Lewis drove him home. Parked in front of the Kelly's house, he pulled out his wallet and extracted four ten-dollar bills. "This is for eight hours' work." Then he removed a twenty and gave it to Pat, saying, "And this is a tip, for services rendered. Almost." And he laughed. Pat crumpled the money and shoved it into his coat pocket.

Inside the house, Pat begged off dinner with the family, took a scalding bath, and went right to bed.

❖

The next morning, still hung over and feeling fragile, he called Frankie while his family was at Mass. As soon as she heard the crack in his voice, she said, "I'll pick you up in ten minutes." Back in a booth at the Longhorn Diner, Pat haltingly revealed what had happened the day before, and when he got to the part of being led into the bedroom, "like a lamb to slaughter," his eyes flooded with tears. Frankie's face was the perfect picture of rage.

"The dirty bastard," she said. "The dirty bastard!" loud enough the second time to raise heads in the adjacent booth. "He should be criminally prosecuted. But you aren't underage, and he'd lie his way out of it." Mimicking the doctor's affected speech, she said, "Oh, I'm so sorry for the dear boy. He was probably hoping for a higher grade."

Pat couldn't help but laugh. Then, serious again, he asked, "Do you want to hear the gory details?"

She thought for a moment. "I don't think so, Pat. I love you too much." He reached for her hand, and she began to cry.

"Well," he said, "I'm relieved to say I don't think he got what he wanted."

Frankie wiped her eyes. "Let's make sure he doesn't get the chance again."

❖

Dr. Lewis didn't show up for office hours the next week, claiming to be busy settling the new house. They did speak on the phone, and Pat took directions for getting Dr. Lewis's grades into the Registrar's office. There was no chitchat. Since the professor's classes were all done in performance, there were no written exams to be graded. Pat extracted the class lists from the file, noting the A he had received in Oral Interpretation of Literature, and submitted the grades.

His last scheduled day in the office was Wednesday, December 17, when the University closed for a month-long semester break. Pat sat in his chair looking out the windows, realizing how rarely he had actually taken in the view of the park. Snow was falling softly, and he could hear the school choir practicing on the stage in the auditorium.

Finally it was time. He turned to his typewriter and wrote the following message:

Dear Doctor Lewis,

Due to a change in plans, I will not be working for you during the spring semester. I hope you will find someone who better meets your needs.

I have already changed my major to English, so I will not be taking the second semester of Oral Interpretation of Literature.

I assume you found the shattered bowl in the front of your station wagon. I'm leaving this money for a replacement. I hope it will compensate for what was broken that day.

Pat removed the letter from the typewriter and, without signing it, laid the note and the crumpled twenty-dollar bill on the desk, locked the door, and put the key through the mail slot.

WHILE TRYING TO ESCAPE
SCOTT POMFRET

The moment my dark boat-friend and I stepped onto the levee, a Freedom Agent greeted us at gunpoint. Pistol cocked, eyes narrowed, hand firm, brass buttons shining, he demanded my boat-friend's papers.

Me, I'm a small man. I shrieked and cowered and acted nothing like a manly and proper sailor.

My boat-friend? He extracted papers from his seabag with the dignity of a newly elected Pope.

Made uneasy by my boat-friend's confidence, the Freedom Agent's moustaches twitched. His eyes bulged. His face dripped sweat like a turnip unearthed from the soil at high noon.

Refusing to examine the unexpected papers, he demanded instead an accounting of my boat-friend's history and his business in New Orleans.

"I've no business yet," my boat-friend cheerfully replied. "But history? Of that, sir, I've plenty."

No man in all the world had such a tendency toward hyperbolic amplification as my boat-friend, and, calling himself Ulysses, he described a blasphemous and unbecoming life consisting equally of bits of African kings, ancient libraries without end, blinding riches, catamite service, flesh rites, epic battles, mythic beasts, and marvelous escapes.

Flummoxed, the Freedom Agent dropped my boat-friend's papers in the mud as if they were infected by yellow fever. He jerked a thumb to the registry shack at the levee's end, where my boat-friend was to declare himself like a load of cargo at the counting house.

"No free Negro can stay in Louisiana longer than thirty days," the Freedom Agent warned. "I'll come find you myself and see if you're in the mood for stories then."

Stories of the Freedom Agents' rough welcomes had made their way back across the ocean to my own Cork City. Originally known as Fever Agents and formed during the epidemic of 1848, their original task was to prevent new immigrant ships from landing and corralling Irishmen already arrived into the neighborhood of the Irish Channel, where a mix of Irish and slaves were compelled at rifle-point to build a wall around themselves in a futile effort to check the fever's spread.

For two years, the agents kept the quarantine, and when the fever finally ebbed, the agents nevertheless persisted and were their own form of pestilence. They found new work at the ports and new champions in the city hall. Persecutors of every difference, they turned from preventing fever to ferreting out every anarchic Continental tendency, membership in Hibernian Societies, sexual perversion, Negrophilia, and abolitionism. In the 1850s, the Know-Nothing Party, who were great supporters of the agents' work, secured power and every patronage post was filled with one of theirs.

One apparent happy beneficiary of the Know-Nothings' political largess was the hostile clerk we met in the registry shack at levee's end to which the Freedom Agent had directed us. He demanded every last bit of data from my boat-friend but the length of his shillelagh, though I readily suspected that latter datum was of greatest interest.

All the while he scribbled in his ledger, the clerk stole sly and appraising looks at Ulysses and no wonder: my boat-friend was a prepossessing specimen. Twice my weight and height. Skin the color of copper. A high forehead that gave him an unearned name for honesty. Cheekbones like a king. The words *I regret this already* tattooed on his right shoulder blade. And strong? It was nothing for Ulysses to carry a barrel of flour under each arm and another on his head. For every man he had killed or maimed,

Ulysses had added a bead to his necklace, which was by that time nearly thirty feet long, and longer still it might have been, but he counted only the white men for victims and not the coloreds of any race.

Setting aside his ledger and brandishing a magnifying glass, the clerk demanded Ulysses strip to his skivvies, so that he might inspect him for signs of fever. Ulysses gave him something to inspect that was much more satisfying to both parties, and Ulysses and the clerk detained us no further.

Free to proceed, we encountered pure chaos. Choked with the offscrapings of scuppers and casks, the Mississippi River burned fierce as a dose of the clap. Plumes of black-and-white smoke from the funnels of a hundred steamships made columns into the sky, as if so many colleges of cardinals couldn't make up their minds about the next pope and selected many all at once.

Hawkers and draymen and speculators and dockworkers and slaves and mules jammed the streets and byways. Precariously balanced goods of every description were stacked as high as mountains: bales of cotton, hogsheads of *poitin*, bags of produce, sacks of grain, hams, bar-iron, bundles of coarse linen, casks of butter, crates of Pittsburgh bottles. Each instant, we were jostled and run against and in danger of having our legs broken by machinery or the head smashed by swaying hardware at the end of a crane's hook.

After the ocean's isolation, the tumult was like living beneath a bell and every moment dodging the clapper, but never escaping the clamor. I'd have turned back to the safety of our vessel, had Ulysses not seized my collar and held me fast.

Overcome with glee and terror on account of everything's novelty, I threw myself at my boat-friend again and again. Each time, Ulysses fended me off, yielding neither ground nor affection, until at last I broke through his defenses and clambered up his backside, for I was but half a man tall and he a monster.

I threw my arms around his chest and buried my face in his neck. He smelled of barely broken sweat. I kicked to prod him as a man spurs a mare, and he cheerfully caught up my legs and marched into the madness without further encouragement.

Here before us were a thousand delights heretofore unknown to sailors like us: awnings and gas lamps and steam engines and omnibuses and telegraph poles.

Here were balconies and gay females. And here just a door away were more balconies and more gay females. And then more of them still, and each group hallooed and sang ribald songs and invited us to join them in their rooms, fees paid strictly in advance.

Here was a great stuffed chickencock nearly seven feet high followed by prettyboys holding posters of pale men and slogans about senators and divided houses and unions and half-slaves and freemen.

In a square just beyond the port was a soapbox *maneen*—a great orange-skinned sack whose figure no clothing could flatter, with an enormous quantity of chins and a mass of straw-colored hair—who promised to pave Rousseau Street with pancakes and let molasses run in the gutter so that the poor were never hungry.

Proud as ten peacocks, he proposed great public casks of *poitín* on every street corner from which the *tafia* would issue more cheaply than river water. He offered to supply whores prepaid by the city treasury and personally quality tested by him.

Heralds relayed this speech back to the square's furthest reaches. Fists shot into the air and such a roar you never heard, even from the winds over the North Atlantic.

"Is it the Mardi Gras?" I gasped, for Ulysses had described the *feis* to me aboard our vessel, and I had imagined it as noisy as all this.

"Mardi Gras? It's *June*, fool," Ulysses replied. He explained these antics were all part of the strange custom of selecting a new high king of New Orleans. "If you think this is something, just you wait until they pick the President! That's in November."

Perhaps because Ulysses and I towered above the crowd, the *maneen* singled us out for abuse. Infuriated that his words won no notice, he forced himself in our path flanked by a pair of Freedom Agents.

Fast as pistons on a steamship, my boat-friend knocked the *maneen* and both Agents flat. He snatched the Agents' loose pistols from the air, pointed them toward the sky, and fired twice.

These deeds were unwise, reckless, foolish, and absolutely delicious. Even if they wrecked us, I decided, they'd made us undeniable as a stubbed toe, and I loved Ulysses all the more.

❖

Ulysses was as fixed and fearless as stone, but mine is a split and skittish nature. A mere bone chip of a baby, I'd entered the Irish countryside on Candlemas with a head of golden curls that turned black as blindness after just seven days and then again flame-red seven days later. Left for dead, I was named Ciaran Leath by boys who found and knew me well, because in Irish *ciaran* means "dark" and *leath* means "half."

I've always been the dark half—half day and half night, half this and half that, half woman and half man, half Catholic and half pagan, half here and half one foot in the OtherWorld, half human and half Faerie, a cross between the Good People and the rest of us. I am a borderman, caught mid-stride between this place and that. I'm blessed and cursed and it's no surprise that in Irish, the words for *curse* and *gift* are very close.

My two-sidedness made it easy for me to adapt to our adopted city; I could see its good sides and bad. We spent our first days in New Orleans washing away the ship's stench with great quantities of *poitín*. As God intended the body for use, sundry frolics and a quantity of wrestling and shedding of pantaloons we had, and a few fist fights from those not content to leave Ulysses's strength untested or my puniness unmocked.

In rooms or alleys too dark for my ugliness to show, our bed-companions included the cornmeal man, the hot pie man, the waffle man, the candy man, the broom man, the clothespole man, the chimney sweep, the bottle man, the knife sharpener, the umbrella man, the Jesuit Père Bonseigneur, and Zozo La Brique, who sold brick dust for scrubbing stoops--and some of these twice. The experiences made an accord with my general view that shillelagh-sucking generally ought not to be suppressed but rather encouraged as an occupation not half so good as some but better than many, with a commensurate diminishment in feelings of conflict, so that if we all had ever dedicated ourselves full-time to this engagement, we'd be nearly as happy in this world as in Faerieland, where they were fucking all the while.

After these frantic first days, Ulysses and I found digs advertised in the Irish Channel, a place to which we were drawn even though most quarters in the city were again open to Irishmen and Negroes after the scare of 1848.

Our stout white Protestant landlady was at first ill-disposed to our custom. Madame Olympe muttered darkly about Negrophilistic tendencies and sailors' vices and her associations among the captains of the Freedom Agents.

Being pale as a radish, I assured this leviathan quite firmly that Ulysses was but slave to me. Wages from the ship's quartermaster and other compliments smoothed any further embarrassments of our companionship, which she overlooked with a very modern grace.

As soon as she set off to count her coins, Ulysses cried, "Your slave, my arse! I'll show you who's in charge, little man!"

There followed some letting down of bags and drawers, some wrestling and what-what, still an appetite in us two like we hadn't just spent three months at sea doing much of the same, and then a profound and welcome sleep.

During the long passage from Liverpool, I thought I had heard every story my boat-friend had to tell, and most of them twice, but our first full day in our new digs, Ulysses confounded me with something new. He produced a *papier-mâché* head from his bottomless seabag. Fitting a net foundation to the head and securing it with pins, he attached folds and frills of lace and tastefully scattered little pink rosebuds until he had fashioned a very comely bonnet. This bonnet he fixed on his head atop a blonde feathery wig, the ends of which had been wound on a slate-pencil into stiff little curls.

On each earlobe, Ulysses hooked bangles. On his broad rough hands, he pulled nankeen gloves, which well-covered the wrist and had a hole for the thumb and a deep flap to hide the size of his palms. The face he painted and plucked.

Soon he squeezed all the broad shoulders of himself into a magnificent dress. It had multiple skirts and a plunging décolletage that he wore over a whalebone corset laced within an inch of his life. Gold-dipped sleigh bells had been sewn into the lace flounces on the shoulders and sleeves. The narrow black ribbons of his black, heelless slippers wound over the instep and crossed and re-crossed from ankle all the way up over white stockings that reached as far as his shillelagh.

Finished, Ulysses shook his shoulders, rattled his sleighbells, curtsied primly, and pronounced himself Yulia.

"Yulia Bienville, *merci beaucoup*."

I bowed deeply and said I was pleased and honored to make Miss Bienville's acquaintance.

Flattered by the attention, Yulia bade me sit on the edge of my straw for instruction. For my benefit, she demonstrated the fine art of holding out skirts with thumb and forefinger. She painted my face and doused me in rosewater. She demonstrated how to sit stiffly on the extreme edge of a chair, how to fold the hands on the lap, and how to droop the eyes in a pensive and flirtatious way.

Though a thorough flit, I proved a hopeless student of the ladylike arts, and to my immense relief, Yulia soon abandoned any idea of my joining her in public on a *Lughnasa* promenade in a well-made dress. She went out on her own.

I calculated the *feis* would be over on the morrow and the wigs but a passing fancy for its celebration. But when Ulysses persisted in his disguise, I did warn him against furthering the rash practice. I reminded him that a rich bounty had been levied on us for having laid out the soapbox *maneen*, and if the *gardai* ever discovered Ulysses beneath the wig, he wouldn't be long for the world.

"For such a purse, and smaller still," I said, "men will do almost anything."

"You're just afraid I'll find a full measure of a man out in the streets, and not a half-specimen like you, and trade you for him."

"No jealousy motivates my warning," I insisted. "I know what I am, and what's good for me is equal good for another, and your shillelagh never once got used up because someone else had a taste of its knob. That's my philosophy and none other, so help me God."

No, rather, what I feared (and scarce dared tell my boat-friend) was the crack of Ulysses's skull from Know-Nothing mobs, or the bounty hunters pressing Ulysses back into a sugar plantation slavery he had never known, or the knife parting him from his shillelagh and leaving him a lady for good.

These were real and present dangers in 1858 in New Orleans. Indeed, each night its streets overflowed with rowdiness and gunfire and fisticuffs and blood in relation to the electing of kings. My fellow Irishmen were on the one side and Know-Nothings on the other, and none of the bastards with so much as a chamberpot to piss in, but they were denouncing one another and tearing down banners and portraits and wearing chickencock suits and forming new societies and tossing men from the Wall around the Irish Channel and every once in a while stabbing one another and leaving a man bleeding on the banquette for the braver sort of *gardai* to haul away to hospital or grave.

Yulia, though, was entirely heedless of such dangers, or even enjoyed them, or perhaps just enjoyed tormenting me.

Having lost near everything in the Great Famine back at home, I hadn't come clear across the ocean to lose more, and, so help me God, I almost quit Yulia entirely just to avoid the complete loss of her.

For all of us, it'd have proved better if I had.

❖

We soon acquired a hundred friends to fawn over Ulysses and squeeze his muscles and squeal—some bumboys, some putains, some poets, some priests. Each had tales to tell of abuse by Freedom Agents and Know-Nothing mobsters, but none was so passionate as our compatriot Zozo La Brique, who was often taken for a red Choctaw or Natchez on account of the brickdust of his trade and beaten like a carpet until all the dust fell off him and the mob realized he was white.

Impressed by my boat-friend's open defiance of the soapbox *maneen*, Zozo proposed a hundred other obstructions to the injustices of the Freedom Agents: bomb the Wall; set loose the steamships at night; burn the Negro registry; march a stuffed manikin in the image of a baby in a nappy but wearing the soapbox *maneen*'s face.

"There's no other way to wake this sullen mass of Channel Irishmen," Zozo proclaimed. "All of them crowded upon one another with shoulders drooping, tongues still, and tails between legs. They'd neither spine nor spark in them, and unlikely either to banquet or build bonfires, but on Lughnasa or Samhain and other *feiseanna* only to pursue the same dull daylabors, which makes me think the chief work of my people here in New Orleans was to dig hollows out of themselves as you'd peel a *pratie* from its jacket. Is it not so, Ciaran? You're one of them."

I reminded our rowdy guest that on account of the encounter with the soapbox *maneen*, Ulysses and I were wanted men. We couldn't go abroad from Madame Olympe's apartment without unacceptable risk. Posters promising reward for our capture were pasted on every lamp post.

But Zozo and my new friends pointed out that the transformation to Yulia had rendered those posters powerless, and indeed, Yulia did regularly promenade without excessive molestation.

In fact, our landlady Madame Olympe, who had a solid reputation for her taste in Negro bucks, had taken a special shine to my boat-friend. As it was the fashion that year for a white lady to take on a colored Creole companion, Yulia and Madame Olympe made their liaisons under this guise. Accordingly, my boat-friend only reluctantly participated in Zozo's plottings, but such was the violence of the times that the string of beads around her neck grew longer and longer, enough rope to hang her, even as she was developing other, more domestic dreams.

❖

In addition to her interests in real estate, Madame Olympe was the proprietor of a milliner on Chartres Street called Provençals, which catered to all the finest ladies of the Quarter. Its windows teemed with beautiful *barèges,* Marcelines and chiné silks, organdies stamped in gorgeous designs, *mantillas, visites, cardinals* and imported French calicoes.

My boat-friend became enamored of this place and spent many hours with her face pressed to the glass. She imagined and recounted to me in great detail all the balls she'd never attend wearing the clothes she couldn't afford.

Noticing her interest, Madame Olympe hired Yulia at Provençals to assist her in servicing her clientele.

After a day of such work, intent on her own improvement, Yulia lugged home a power of the silliest titles from the adjacent booksellers and had me read aloud from them under candlelight: *The Imperial Letter Writer. A Guide to Domestic Bliss. The Sphere of a Woman: A Manual of Elegant Recreations, Exercises and Pursuits. The Bazar Book of Decorum; The Care of the Person, Manners, Etiquette, and Ceremonials. The Lady's Guide to Perfect Gentility. The Mirror of Graces, or the English Lady's Costume.*

Much I learned from these scholarly works that I never knew, and all of it perfect balderdash, but they inspired Yulia, who began to boast that she would one day be the proprietor of Provençals and raise a house full of children and cook for a good man and occupy a pew at the Saint Louis Cathedral and enjoy gossip and black tea with a few close lady friends.

"You know," she said, "*Normal* stuff."

"Well, I'm not like you, Yulia," I argued, "what with all the reading about the fine ladies and elegant recreations and *The Mirror of Graces.* I know who I am, and content with it, too, I'd say, so long as there be a shillelagh available for sucking."

Yulia explained that she wasn't unsympathetic to the injustices against the Irish and her own race and even Zozo La Brique, but she wanted just this one chance for a more mundane life.

"Must it all be misery?" she asked, sounding decidedly highfalutin and not the sailor I'd met, who'd drawn down his pants within thirty seconds of meeting me.

Hurt and disappointed, I willingly threw myself further into Zozo's plots. We two regularly instigated fights with the Freedom

Agents and Know-Nothing mobs from which Yulia had to save us.

Each time, Yulia said would be the last, and yet Zozo and I provoked another scene and there she was.

We ought to have stopped, I suppose. We ought to have honored her choices. Yulia could pass as a lady far more than a bumboy like me might ever pass for a man. I was a mustard pot and jasper and molleen and flit and polly and moffie and ponce and poofter and nelly and gobbler and swish. I was pale as a radish, tattered as a flag, half the height of your average fellow.

And this, no doubt, was what I grudged Yulia. Not the trysts with Madame Olympe or with the myriad bumboys of our acquaintance. Not her impatience with our grubby apartment just under the Wall in the Irish Channel, which forced her to brave a gauntlet of Freedom Agents at the checkpoint every time she wished to venture to Provençals.

No, what bothered me was her desire to be what I never could.

❖

Madame Olympe was ostensibly married, and her estranged husband proved to be none other than the soapbox *maneen* of our prior brief acquaintance. Recovered now, the *maneen* had developed a certain suspicion of his wife's particular Creole companion. According to the housemaids, who told us everything, the *maneen* hadn't yet put his finger on what was amiss, but he stared at their frequent visitor with narrowed and blazing eyes. He questioned Yulia relentlessly about the beads on her necklace, the likes of which he was certain he had seen before.

With the help of her books of improvement, which had much gilded her native art and guile, Yulia deftly turned aside the *maneen*'s remarks. She steered conversation to his preferred topics—the perfidy of the Irish, the disloyalty of slaves, the disease-spreading of immigrants, the oppressions of the North, the ignorance of the Negro, and, most of all, the shenanigans of Zozo and the lower classes. On these matters, the soapbox *maneen* droned for hours in Yulia's presence and not a single word my boyfriend said in our defense, according to the housemaids.

"Yulia's no friend of ours," I confided to Zozo after hearing yet another such account, but each night, I welcomed my boat-friend home. I threw myself on her as I'd always done. I told her I wanted to be the sheet on top of her. I wanted to be the golden wig-tresses on her head.

"You love me," I crooned in her ear. "As much as two pints of beer. As much as the moon. As much as a lamp needs its wick. As much as a lottery prize or a bonnet from Provençals."

❖

I didn't aim to betray my dear Yulia, but a thing always acts ultimately according to its nature. A knife is sharp; its nature is to draw blood. A hammer is heavy; its nature is to dash out brains. Me, I'm two-sided, half this and half that. My nature is to betray.

I reached out to the clerk at the Negro registry, who in his shame was only too happy to pass a message to the soapbox *maneen* as to the truth of his wife's relations with Yulia. The *maneen* assembled a ready mob, and when it had finished with her, Yulia was bruised and mutilated, the white teeth only stubs, having been knocked out one by one with a pistol butt.

The thugs hauled her corpse to a lamppost along the Wall and strung her there by her own necklace. By order of the Know-Nothing mayor, all were forbidden to pull the corpse down on pain of death. Yulia was to serve as a message to all foreigners, whether black or Irish, not to defy the authorities, and two armed Freedom Agents kept a careful watch.

Three days later, not through the agency of any hero, but only at the instigation of a light breeze, the necklace broke. Beads pinged like gunshots, and her body fell heavily to the cobbles. The Freedom Agents riddled her corpse with additional bullets.

"Shot," they joked, "while trying to escape."

When they grew tired of the game and went in search of further sport, Zozo and I crept from the shadows of the Wall and retrieved the corpse. We dragged her through the checkpoint at the Channel gate and hauled her up three flights of stairs to our digs.

I did my duty. I laid out the corpse on a cooling board stretched between chair and chamberpot with feet pointed toward the door. I fitted her in a white dress, white silk stockings and a new pair of white heels freshly purchased from Provençals that were better than any funeral society could provide.

I lit white candles and threaded a rosary with white beads around Yulia's long fingers. From sashes and door and across the looking glass, I hung black crêpe, and over the eyes of saints and icons, I hung handkerchiefs. I even placed picayunes on my boat-friend's eyes to pay her passage to the Other World.

All the rest of night and all the next day and into the next night, I sat a steady, lonely vigil.

"Why," I asked the corpse over and over, "did you make me do this?"

❖

Everyone knows it's bad luck to count the guests at a funeral, but among those come to pay respects were all the bumboys, putains, poets, and priests of our extended acquaintance. The mourners knelt at Yulia's deathbed, and if one of them did steal the coins from the corpse's eyes, still they said kind things about her. They praised the whiteness of dress and stockings and heels, and they regretted that she would never stand behind the counter at Provençals or win her lottery or raise her brats or gossip with *les femmes* like a proper lady.

A swallow-tailed kite flew in the window and became trapped. After some manic fluttering, it alighted on the curtain rod and became still as porcelain, as if trying to persuade us it wasn't present at all. But its heart thudded so hard, it might as well have been a tiny, rapid funeral drum, and we all stood to attention at the exits and saluted as it again flew free, as most of us never would.

When the hour came to transfer my boat-friend to a waiting dray, the mourners grunted and tugged and strained without success. Others volunteered, and still there was no moving her.

To put a little life in the corpse, I emptied an entire bottle of *poitín* down her gullet, but this produced no discernible improvement in her condition.

Only when appeared at the door a dozen exactly like my boat-friend—seeming to my weak eyes half one thing and half another but entirely themselves—was hope found. In their care was the corpse at last hoisted up and into the coffin and the coffin placed on the rented dray. Even the Freedom Agents didn't trouble us at the Wall around the Irish Channel because everyone in New Orleans loves a funeral.

Mules were prodded. Dirges were sung. Heaven wept. A one-armed boy with sleeve pinned up observed us from the curb with a greater hunger than the world could fill.

At La Cimetière Lafayette No. 2, Zozo La Brique punched holes in the coffin to keep it from floating during floods. *Putains* of our acquaintance spoke at length, and—despite their bitter competition with the deceased—particularly praised their sister's every part: tongue, cheeks, eyes, nose, and shillelagh.

Entrusted with a dollar, Père Bonseigneur put a blessing on the coffin. Madame Olympe had to be pried from the boxlid, on which she sobbed and beat for an hour, before the mourners could slide the coffin into the casket-sized niche in the graveyard's walls.

Throughout the ceremony, a volatile stew of superstition, suspicion, goblins, ghosts, haunts, fatal spirits, swamp gas, mist, heat, humidity, Laudanum abusers, women in trousers, and rouged men swirled—an unhallowed and roiling cess of tricky spirits and roving undead; fragments of old indigo vats; fireflies flitting over fresh graves; piratical and cursed treasures buried; and hexes and spells to which I'd previously been blind, but as busy as the levee.

Here were Faeries, a fifing lot and familiar to me, all shiny buckles and red hats, but their leather shoes did still kick.

Here were native haunts, dark-shuffling and moss-draped, rattling chains and brandishing canal shovels, all color leached from them by the swamp, dancing a singular dance that looked like a chain-gang shuffle, yet they flew fleet as wind when summoned or sent.

Spirits abounded: Irishmen who had labored on and fallen from the Wall; slaves whipped to death and all the skin of the back fallen off them; syphilitic whores; children crushed by rushing drays; an immigrant waylaid at the polls and skull crushed under the kicks of the Know-Nothing mobs.

Some spied on the proceedings as if alive. Some smothered the mourners in kisses. Others were grasping and full of curses.

A small few attempted to whisper my betrayal into the ears of Zozo La Brique and my other bed-companions, but God gave these innocents no ears to hear me maligned and no doubts as to who I was at heart. And despite this attempted assassination of my good character, all the spirits, each and every one, were grateful to me for my witness: I saw them for what they were, when in all the world, no one else did.

A Sneeze
K.W. Holland

During his third month at home, someone broke into the house while Carter napped.

"They didn't break in," his husband, Jason, corrected later that evening. "They just opened the door and walked in. It was more like a walk-in. They might have even sauntered."

Carter was eating a banana because it had been safely ensconced in its peel during the invasion and thus hadn't been touched. "You keep saying 'they,'" he said through a mouthful of mush. "Do you think there was more than one? I think there was only one."

"Well, it could have been a he or a she or an it, for all we know. We don't know how they *identified*." Jason bent down and reached into the recesses of the refrigerator for a yogurt. He was still dressed for the office. Usually he came home, dashed into the bedroom, and re-emerged wearing sweats. Tonight, though, the police had been there when he arrived.

"You still think I'm making it up."

"I never said you were making it up. Not once did I say that."

"There was someone here. In the house."

And there had been, Carter was sure of it. Yes, he'd been groggy and heavy-eyed when he stumbled out of the bedroom to investigate whatever sound had stirred him awake. But the key word here, he thought, was *awake*. He was awake.

He was awake when he saw the front door swinging half-open. He was awake when, through the picture window next to that door, he saw what could have only been a human figure race through the yard, a blur beneath the aging willow trees that shadowed their lawn. The blur reached the sidewalk and vanished before Carter's mind was clear enough to recognize what was happening.

But he'd been *awake.*

Hadn't he been?

"Well, we're lucky they didn't take anything," Jason said. Then he scooped yogurt into his mouth with a spoon like a hungry robot, one quick sweep after another.

"Yes, we are lucky. I scared them away before they could take anything. The police said so." Well, one of them, the nice heavy-set ginger, had said so. The other, a woman whose blonde hair seemed as brittle as her dark eyes seemed hard, kept smacking her lips and asking about the noise that had woken him up.

"Nothing broken? Nothing knocked to the floor? Did the intruder say something, perhaps, call out a warning, or a greeting?"

"Him," Carter said now, after he swallowed the last of his banana. "I scared *him* away. Before he could take anything. There was definitely only one of them, and he was definitely a man. I think."

"Really?" Jason placed the empty yogurt container next to the banana peel on the granite-topped peninsula, which was otherwise, like the rest of the kitchen, completely clear and scrubbed to the point of glossiness. Since the cancer had taken away Carter's ability to continue working, he felt it was now his job to prowl around the house with a bottle of surface cleaner, like Mommie Dearest on a bender. (He thought of "the cancer" as an entity with a mind of its own, fighting for its own life against his, and winning.)

Jason continued, "You're *definite* about this? Did you remember something else? Something we should tell the police? Should we call them back?"

"No! No. It's just a feeling I have."

"Alright, alright." Jason put an arm on Carter's shoulder, and smiled at him in a way, Carter thought, that was meant to reassure. "Sorry you've had such a day, hon. At least now we know to keep the doors locked. Even when we're home, it seems."

When people asked Carter how he met Jason, he always said, "Through a friend," and then changed the subject. Jason had no qualms about having met online, but Carter felt squeamish about sharing that fact. "It's not like we met online and went on a date," he said, explaining his reluctance. "I wasn't waiting for you in a restaurant with a white rose or something."

"Good Lord." Jason could actually verbalize an eye roll. "You don't have to tell people we met online and met up for a quick fuck. Just say we met online and people can draw their own conclusions. Though I doubt most of them will picture a white rose, for goodness' sake."

Is that what it was, Carter thought, a quick fuck, and then: yes, it was. As quick as the flush on his face, as quick as he went down on his knees (his gaze turned up at that handsome, smooth face), as quick as the thrust of Jason's hips, as quick as the shy smile and the peck as they went their separate ways.

As quick as the way they arranged to meet again the next night, and the next, and somehow six months later they were living together. As quick as the years accumulated, until that day two years ago when Carter received his bad news. (*Our* bad news, Jason said—it had always been *his* diagnosis, too; *our* fight, *our* cancer.)

Later, Jason took a shower while Carter sat on the couch in the living room, which faced the front door. The picture window, through which he had seen the blurred intruder earlier, now looked like a frame around a black canvas.

When they first moved out here a couple of years ago, they discovered on the very first evening just how dark it was, due to the complete lack of any street lighting in their section of neighborhood. Carter, who had been the one most enthusiastic about their move from city to suburb, was also the one most unnerved by the shadowed solitude, and he immediately declared their need for some sort of outdoor lighting plan. Jason agreed, and the two of them often discussed options and ideas, but the plan itself, not to mention the lights, never materialized. It was their routine, to imagine things they would like to do someday.

We really *should* install some lights out there, Carter thought again, and then, suddenly: *Someone could be standing right outside that window, for all I know.* Enveloped in the night, someone could be watching him, and he wouldn't even know it.

He stood so fast it was very near to a jump.

Even though he'd been relieved when they left, and regretted having called them, he wished the cops were there now. Even the bitter blonde. "Why were you home this afternoon?" she asked. "What do you do for a living?"

It was *the question,* the one Carter dreaded—the reason he hesitated before contacting the police in the first place. There's no need to call the police, he had argued with himself: nobody here, nothing missing, and if I don't call the police, I won't have to answer *the question.* It was only when he tried to open a closet door, and found he couldn't, because of the clear image that formed in his mind of an intruder waiting on the other side, that he decided to make the call.

He called the police (the non-emergency number, of course, and he'd been very apologetic about it), but didn't contact Jason, which was his first instinct but one he had successfully resisted. I shouldn't bother Jason, he thought, Jason's too busy; and beneath that thought, buried but rumbling, lurked a fear that his husband would assume that everything had merely been a figment of Carter's chemo-fueled imagination, that maybe he'd be right to do so.

Two officers responded to his call, eventually, the man and the woman, the man kind-faced and nearly handsome, the woman—well, she was the one who asked *the question.*

"What do you do for a living?"

It was obviously her job to ask, but in the DC area, even way out here, it was a question to which everyone felt entitled to an answer, an answer they also felt entitled to judge; but his truthful response now, Carter felt, could only invite pity, or further scrutiny. So he'd spent the last three months at home, avoiding conversations with anyone he didn't already know, leaving only for doctor's appointments and grocery runs.

He hadn't needed to answer *the question.*

Until now, finally faced with the direct query, and from an authority no less, Carter stammered out the reason he was home in the afternoon, the reason he no longer did *anything* for a living. The cancer. The chemo.

The cop pursed her lips like she was kissing the air and arched one eyebrow higher than the other. "You don't look disabled," she said.

Carter's face flushed and he said, with a force that surprised even him, "You can't *see* it. You can't see it growing inside me. You can't see it taking everything away."

The other cop, the nice one with the reddish hair and soft build, placed his hand on Carter's shoulder, which is when Carter realized that his voice had sounded like a sob. "It's alright, sir."

Carter shook him off, then felt ashamed; the guy had only been trying to help.

And now he wished both of them were there because there was, he decided, someone standing outside the window, watching him. It started as a wild-eyed hypothetical (*someone could be standing out there, for all I know*) but had somehow turned into a certainty in his mind.

He came back, Carter thought, he came back to finish the job, and, and—and what job? What job could he/they/it have possibly come for in the first place?

He glanced around the living room and thought, well, we *do* have nice things—nice vintage Danish furniture; nice art, mostly by friends, hanging on the walls. Nice big, heavy, unwieldy things. We're not the jewelry sort, he thought, not electronics types, and he couldn't remember the last time there was any cash in the house. So why would anyone be so determined to get back inside? What could they be after?

At least the door is locked this time, he thought.

It is, isn't it?

He stepped hesitantly toward the front door, his eyes flitting to and from the window, and when he reached it, he touched the knob, twisted it slightly—

And the door opened toward him.

Carter gasped and pushed it back into place as quickly as he could.

It hadn't been locked. The deadbolt hadn't been turned. A key was required to lock it from the inside (*fire hazard,* Jason always said, and he was right, but it was something else they discussed and never followed up on). Carter always locked it in the evening after Jason came home—had he done so tonight as well? He thought so.

Although, the police had been there when Jason came home. There'd been much confusion. Concern from Jason: "What happened? Are you okay?" Confusion from the cops: "You're married? You hadn't mentioned." (And was that a slight roll of the blonde officer's eye when she used that word? Did she place mental quotation marks around the word "marriage"?)

But after the police finally left, making only the vaguest of promises regarding a potential investigation, Carter used his key to lock the deadbolt behind them.

Hadn't he?

Well, he did so now.

A light drum against the window meant that outside it had started to rain. It was not, he told himself, the sound of tapping fingers.

In the bedroom Carter found Jason, still damp from his shower, already in bed with a book. It was the same collection of Donald Justice poetry he'd been reading—or rather, looking at—since Carter gave it to him months ago.

"Did you turn off all the lights this time?" Jason asked.

"I did. And locked the door. Double checked it."

"Yes, I locked it earlier," Jason said, "after the police left."

"You did?" Carter dropped his pants into the hamper he kept on his side of the bed. "You did." He remembered, now: Jason was the one who led the police to the door, thanked them for coming, an apologetic grimace on his face; Jason was the one who slipped a key in the deadbolt and turned it.

Carter slipped beneath the bedsheet and wondered why, then, the door had been unlocked just now. Jason set his book aside and placed his hand on his husband's forearm. "I'm sorry you had such a stressful day," he said.

"It's okay," Carter said.

Okay okay okay. It was his mantra, an admittedly unimaginative one. *Okay okay okay.* That's what he repeated those nights he woke up and couldn't fall back asleep. It's what he repeated the two times he'd been wheeled back into the operating room for major surgeries, once to remove part of his colon and once to remove part of his liver. *Okay okay okay.*

He said it last week, during his visit to the oncologist. A routine visit, he assured his husband, and told Jason not to bother missing work to come with him, like he had done so many times.

Okay okay okay, he thought, when Dr. Zhi told him the news wasn't good. *Okay okay okay,* he said, when she said that there were now tumors in the peritoneum, a part of his body he had never heard of before. Apparently, unlike the other parts of his body they'd chopped into pieces, this wasn't an option for the peritoneum, some sort of tissue around his abdomen. Dr. Zhi explained it further, but Carter found it as hard to focus on her words as it was for him to focus on pretty much anything these days. He left the appointment knowing only that the chemo didn't seem to be working anymore, and that their options were narrowing, as narrow as the thin line that had replaced Dr. Zhi's usual gaping grin.

This will be a good project for Jason, Carter thought on his way home. Jason loved to research, loved to spend hours online studying things like *peritoneal metastasis* and *open clinical trials.*

Instead, when Jason asked how everything went, Carter simply said, "Okay."

Okay okay okay.

Later, Carter lay awake next to Jason's sleeping body and thought about his experience that afternoon. Three months of quiet routine, daily naps brought on by the oral chemotherapy he administered to himself morning and evening, shattered in one second by—by what? What was the sound that had blasted him from sleep? As the blonde officer suggested, did the intruder say something—a warning, a greeting?

Of course not. It must have been a sneeze, or a cough, he thought, and he tried to remember the moment of his awakening while he drifted into sleep, and slid right into dreams that were painful in their dullness.

In one dream, he was in bed, but awake, and while Jason slept, Carter counted down the seconds until he had to get up and go into the office, an office he had not seen, in waking life, in months.

In another dream, he also lay awake in bed, also next to a sleeping body, but he knew—just somehow *knew,* without even looking—that it wasn't Jason's body, and then he also knew that the body next to him was no longer asleep.

Perhaps those were both different parts of the same dream.

This time, it was definitely a sneeze that woke him. A loud, sharp burst. Followed, very quickly, by a second one.

Tension seized him and dragged him out of slumber.

Someone sneezed, he thought, someone in my house. Jason still slept; his snores, which Carter usually found deep and comforting, were raspy and ragged, like the noise was being pulled out of his body by a—by a—what do you call those things you pull to start a chainsaw, he wondered.

He shook his head and lifted his upper body up to rest on one arm. Focus, he admonished himself. His focus faded out of his control soon after the chemo started, and only got worse as the doses continued. His tongue reached for words his mind had forgotten; he was often sidetracked by meandering thoughts that slid like sled runners on a muddy hill.

Carter tossed off the sheet, damp with his perspiration. (*Night sweats,* the nurse had said, *sometimes a side effect of the chemo,* and he remembered that old Thom Gunn poem, about AIDS, and thought, not for the first time, of all those years of self-denial and fear, how he'd managed in the end to avoid HIV only to one day be roused from a colonoscopy and be told by a grim-faced doctor, *I don't have good news.*)

Carter stood out of bed. He wore only a pair of red briefs. His legs quivered. Was that neuropathy, he wondered (another potential side effect of the chemotherapy), or was it mere fright? (Also a side effect, really.) He glanced down at his husband's sleeping form, barely distinguishable in the darkness. (His earlier dream, about sleeping next to someone who was not his husband, shifted briefly into his consciousness, then back out of it.)

I should wake him, he thought, but what if I'm wrong—what if I wake him, and he makes his way through the house, and there isn't anyone here at all? Jason would be so kind about the situation, so *understanding*, and right now Carter felt that he couldn't bear any more understanding. So he chose to let his husband sleep, and made his way toward the open bedroom door to determine if his intruder had indeed returned.

(Let's be clear, he told himself: *there is no intruder.* It would not make any sense for there to be an intruder. This is still a rational universe, even random things like cancer happen for rational reasons, and it would not be rational for someone to break into our house this afternoon, or walk in as the case may be, and then return in the middle of the night. We don't have valuables or enemies; we aren't secret agents or criminal masterminds; we are a smart young accountant and his slightly older, dying husband.)

He must have forgotten to leave the light on in the bathroom, which usually served as a beacon. Instead the hallway was completely black.

(Describing himself as "slightly older" might have made him smile under different circumstances. Was ten years slight? When they met, Carter was barely in his forties, and Jason in his thirties, and the age difference had seemed slight to both of them, unremarkable. They both knew couples with larger age gaps than that. After his diagnosis, when he felt years crash on top of him like a collapsing shelf, Carter suddenly felt much older, as if the possibility of mortality had caused him to age when in fact it merely made him realize just how old he already was. A man in his fifties; a man of a certain age.)

Their bedroom was at the end of the hallway, and the light switch was at the other end, which opened into the living room. He made his way past the other doors, all along the right side of the hallway, and reached out to touch them as he did, as much to steady himself as to count them: the guest bedroom, the bathroom, the other guest bedroom they called the library because of all the bookshelves Jason had built into the walls. This, he thought as he passed the last door and reached toward the light control, is the mistake people make in horror movies, wandering through gloom, investigating strange sounds.

He imagined, for a fragment of a second, that the light switch wasn't going to work: that the power was out, had been turned off, or he'd woken in some alternate dimension where there was no such thing as light.

But with a flick everything worked as it should, and the overhead lights splashed on. His eyes tried to blink the glare away as it flooded the hallway and spilled into the living room. He stretched his face in an effort to adjust his pupils so he could make sense of the scene before him—which was, in fact, the same scene he'd left earlier, when he went to bed.

With one important change.

No, there was nobody else in the room, no intruder waiting, no source of the sneeze he thought he heard just moments before.

But the front door was open.

When Carter was a child, he suffered stomach aches and headaches on a regular basis. His parents never took him to a doctor because these ailments never seemed, to them, to be that serious. *All in your mind,* his mother told him. When he grew older he decided that, though he hated to admit it, they were right. It seemed the headaches and stomach aches were rooted mostly in the near-constant stress and terror he felt growing up.

What he remembered of his childhood was mostly panic. Panic that he would be left alone; panic that he would never be left alone; panic that he was different from everyone else, panic at the thought of being the same. Panic when he realized he was gay; panic that he was sick, and that he would become diseased, and would get AIDS and die and then, worst of all, go to Hell, or something. He would lie in bed while his stomach clenched and groaned, like the panic was alive inside him, stretching malevolent tendrils through his guts, and then up into his head, where they beat against his temple in a rhythmic pounding.

In adulthood, he settled into a quiet career, spent more time with computers than people, avoided situations that made him uncomfortable, and over time the panic dissipated, and so did the strange ailments. He barely remembered the pain he used to feel, in response to the fear that used to grip him. Despite even the cancer, despite what the doctor told him last week, Carter had tamed the fear that used to rule his life, had proudly beaten its sharp edge down to something dull and harmless. Carter had almost forgotten what panic felt like.

Until now.

The door waved a bit in the wind, as if beckoning him over. He'd locked the door before bed, he was sure of it, and it could only be unlocked with a key. So someone was, or had been, in the house; if not in the living room right now, perhaps the intruder was in the kitchen, or the family room, or (and at this thought Carter stumbled to his side, to lean against the wall) behind him, in one of the other rooms he had already passed on his way to where he stood.

The old panic roared awake, stretched as from a long slumber, cold hands reached out and twisted his insides like a wet rag.

He lurched toward the open door, almost an automaton, not able to think of a plan or even of anything beyond putting one foot after another. It wasn't until he reached it, and felt the cool night breeze wick his skin (I'm in my *underwear,* he remembered), that he thought of calling for his husband.

Instead he grasped the cold metal knob and forced the door back into its place. He almost fell off balance as the sound of the slam split the quiet.

They kept a carved wooden pedestal beside the door, something Jason found on one of his thrift shop excursions; its flat top was about as high as Carter's waist, and on that top he usually set down the day's mail. It piled up until it bothered him and then he threw it all away. It still hadn't quite reached the point of aggravation, so the pile that sat there now—a couple of catalogs, neighborhood coupon flyers—wasn't that large, and didn't draw his eye. What *did* catch his notice was the set of keys that sat on top of the pile. His own keys, one of which was required to lock, or unlock, the front door. This wasn't a place he usually placed his keys.

He grabbed them now, found the deadbolt key, fumbled it into the appropriate hole and twisted the lock shut. Then he threw the set back toward the pedestal (he missed, but didn't notice them jangle to the floor) and practically danced back away from the door on the balls of his bare feet.

"Okay okay okay," he whispered to himself.

Again it occurred to him that, if someone had been in the house and then left, and if they (he?) were outside in the front yard standing beneath the trees, then Carter could not see them, but they could see him, at the very least silhouetted against the hallway lights shining in the background. He turned, shuffled rapidly back to the switch and flicked it into the off position.

He stood for a moment, and let his eyes adjust themselves, and listened to the sounds around him. There weren't many. Jason's snores continued from the bedroom, more calm than before; the door's bang didn't seem to have disturbed him. He could also hear that mechanical hum that always droned beneath everything else, something he'd only begun to notice the last few months, after spending so much time alone, and then only when he stilled himself to hear it.

If someone else was in the house, they were being very still themselves.

"Okay okay okay," he said again.

Carter tried to remember locking the front door before bed. He had pulled it open, and been surprised that it wasn't already locked, he remembered that. Didn't he then push it back into place, close it, use his key to lock it?

Probably not, he thought, that must be why the door is open. That's why he'd been awakened by a sneeze, or something; some noise that must have come from outside while the door, left ajar, swayed in the wind. I must have meant, he thought, to close the door and lock it, but my attention is so easily diverted. The chemo pills he ingested every day had coated his brain until he saw everything as if through syrup.

Self-blame weakened his panic. His insides released themselves and he exhaled deeply, then breathed in just as deep.

He thought *okay okay okay* and then he thought *I should check these rooms along the hallway* because, well, he didn't expect anyone to be in those rooms now, so they were safe to enter, right?

In the room they called the library, he wondered how long it would take them to fill the few remaining empty shelves, given how many books they both regularly acquired. Jason scoured used book stores, and Carter surfed Amazon, but their compulsions were similar. Maybe two years left before we run out of room in here, Carter estimated, and then he wondered what might be the last book to place, and who would be the one to buy it.

"It won't be me," he said aloud, surprising himself with the plain-stated *factuality* of the statement, the *finality*.

He wouldn't be here in two years, not even one. Those last few shelves would remain empty, as far as he was concerned. They'd be a legacy.

Perhaps, Carter thought, I should sit down at the computer and compile a list of the books I would have liked to have read, a suggested list for Jason.

But, no, that's a void for Jason to fill, he thought, and instead he left the library and continued down the hall.

In the bathroom, he turned on the light and its brightness smacked him in the face. The medicine cabinet mirror was cracked. They'd discussed replacing it, but that only led to the planning of a complete bathroom remodel. "We might as well do everything at once," Jason said, "when we get around to it."

I wonder what the bathroom will look like, Carter thought. His own image in the mirror was drawn, pale and puffy—in need of its own remodel. Most people found it hard to believe he had cancer, or was on chemo, because he wasn't bald, and he certainly wasn't thin. "You look great," they said. (Before he was sick, nobody ever told him he looked great. Except for Jason, he admitted.)

In the guest bedroom, the small cushioned chair in the corner had been overturned. (Jason called it a "grandma chair" when Carter picked it out at the rummage sale, but bought it for him just the same.)

I did that, Carter remembered, earlier today, when we explored the house, the police officers and I. "Should we look under the bed?" the blonde officer asked, sarcasm practically bleeding from her mouth.

"Yes," Carter replied, angry about her subtly accusing tone, "I will," and he accidentally knocked over the chair when he got down on his hands and knees. He knew there was nobody hiding in the cramped space beneath the bed, unless his intruder happened to be a child, or very small-statured adult.

Oh, the *police*; that woman was right all along, wasn't she? He thought of the swinging door, both that afternoon and tonight, and how, if he'd accidentally left it open the one time, it was likely he'd also done so the other.

His earlier denial, his insistence on the accuracy of his memory and the necessity of there having been a home invader, made his face burn. The police woman was right to be skeptical. And Jason, who had tried to hide his own disbelief (but Carter knew it was there), was also right. (As always, he thought, Jason was *always* right, and Carter wondered why that felt more like an accusation than a compliment.)

In a way, he'd always known they were right, but only now did it *feel* like the truth. I'm a fool, he thought, a diseased, chemo-addled fool. The medicinal poison had fogged his perceptions so much that he had turned into the sort of embarrassing invalid who calls the police for literally *nothing*. And in the end—just thinking this made him snort a dry, bitter laugh—in the end, the chemo hadn't even worked!

He left the guest bedroom, shut the door gently behind him, and returned to his own bedroom, his and Jason's.

Jason was not alone in bed.

Carter would have gasped if he could have caught a breath, but instead he stood in the doorway and tried to make sense of what he could make out in the dimness. There was Jason, asleep, mouth open, each inhale a raspy buzz. He was on his back.

And lying next to him—someone else? Another figure, but the blanket pulled completely over its head.

A trick of the non-light, Carter thought, but the shape—there was no mistaking it, was there? That afternoon he'd seen a figure darting through the yard, away from the house. Was it the same figure he saw now, lying in wait, beneath the bedding, beside his husband?

Instead of screaming, calling out Jason's name (like he *wanted* to, like he probably *should*), Carter drew closer to the bed. The hidden figure did not move. Carter reached out, but stopped before touching it. His hand remained suspended in the air, as if something held it back, as if he wasn't responsible for moving his own hand forward and backward, like his hands were responsible for their own choices.

He thought of that kid, Rodney, a year or so ago. (He wasn't a kid, Carter thought, he was in his twenties.) (Very *early* twenties, he countered himself, so yes, a kid.) His hair was dyed white and there was a small ring in his nose and his face was hairless, unwrinkled. "Hello, Daddy," Rodney said through his grin, and Carter's greedy hands stretched out to stroke flesh both soft and firm. Later Jason asked him how his day had been, and Carter said, "Okay."

Okay okay okay.

Now Carter closed his eyes and pushed his hand down with a sharp thrust, expected to grab the figure under the blanket, perhaps by his shoulders, but instead there was *only* blanket, nothing beneath it. His eyes flew open in bewilderment, he veered his head back and forth to see if the intruder had slipped behind him or beside him, then grabbed the bedding and overturned it.

Still nothing.

The figure he had seen (it was *there*) was not there.

"What's happening?" That was Jason, his voice crusted with thick sleep. (*Now* he wakes up.)

"Nothing." Carter's reply was a loud blast, like a sneeze, and unlike his body, did not shake. He'd been quivering since he came into the bedroom, and with the disappearance of the figure that may or may not have been in the room next to his husband, his shaking did not fade, but intensified. He trembled like he'd just been doused with ice water.

"Alright," Jason mumbled, and rolled over, his breathing almost instantaneously finding a slow rhythm. His sleep hadn't really been interrupted, Carter knew; he wouldn't remember the exchange in the morning. There had been lots of exchanges Jason didn't remember in the morning.

Carter considered lying back down in bed, but the intruder had left an indentation in Carter's mind, if not in the mattress; he stood and waited for the shivering to subside. When it slowed, he turned and walked out of the bedroom, strode to the end of the hallway and back into the living room.

This time, he almost wasn't even surprised to see the door swinging open, once again.

Since the lights had remained off for so long now, his eyes felt at home in the darkness, and he walked up to stand in front of the open door. Beneath the clouded night skies he made out the trees that made their front yard feel like a park (it's why Jason fell in love with the place), their two cars in the driveway, the home on the hill across the street set far back from the empty exurban road.

The road…was that someone standing there, in the middle of it?

He thought again of Rodney, the kid from a year ago, and how he kept texting afterwards, but Carter stopped responding. He felt guilty, pure and simple, and feared that one day the kid might just show up at the house. Oh sure, he and Jason had discussed being open, sleeping with other people—what gay couple these days hadn't at least *discussed* it?—but Carter had been the one adamantly opposed. It's a *marriage*, he said; that means something, doesn't it? Shouldn't it?

It wasn't an argument, or even a disagreement, just a discussion. Jason agreed, and it never came up again.

Since the diagnosis, Carter wondered if Jason still agreed. Every time Jason was late, or out of town, Carter wondered if he was with someone else, and sometimes the idea of such a betrayal would work him into a jealous frenzy. I have *cancer*, he'd think with self-righteous fury; how *dare* he?

Then, he'd eat ice cream and calm down, and think: I have *cancer.* Doesn't he deserve to be with someone who *doesn't?*

How *dare* I?

All this time, of course, Jason never failed to treat Carter with kindness and, yes, even desire. It was Carter who begged off of sex, who blamed his treatment and surgeries for his lack of lust—and for good reason, he thought; he really didn't feel inflamed most of the time.

(*Hello, Daddy,* Rodney said.)

I wonder who he'll wind up with, Carter thought, who Jason's next husband will be. Someone who deserves him, I hope; someone he deserves. He thought of the empty shelves in the library, waiting to be filled, and considered, again, sitting at the computer to make a list, not of books, but of the qualities he felt Jason should look for in his next partner

But, no, he thought. I won't be filling that void, either.

He wondered if Jason thought about these sorts of things, if he wondered what life will be like if (*when*) the cancer won its petty little war, and he felt sad that they'd never been able to talk about it with each other. (The one time he tried, Jason walked away; *feels too much like defeat*, he said.)

Was the figure in the street waving?

Or was that a shadow, part of a tree?

Quiet lay over the house like a veil; suddenly, a sneeze ripped through it.

Carter asked his mother once (he was in the third grade) why people said *bless you* when other people sneezed. Well, she said, your heart stops when you sneeze, so people used to think if they gave you a blessing, maybe it will start again. He was already old enough to know that the idea of a heart-stopping sneeze was almost as silly as the idea of a heart-starting blessing. But still, the concept of both took root in the cellar of his brain, like a forgotten and deformed potato, and since then whenever he sneezed, and other people said *gesundheit* (instead of *bless you*), he always felt slighted, as if they didn't care if his heart started again or not.

This time, he recognized the sneeze.

Imagine, recognizing something like a sneeze! But that's what comes of a marriage, he thought; I know his sneeze as well as I know his snores, his farts, the sound he makes when he clears his throat, the sound he makes when he comes.

"Bless you," Carter whispered, then wondered, will whoever's next say *gesundheit*?

I hope not, he thought. I hope that, whoever it is, he offers a blessing.

It wasn't as cold outside as he feared it might be. Especially since he was only wearing briefs, a thought which would have usually made him retreat back into the house in shame, but now it just seemed like an item of interest, something to note: *Oh, it's not as chilly as I thought it would be, what with only being in my underwear.*

He made his way into the yard, ignoring the squish beneath his bare feet, until he stood under the willow trees that loomed over their house. Jason loves these trees, he thought, and so should I. ("When we get married," Jason said once, "we should have the ceremony right here, underneath the willows." But Carter preferred something simpler, and they were married in a courthouse. They signed documents, then had lunch. The best lunch of his life, Carter realized now, though he couldn't remember what they ate.)

Carter walked toward the road, or toward where the road should have been, but the yard seemed more expansive than he expected. More trees to his sides, more branches above looming like aerial shadows, and the road, where was it now? It must be right here. It must be very close.

We don't even own a yard, he thought, so much as we own woods, and is it even possible to *own* woods? Possible to even, really, own anything?

Something, someone raced past him.

A blur in his peripheral vision, a rough brush against his side.

But Carter didn't fall, or turn, or slow his steady pace, not even when he heard the sound of a door being closed, slammed.

When all is said and done, Carter thought, Jason will probably be relieved. Won't he? It's like a second chance at something. A fresh start. Yes, that's what it is.

Behind him, distant, perhaps muffled by the now-closed door, another sound started low and then rose, increasing, long and steady like a siren—no, not a siren, Carter thought, more like a howl, a wail, a swelling drawn-out sob. But he shook his head and ignored it, continued on his way, and wondered when the sun might come up, when he might finally reach the road that must be there.

UNE TRANCHE DE VIE
GARY SMITH

For the first few days after he retired, Lawrence Kline continued to get up at six o'clock so he could sit at the table with his coffee and watch the cars speed down Chatham Road. "Have a nice day," he'd sing out when traffic was at its heaviest; and he'd lift his mug in a toast, happy that he was no longer part of the rat race.

But he soon tired of that, and while the traffic whizzed by, unnoticed after a glance, he'd worked the crossword puzzle in the morning newspaper instead. The puzzles weren't very hard. He didn't have to cheat until he came to the clue for 34 DOWN, "slice of life," which needed to be filled in before he could complete 37 and 44 ACROSS, both acronyms, which he'd never been good at. Finally giving up, he rose from the table and went to his study to look for the answer on his computer.

"Slice of life," he discovered, was an expression used by writers, referring to an apparently arbitrary series of events with no plot, no in-depth characters, no conflict, no denouement, and no ending. None of that gave him the word he needed for the puzzle, which turned out to be "incident," but he thought about the phrase for several days as he drove to and from Road Ranger for his ten o'clock cappuccino or sat at the table eating the fast food takeout he regularly picked up for dinner on his way home from Cherchez-Vous.

At first he wondered if enough slices of life would make a whole life and decided, no, they wouldn't. Someone at the office had once brought in a cake consisting of twelve pieces from twelve different cakes, the latest gimmick from a chain grocery store's bakery department. But the way Lawrence saw it, that wasn't a whole cake. It was just twelve separate wedges put together.

He went back to the computer and looked up the definition again: an apparently arbitrary series of events with no plot, no in-depth characters, no conflict, no denouement, and no ending. It had such a boring, limiting connotation. And that's when, slightly amused, he realized that it was a perfect description of his life.

He pronounced "slice of life" aloud in French: une planche de vie. Everything always sounded so damn much classier in French. He checked the computer to make sure he had it right and found that it should be tranche instead of *planche*. Well, hell, he hadn't had French since his freshman year of high school in—what?—1963?

He'd had to change schools twelve weeks into his freshman year after his parents found a cheaper rental house in the country. He'd been taking art, but they didn't teach it at the new school, so he signed up for French instead. In six weeks he'd caught up with the rest of the class and made A's on all the tests. Word spread that he was a brain, which surprised him because all he'd done was memorize, which was the way he'd always learned his lessons.

There were 22 students in the freshman class, kids who'd been together since first grade. He had the feeling, all the way through high school, that they'd never stopped seeing him as a new boy—a visitor they were nice to.

After graduation, he moved to San Francisco for the Summer of Love. The zillions of kids dressed in outlandish hippie garbs, wearing beads and bells, fit in perfectly with the psychedelic shops and brightly painted Victorian houses of the Haight Ashbury district.

Too insecure to be totally free, Lawrence found a job at a head shop working part-time for minimum wage. He slept on the floors of crash pads with groups of homeless strangers; sat under the eucalyptus trees and ate food supplied by the Diggers, free for the asking, in Golden Gate Park; listened to concerts in rooms hazy with marijuana smoke; yet he never felt like a real hippie or connected to any glorious movement.

He tried to fit in, to be as uninhibited as they were: long-haired girls, eyes closed, hands reaching up to the sky, slowly turning, turning, turning, lost in a world of their own; couples embracing on the sidewalks, eyes closed, swaying to some tune only they could hear and never moving their feet; a girl's thin, high voice suddenly breaking into song—"If you're going to San Francisco, be sure to wear some flowers in your hair"—with first one and then another joining in, holding hands, until there was a whole chorus assembled, sometimes so many they blocked the traffic. Lawrence was too self-conscious to sing. He'd never been able to carry a tune, and he'd always felt awkward trying to dance, never able to detect the rhythm that others seemed to find so naturally.

He had no courage, no boldness. Too leery—not the best word to use, he thought wryly. Too wary, then—to try marijuana or LSD or any of the other dope shoved under his nose by stoned, happy strangers.

So he mingled, an unconnected part of it, an observer, until it palled. The familiar strangers moved on: went back home, migrated out of town to join the communes, returned to college, found jobs... Lawrence hung on for several more years. He left just as the Manson trial began down in L.A.

After San Francisco, Lawrence moved around the country, working just enough to get by. His mother had provided him with an abundance of stamped postcards, insisting he mail one every week so she'd know he was still alive. She sent her letters to his last known address, always mentioning whatever news she'd heard at the grocery store about the kids he'd gone to school with. Several were almost through college now, she wrote, causing Lawrence, who'd been valedictorian, to feel a vague sense of his own failure. Sherry Eshelman's dad had died, she said. John Nagle was working at the hardware store. And Brian Ackerley had gotten married.

❖

Lawrence hadn't really been friends with Brian—if that's what you could call their relationship—until toward the end of their senior year when Brian started spending the night at his house so Lawrence could help him study. He was flunking three of his courses. If he could pull a C minus on his finals, the teachers told him, he would pass.

Brian rode the school bus home with him and as soon as they'd eaten and Lawrence's mother had cleared away the dishes, they'd spread their books out on the table and study. Lawrence mainly fed him the answers to questions that he suspected would be on the tests and went over them until Brian had memorized them. It didn't take much to figure out that Mrs. Alexander would ask about Macbeth's tragic flaw and the witch's three prophecies or that Mr. Bromley would have multiple choice questions about the Dred Scott Decision and the Missouri Compromise.

After they finished studying for the night, they'd go up to Lawrence's room, undress down to their underwear, and sit cross-legged on the bed talking. Brian wore jockey shorts that were the whitest white Lawrence had ever seen. Lawrence's mother bought boxer shorts for him. Sitting there, he had to be careful the pee hole didn't gape open.

One night Brian told him about going out with a girl and putting his finger up in her. It sounded more like what Brian had heard the other boys bragging about in the locker room than something he had actually done himself. Lawrence questioned him for details. His vague answers made Lawrence realize that Brian hadn't done much more than he had himself—which was nothing.

After a while, they turned off the light and lay under the sheets, the room dimly lit from the pole light his father had installed outside after someone had siphoned gas from his tank. A Jesus picture with a big halo and a heart outside the body, looking ghostly in the half-light, peered down at them from the wall where his mother had hung it. Lawrence quizzed Brian again to see if he remembered the answers, their voices overlaid by the faint sounds of crickets and frogs and the distant bursts of TV laughter from the Johnny Carson show his parents watched every night. Finally, they fell asleep.

After graduation, they no longer saw each other. That's when Lawrence, dimly aching inside, realized he'd had a crush on Brian. He wondered what would have happened if he'd reached over and—and what? He wasn't sure what two guys could do. Hug? Press against each other? Maybe touch each other down there? He couldn't see them doing that. He wondered if Brian had had a crush on him.

He'd probably never know.

Lawrence eventually landed in Ohio, where he worked as a janitor at the University of Cincinnati. One of the students, a spoiled only child named Cynthia Louise Porter, pursued him until he proposed to her. Her father, a bigwig at Proctor and Gamble, hated him—which, Lawrence learned later, was why Cynthia had married him. Her mother, a pretty woman who wore her blond hair pulled back in a severe bun and who favored black pantsuits and low heels, smiled a lot and was always pleasant to him. Lawrence thought she liked him until he overheard her tell Cynthia, "Your father sent you to the university so you could meet a man with a future. Not a janitor, for Christ's sake."

They stayed together long enough to have a kid he never saw again after the divorce. If Cynthia tried to contact him for child support, he never knew about it. They were probably just happy not to have him in the picture.

When Lawrence's parents retired to Florida, he moved back into their house and took over the rent payments. He worked part-time and returned to school, mostly night classes, until he got his degree. Then he moved to the state capital, where he became a CPA, finding loopholes for politicians to protect their money from the IRS.

And there he stayed for the next 32 years, years that lay like a huge, gray stone on the timeline of his life, the only saving grace being that, as long and as painfully dull as it had been at the time, looking back now, it seemed but a blip, hardly thought of or remembered at all.

❖

After he retired, Lawrence started going to Cherchez-Vous, a lavender stucco building located in the middle of a large parking lot in a mixed commercial and residential area. He went there the first time mainly out of curiosity and boredom. He wasn't overly obsessed with pornography, though he'd checked out a few X-rated sites on his computer until he ended up with a virus. The man at BLH told him that's probably where he got it.

He often wondered if anyone he knew had ever seen him go into Cherchez-Vous—maybe Louise, one of the secretaries from where he'd worked, glancing up from washing dishes at her kitchen sink. She could see the parking lot from her window. He'd heard her laugh in the break room about the way men slunk into the place, averting their face from the nearby houses.

There was a door as soon as you came in the main entrance that you took if you wanted to see the strippers or get a lap dance. Lawrence had never gone into that part of the building. At his age, he'd feel ludicrous around all those young, half-naked girls.

Past that door, you came to a small area where erotic aids were sold—dildos, pornographic videos and magazines, sex dolls... If you bought anything, you'd pay a man at the counter. He also sold tokens to those using the booths and collected five dollars from the men going into the theatre.

Lawrence always went to the theatre. The door opened onto a small room with two short rows of seats and a TV screen mounted on the wall. A black curtain over a doorway led to another room with more seats and another TV screen showing a different movie. It was on his third visit there that Lawrence sauntered into the back room for the first time. Three old men watched the movie while two other men stood in the far corner, one—no, that couldn't be right, but it was—one giving the other a blow job. Lawrence sat down, stunned. He kept glancing at the old men, who actually weren't that much older than him. Couldn't they see what was going on? About that time, the men in the corner finished, one turning, zipping up his trousers, and exiting through the curtain; the other—Lawrence later learned his name was Danny—stayed and watched the movie as though nothing unusual had happened. What amazed Lawrence, even more than the two men engaged in the act, was the three old men totally ignoring it.

Lawrence set his cappuccino on the coaster and rummaged around in his desk drawer until he found the stamps to stick on the three bills he'd just written checks for. He affixed three of the return address labels he'd been receiving from Médecins Sans Frontières ever since he'd donated to them over 15 years ago.

He laid the letters on the edge of his desk and glanced at the balance in his checkbook. It had grown too large again. He needed to buy a CD to get a higher interest rate. Maybe he'd call the banks later and find out how much they were paying.

Being as alone in the world as he was, with neither friends nor relatives, he needed to start getting his affairs in order, make some arrangements for when he died. If he didn't, he wasn't sure what they would do with him. He supposed someone would bury or cremate him, if not for love, as his grandfather used to say, then for stink. There wouldn't be a wake or funeral. Who'd come to it? No one would even know he was dead unless the newspaper published a list of deaths automatically. He needed to start thinking about who he'd leave his property and his money to. Maybe a charity, an animal charity for cats, like the one Doris Day ran. He'd always liked Doris Day.

He returned his checkbook to the drawer. After he mailed the letters, he'd drop by Cherchez-Vous for a few hours. He vaguely wondered how much money he spent there every month, but he could afford it. He didn't have any other extravagances. No hobbies. Just Cherchez-Vous.

He didn't go for the movies. They didn't even titillate him anymore. After all, there were only so many ways to do it. But he did like sitting there in the darkness. It relaxed him. A psychiatrist would probably say he was trying to crawl back into the womb, but the way Lawrence saw it, it was no different than people who enjoyed going to the beach and lying in the sun all day long. There was a name for that kind of comparison—things that were opposites but really the same—but he couldn't remember what it was. A negative image, maybe?

He saw the same faces at Cherchez-Vous. Familiar strangers. He liked that they never said much. A vague comment thrown out now and then. You didn't have to reply. "That Danny practically lives here," a man sitting near him had once leaned over and whispered. "Danny's saying his prayers," he'd heard another man tell his neighbor, chuckling.

His initial aversion to Danny had gradually diminished. After seeing something so many times, you became inured to it. It wasn't that much different from what was on the screen, but he did wonder what would possess someone to have such a public need. In his own mind, he had jokingly dubbed Danny The Good Samaritan, but he had recently come around to feeling sorry for him more than anything else. Even a bit protective. Not so protective that he would openly advocate for him, but his reply to any comments he heard now was a disinterested shrug and a throw-a-way "live and let live."

❖

He'd just finished the morning crossword puzzle when Ruth Ann Quigley called to invite him to their 50th class reunion to be held in August. She called from Las Vegas where she'd been selling real estate for the last 28 years. He didn't know how she'd found his number. They talked for almost 30 minutes. It surprised him that he enjoyed her call so much, hearing about the others who'd been in his class. Ruthie named the ones who'd attended college, the same ones his mother had mentioned, except Nancy Mason had gone on to get her masters and Barb Stahlberg her Ph.D. Plain little Grace Smith had moved to Chicago and become a nurse. Three of the 22 were dead. After graduation, Howard Fogel got a job as bag boy at the A&P Grocery store. He'd worked himself up to the manager's position and then two years later died in an auto accident. Pete Bedford and Sarah Kennedy both had cancer. And then she told him about Brian.

Not long after graduation, Brian got engaged, but when his fiancée discovered that his friends had taken him to a strip club—probably Cherchez-Vous, Lawrence thought—for his bachelor party, she canceled the wedding and vandalized his Volkswagen Bug, the one his parents had bought for him after they found out for sure that he was going to graduate. It was the first Volkswagen Lawrence had ever seen. Brian had taken him for a long drive in it. Along the way they'd met two other Volkswagens. Each time Brian and the other driver beeped in recognition, which, Brian said, was what people with Volkswagens did when they saw each other on the road.

Brian and his fiancée eventually made up and got married, Ruthie said, but he should have stayed away from the crazy bitch when he had the chance. He went out drinking just to get away from her. One night when he came home drunk and sat down at the table, she threw gasoline on him and then picked up her cigarette out of the ashtray on the counter and flicked it at him. He survived but was horribly disfigured.

Lawrence felt himself zoning out as Ruthie went on about burns over three quarters of Brian's body, scars over most of his head and face… He'd never fainted in his life, but for a moment, he thought he might. Finally, telling Ruthie there was someone at the door and promising to see her at the reunion, he hung up.

He went over to the sink and splashed cold water on his face before sitting back down at the table. A perfect picture of Brian, the way he'd been years ago, formed in Lawrence's mind: the lopsided grin, the mischievous twinkle in those dark eyes, the brown curls that stuck so tightly to his head, the white jockey shorts. My God, Lawrence whispered. To have to go through life looking like some awful phantom of the opera.

Why hadn't his mother told him? She had to have known. She always had avoided anything unpleasant. He should have asked Ruthie more questions before he hung up, but he'd been so taken aback. Had she kept in touch with Brian over the years? What kind of work had he done? Was he still living in the area? What had happened to his wife? Hopefully, she was rotting in prison or an insane asylum. Lawrence went to his desk, and pulling out a pen and paper, wrote down the questions before he forgot them. What is Brian's address and phone number? he added. He paused. What the hell would he say: Ruthie told me your wife set you on fire? He stared down at the questions he'd listed, then folded the page in half and stuck it in the drawer.

For a moment he was both sorry and relieved that they hadn't kept in touch. He wouldn't have wanted to watch what Brian had gone through: being pointed at by little kids, their parents shushing them even while they stared themselves. They would have stared at Lawrence, too, if they'd seen him with Brian. Brian's problems would have become his problems. He would have been sucked into Brian's life.

❖

Lawrence sat at the table. It had been snowing since six o'clock, huge, fluffy flakes that stuck to the tree branches and didn't melt when they hit the ground. Everything white, except the dark line of Chatham Road, where the traffic had kept the snow melted. If it got colder it would freeze into black ice. He wouldn't be able to get his cappuccino, unless he wanted to go out in this weather, which he didn't.

He glanced at the stack of books across from him: *Dell Crossword Puzzle Book, Large Print Crosswords, 500 Crossword Puzzles, Difficult Crossword Puzzles, Amazing Crossword Puzzle Book...*

To keep himself busy after he quit going to Cherchez-Vous, he'd bought all the crossword puzzle books he could find, as well as two 3,000-piece jigsaw puzzles. That had been two months ago, late October. Almost Halloween. Warm in the sun, but nippy enough for a jacket in the shade. White clouds drifting eastward in slow motion stood out against a baby blue sky. The sugar maples had lost just enough leaves to coat the ground in gold, but not enough to be missed from the trees themselves.

Lawrence had paid his five dollars, waited for the attendant to buzz the door open, and gone inside. He sat down, glancing casually at a man sitting in the same row. The man glanced back, caught his eye for a moment, and looked away. My God, Lawrence thought. For a moment he couldn't catch his breath.

The man's face had a warped look to it, the skin mottled, lighter than normal in areas, and shiny, so that it seemed to wetly catch and reflect the light from the screen. Lawrence jerked his eyes away and directed his gaze toward the movie, where a naked man pounded away in an unoriginal scenario while the woman emitted little cries: oh, oh, oh, oh, with not a single variation.

Lawrence shifted in his seat, turning his head slightly so he could get a better view of the man. The scars on his face had a lumpy look to them, some raised slightly higher than others. In places the skin appeared stretched, tightened. *Could* that be Brian? There was nothing in the man's appearance of the Brian Lawrence had known. But would there be? After fifty years of aging, plus the scarring?

He'd seen a YouTube video of an artist molding a head out of clay, shaping it by adding layer after layer of thin gray flaps of clay. That's what this man reminded him of: the clay head before the artist finally started smoothing it out.

Not all of the man's head was scarred. Had he shaved the rest of it to be consistent? A few years ago, Lawrence had thought about shaving his own head, or the horseshoe of fringe he had left. Be in keeping with all the younger guys with male pattern baldness who were trying to look virile instead of old.

If that *was* Brian, would he recognize me, Lawrence wondered. And if he did, would he say anything? He'd surely keep looking to make sure. Out of the corner of his eye, Lawrence saw the man glance at him and look away.

Not able to take anymore, but not prepared to leave either, he stood up and went into the back room, empty except for Danny, kneeling in front of a stocky middle-aged man. He should have known. Lawrence stood there, irritated, not knowing what he wanted to do. Before he could decide, the man with the scars came through the curtain, halting beside Lawrence and staring at Danny. Didn't expect that, did you? Lawrence thought. The scarred man looked over at Lawrence, almost as though he were waiting for Lawrence to give him an explanation. Lawrence looked away.

The man with Danny finished and left the room. Danny stayed where he was, looking up. Lawrence took a step back, looked at the man standing next to him, and jerked his chin toward Danny. The man moved forward slightly and then hesitated. Lawrence put his hand on the man's back, urging him another step closer to Danny. Then he turned and left.

❖

Lawrence stared out the window. The lower boughs on the pine trees in the back yard brushed against the ground from the weight of the snow. And it was still coming down.

His eyes lost focus and he closed them for a moment. He imagined two old men sitting Indian style on the bed, one scarred over most of his body. I could have gotten used to those scars, he thought. He stood up, and going into his study, sat down at his desk. Tropical fish moved slowly back and forth on the screen saver. What if, all those years ago, he had gone to Brian and said, laughingly, Did you know I had a crush on you? Or what if, two months ago at Cherchez-Vous, instead of pushing Brian toward Danny, he had said, "Is your name Brian?" even though he'd been sure it was after Brian had followed him into the other room.

He reached into the drawer and pulled out the paper he'd written on after talking to Ruth Ann Quigley. He unfolded it and read through the questions. When he finished, he slowly wadded the paper up into a tight ball and dropped it in the waste basket.

Runner-Up

MESOPOTAMIA
LEWIS DESIMONE

I was still fumbling in the kitchen when the doorbell rang. The clock over the refrigerator said 6:35, so I immediately knew who it was. Brendan had a nasty habit of arriving early for everything.

I buzzed him in and double-checked the oven. The cassoulet was simmering gently, the smell of fennel lingering in the air as I closed the door. Everything was under control, so I could rest for a few minutes, until the others arrived.

Brendan greeted me with a bottle of Côtes du Rhône. "I wasn't sure what you were serving," he said with a shrug, apologizing for bringing a $50 bottle of wine.

"This will be perfect," I said. "Shall I open it now?"

"Just decant it. In the meantime, can you get me a Campari and soda?"

I searched the bar. The alcohol was organized according to frequency of use—gin and vodka in front, a variety of whiskeys and rums next, and everything else cluttered haphazardly in the back.

Behind me, I could hear Brendan settling into the chair. "It's got good bones, this place," he said, an odd gruffness in his voice.

I finally found the Campari, the bottle mottled like it had caught a case of glass-borne measles, still half full of potent red booze. It looked like cherry cough syrup but, as I remembered, tasted more like arsenic. I was surprised I even had any. It must have been a party gift someone had brought ages ago (someone with very peculiar ideas about party cocktails). I mixed his drink and made myself a gin and tonic. When I turned around, drinks in hand, I found Brendan gazing at the room, neck contorted to take in the far corners of the ceiling.

"Have you ever had it appraised?" he continued.

"What, the apartment?"

"I could easily get you 800 for it. The market's insane right now."

A one-bedroom on the edge of the Castro, worth that much? I shook my head in disbelief and took a seat. "I only paid 200."

"Yes," Brendan said, "twenty years ago. It's a whole other world these days."

Handing Brendan his drink, I studied the crown molding above his head, the still gleaming hardwood floor beneath our feet. I'd installed the brass curtain rods myself—half a day spent standing on a chair with an electric drill in my hand and a pencil in my teeth for marking the holes. That had been my first major household chore when I'd bought the place. Now I was a regular at Home Depot, a handyman manqué. Owning property had turned me into my father.

"I couldn't sell," I said. "Where would I go? If this place is worth that much, so is everything else. It's not as if I can afford to upgrade."

Brendan gazed sheepishly into his glass. His dark hair was still thick and curly. At this point, he was probably fixed for life. "I could find you something. Believe me."

Brendan had stumbled into the real estate business at the perfect moment, just when the city was starting to recover from the dot-bomb. He'd been a bartender in the early days and then a teacher, but the kids got worse and worse each year and he was never going to get rich off an annual cost-of-living increase that barely kept up with his rent. He quit and started studying for his real-estate license. He said it was the best decision of his life. Even in the off years, when commissions were thin, he at least enjoyed his work, and no one at the office was shooting spitballs at his back.

"Maybe not in this neighborhood," he said, gesturing toward the window with his drink. The Campari caught the light and glowed in his hand like nuclear waste. "The demand is pretty high here, but there are other spots where things are a little slower. Potrero Hill, the Outer Sunset."

"The Outer Sunset?" I repeated, trying not to scowl too obviously. The name sounded like a euphemism for death, and the architecture confirmed it. "Are you serious?"

"There are some great places out that way." Brendan squinted thoughtfully. "I'll take you for a drive next Sunday, see a few open houses."

"Don't rush me," I said. My glass was sweating; I wiped my hand on my pants and gazed over Brendan's shoulder.

"This isn't a surprise party, is it?" he asked, thankfully changing the subject.

"No," I replied. "You can't surprise Oscar. He knows all. And besides, he would kill me if I put him on the spot."

I opened the wine and found a decanter in the cabinet. "As a matter of fact," I added, watching the wine swirl its way toward the wide base of the decanter, "we should probably pretend this isn't a birthday party at all. As much as Oscar loves attention, he's still a little shell-shocked about turning 50."

"How do we pretend it's not his birthday?"

"Just don't use the word," I said.

"*Birthday?*"

"No. *Fifty.*"

Oscar's birthday had actually been a week ago, but dinner had been a scheduling nightmare, with six calendars to contend with. When we were all younger, evenings together could happen at the drop of a hat; now it required an algorithm to coordinate everyone's availability. Thankfully, the gods had aligned around tonight: Oscar had been scheduled to go to court, but the case was unexpectedly settled. Rafe had recently finished decorating a loft for the latest Internet billionaire, and John closed the office early on Thursdays. Brendan and I, the only ones with fairly regular work schedules, were always the easiest to fit in. I didn't really know what Wayne was up to, but, despite John's protestations of true love, I suspected he was only a temporary member of the club and therefore dispensable.

"So where are they?" I asked.

"Maybe John's having trouble getting a babysitter."

"What are you talking about?"

"Oh, is he *bringing* the boy?"

I laughed. "I'm not sure."

"I just hope his heart can stand shtupping a 30-year-old."

I took a sip of my drink. Not enough gin. Not nearly enough gin.

I was back in the kitchen, taking the cassoulet out to cool, when the doorbell rang again. "I'll get it!" Brendan called out.

The kitchen had shrunk on me over the years. When I'd first moved in, I wasn't much of a cook, so room to boil pasta and toss a frozen entree into the microwave was perfectly sufficient. But over the years, my tastes had changed, as well as my desire to entertain. I'd become remarkably skilled at utilizing the tiny workspace between the stove and the fridge. Cassoulet was the perfect dish for a party: it looked impressive, but all the real work was done long before anyone arrived. My guests would have no idea of the chaos that had preceded them.

Brendan pulled open the door and suddenly voices were overlapping and echoing all over the place. Wiping my hands, I headed out to greet them.

"We ran into each other on the street," John was saying, moving a wine bag from hand to hand as he pulled himself out of a caramel suede jacket.

Wayne, his head emerging from a black mock turtle, was squeezed between John and the bookcase. He looked shorter than I remembered, until I realized that he was slouching.

"It was hilarious," Oscar said loudly, bringing up the rear with Rafe.

"What?" I asked, helping him off with his jacket. Beneath it, his white shirt pulled honey tones from his dark skin.

"Manspreading," he said, eyes wide with discovery.

"Sounds like a sexual position." Brendan shut the door behind them.

"Oh no," Oscar replied, leading everyone into the living room, "it's not nearly as much fun as that. It's all the rage these days: complaints that men spread their legs to take up extra space on the subway."

"Like Larry Craig's wide stance?"

"Kind of," Oscar said. "But again, not as much fun."

"This is a new phenomenon?" John asked with a skeptical tone.

"Everything's new to hipsters. They're barely out of diapers and busy creating the world, one reinvented wheel at a time."

I instinctively glanced over at Wayne, but he was too busy looking at his phone to register offense.

"Who wants a drink?" I asked loudly and made my way to the bar.

"What's everyone having?" asked Rafe.

"I have a gin and tonic, and Brendan's working on his isopropyl martini."

Smiling mischievously, Brendan held up his glass, fire-red.

"I'll stick to wine," said Rafe.

There were nods all around. I poured out the glasses. Oscar took one without looking as he continued his story.

"So I get on the M line last night and, much to my joy and surprise, manage to snag a window seat. There I am, tucked in and just about to open my book, when a young woman plops down beside me and—quite deliberately—slams into me, all the way from shoulder to knee. Now look at me—I may be tall, but no one could accuse me of being zaftig. I was barely taking up my half of the seat."

"Was *she* big?" I asked.

"No. Thin as a rail, actually. Clearly, she was making a statement, marking territory. I figured she'd just read some feminist blog and was determined to let me know I was in a no-manspreading zone. She marked me as a culprit merely because I fit the profile—which basically means that, like 50% of the human population, I had been born with, and still wished to retain, a penis."

"What did you do?"

Oscar curled his lips mischievously. "I decided to play it cool. Believe me, I've been profiled before; I know how to turn the tables. I nudged my shoulder forward an inch or so, to give myself some room. Not meeting the expected resistance really threw her for a loop. She jerked her leg away from mine, as if she'd been caught in a criminal act or something."

"Guilt is a wonderful motivator."

"I think I had her completely on the ropes. If she brushed up against me, she was guilty of womanspreading. But if she pulled too far away, she was showing fear of a black man. Her political correctness signals were firing in every direction. And then," he went on, "suddenly, miraculously, there was plenty of room for both of us. I went back to my book and she pulled out hers. I was expecting Andrea Dworkin or something, but it turned out to be Nicholas Sparks."

"Oh, she's a romantic, after all." Brendan batted his eyelashes.

Oscar and Rafe had been among the first couples to get married in 2008, when it was suddenly legal before it was suddenly illegal before it was suddenly legal again. But they'd been together for almost a decade by then, so nothing much changed in their lives. The wedding was largely an excuse for a grand party, and a slap in the face to Oscar's Baptist roots.

The drama of Oscar's story done, we all settled around the table. There was no point in using place cards with this crowd. It was more like musical chairs, everyone fighting for their definition of the best spot.

Brendan turned to Wayne, who had put his phone away and was now gazing into his wine, bereft of ones and zeros. "So, what's new in your world?"

Startled, Wayne shrugged his round shoulders and gave a quizzical look, as if he didn't understand the question.

"Very exciting stuff," John said softly. "There are some VC guys who've expressed interested in his company."

"Viet Cong?" Brendan asked.

Oscar rolled his eyes, but Wayne—earnest, above-it-all Wayne—just smiled. "Venture capitalists," he said. "We're deep into negotiations. With money from them, we can really get the company off the ground—hire the right people, fine-tune the product to make sure it's just right, do all the necessary market research. It's a very exciting prospect."

All I knew was that Wayne had cofounded some techie startup with someone he'd worked with at Google. Until recently they'd been working out of Wayne's living room. "What exactly is the product?" I asked now.

Wayne's eyes lit up as he launched into an answer—a speech dotted with gigabytes, apps, and processing speed. The words flew over my head. It was easier just to focus on Wayne's flawless skin, his thick head of hair, remarkably devoid of gray.

Wayne wasn't just new to our little circle. By most standards, Wayne was new to planet Earth. While the half-century mark had already slapped everyone else at the table—including, finally, the birthday boy—Wayne, barely 30, still looked like he had trouble growing facial hair.

My attention returned when the downward tone of his voice indicated that he was winding up. "So, if all goes well," he said, "we'll be able to launch by the end of the year." He grabbed John's hand perfunctorily before picking up his glass. He'd barely touched his cassoulet so far, mostly picking around the duck and sausage for the occasional scoop of beans.

"How long have you guys been together?" Rafe asked.

"Eleven months," John said. He swirled his glass and looked for legs.

Like a baby's age, I thought, marked by months. "The world certainly moves quickly these days."

"It's the Internet," Brendan said. "It's turned everyone into an Aries: *I want now*. Remember when we had to go to the library and pore through card catalogs?"

"Or engage with a human being at the bank?" Oscar offered.

"Or browse actual books at a bookstore?" I said.

"How *is* business?" John asked.

"I think I counted 40 customers in the store today."

"That sounds good."

"Not really," I said. "Most of them browse the shelves, decide what they want, and then go home to order it on Amazon."

"Bastards," Oscar said in his best Bette Davis.

Wayne cast a quizzical look around the table, as if we were all speaking a foreign language. "Don't you guys like what the Web has given us?"

"Sure," Oscar replied. He dangled a fork over his salad plate, deciding whether to stab a tomato or an olive. "But I think we're also concerned about what it's taken away."

Wayne laughed. "That's probably what people said about Henry Ford, too, when they looked around and couldn't find a horse and buggy."

"Yes," Brendan said with a sneer, "I'm sure it is." He swiveled his head toward Oscar and Rafe. "So, how's the renovation coming along?"

"The new kitchen's going to be gorgeous," Rafe said. "I can't wait for our next dinner party."

I hadn't noticed anything wrong with their kitchen, but they had insisted on an upgrade. Oscar was all about steady progress. As long as something could be improved, it would be. Change was a constant for him. Enough was never enough.

In the old days, that had been his calling card, but then it had referred to men, drugs, parties. Oscar had loved excess. He'd been determined to experience as much as possible as quickly as possible. In those days, no one knew how long anything would last.

To spare more drama, we reverted to small talk, the safe monotony of home design and the latest episode of *Pose*. It was all so civilized: an elegant dinner, designer clothes, fresh manicures, polite conversation that never veered toward sex or politics. Twenty years ago—even ten—the setting would have been completely different. Back then, we would be clumped together in a corner of some bar, talking about how much we hated our jobs or who we longed to fuck. Back then, it was all about what was going to happen next. Now it was about where to put the dishwasher.

"So how's life in the 'hood?" Rafe asked. "I never come down here anymore."

Oscar and Rafe had moved to St. Francis Wood a few years back, seeking a quiet neighborhood and more space. Fog be damned, they wanted space.

"Shrinking," I said glumly.

"Well," said Oscar, "that's never a good thing."

Brendan pushed his plate away and moved his wine glass front and center. "I was just telling Charles he should take advantage of this crazy market and sell this place."

Everyone else started looking around, assessing the room, searching for cracks in the walls.

"And do what?" I asked. "Where would I go?"

"Palm Springs?" John offered.

I sighed. "Palm Springs is where old homosexuals go to die." And even as I said it, a guilty thought jumped into the back of my head: the very phrase *old homosexuals* was something to be grateful for.

Oscar was nodding. "The Castro's dying," he said. "I knew it was over when I saw the first baby stroller."

"The Castro is not dying," Rafe retorted. "If anything, it's younger than ever."

"Point taken," Oscar said. "It's the culture that's dying. Men our age belong in the suburbs."

Rafe shook his head. "If San Francisco can't sustain a gay neighborhood, then what city can?"

"Why do you need one?" Wayne asked.

I glared.

Oscar to the rescue. "You know how you can tell the city's gone straight?" he said, ignoring Wayne. "The gym. The place I go to is in the heart of the Financial District. When I started going, the locker room would be the cruisiest spot in town. No action, of course, but lots of wanton looks." He paused to sip his wine. "Nobody looks anymore. They're too busy talking—even the gay guys. Sports and IPOs, that's the extent of it."

"God help us," said Brendan, reaching for a piece of bread. "We were freer when we were outlaws."

Wayne pursed his lips, contemplating his glass. "Seriously," he said, "aren't things better now? It's like you guys are nostalgic for inequality."

"There's a difference," Brendan said, "between equality and cultural integrity."

"Cultural integrity?" Wayne chuckled. "Like what, drag queens and leather bars?"

"You owe everything you have to drag queens," Brendan hissed.

"Nostalgic memories of Stonewall aside—"

"Memories?" Rafe interrupted, no doubt to lighten the tone. "Just how old do you think we are?"

John laughed loudest. "I think we can agree," he said, draping an arm protectively over Wayne's shoulders, "that life is a little easier for us all these days."

Brendan sighed. "I'm not talking about the Middle Ages," he said. "Gays have had a place at the table, in this town at least, for 40 years. The difference is that, until now, we weren't expected to conform in order to be treated like equals. We didn't have to turn into Ward and June Cleaver to get respect."

"What are you losing?" Wayne asked. "What's the trade-off?"

"We're losing everything that made us special."

"Hell," Oscar said, "even straight people do anal these days."

Wayne grew quiet, close-set eyes focusing on the salt shaker as if to will it, Carrie-like, to fly off the table.

I broke the tension by scraping my chair away and announcing dessert.

"Nothing for me," said Oscar, patting his belly, and the others followed suit.

Anticipating everyone's obsession with burgeoning waistlines, I hadn't bothered to get a birthday cake. But in case anyone asked, there was vanilla ice cream and fresh berries. Now I'd be stuck eating it all myself.

Brendan folded his napkin and laid it on the table with a noticeable flourish. "Well," he said, "if we're forgoing dessert, how about a nightcap?"

Oscar made a show of looking at his watch. "It's getting late," he said, tilting his head to one side. I remembered the gesture from our bachelor days, when Oscar was letting some flirt down easy.

"No no no," Brendan said, "it's barely 9:00."

I started clearing the table. "You know the ritual, Oscar. We've been through it enough times."

Wayne crossed his knife and fork on his empty plate. "The ritual?" he asked, looking up.

I felt like the Statue of Liberty, dishes piled on each forearm. "Every time one of us turns 50, we have cocktails at the Glass Coffin."

"It's kind of like rehearsal," Brendan said. He drew Oscar into a hug.

Oscar squirmed. "Oh, all right," he said, if only to win release.

Rafe helped me gather the remaining dishes and stack them in the kitchen. When we reemerged into the living room, everyone was draining wine glasses and putting on coats. Brendan led the way out the door and down the stairs.

We reached the sidewalk as a limo bus stopped at the corner, the blue glow of computer screens visible through its darkened windows. The bus's streamlined nose looked like something Sigourney Weaver should have been attacking with a flamethrower.

A young woman stepped out, counterbalancing a backpack on one shoulder with a Whole Foods bag on the other. As she approached, I recognized her as my upstairs neighbor, so I held the door open as the others made their way to Castro Street.

We'd never introduced ourselves, though we had passed on the stairs or found each other at the mailboxes from time to time. Somewhere in her twenties, she was renting her unit from Roland, who'd been the longest resident in the building until moving to wine country with his new husband. We'd never spoken, and when she passed she would toss me a perfunctory, closed-lipped smile. I'd never been able to determine whether she was shy or just rude, but I kept testing her—smiling broadly, saying hello only to be greeted by a brief nod.

She did it now as she reached the door, dipping her head, most of her face hidden behind a straight curtain of dark hair, fumbling with the heavy backpack as a nonverbal excuse. She passed into the lobby, hand never touching the door. I felt like a doorman in my own home, but tamped down my resentment. It was her parents' fault, I told myself. My generation, perhaps because we'd been spoiled ourselves, had ended up making terrible parents.

I caught up with everyone else at the corner, falling into line behind Oscar and Rafe. We passed by a storefront where a figure was huddled under a rough blanket, an assortment of items tucked against the wall—a small plastic bag spilling food wrappers, a wadded-up newspaper, shoes with holes worn through the soles. The person's face was invisible, only the long stringy hair at the back of the head showing above the blanket. He might have been a garden gnome or a fire hydrant for the attention his presence garnered.

"Here," Brendan said, grabbing my arm, "I want to show you something." He pulled me toward a real estate office, its windows collaged with flyers advertising various places for sale around the city. "Look," he said, pointing, "one bedroom, one bath, 700 square feet—just like your place. Asking price of 790 grand. Which means it'll fetch at least 900."

The flyer included three photographs—bedroom, living room, kitchen—all taken from tricky angles to exaggerate the space. "My kitchen is nothing like that," I said, noting the sparkling appliances, gray marble countertop, cabinets galore.

"It doesn't have to be just like that," Brendan said. "It has the *potential* to be like that, that's the important thing."

I turned my eye to the description, the flowery euphemisms I'd always found so amusing in these listings, where *cozy* meant Lilliputian and *quiet* meant that the trucks whizzed by every 20 minutes instead of every 10.

"Where is this place?" I asked. "It says Eureka Valley."

Brendan laughed. "It's just around the corner," he said, pointing at the address. "I think that's 19th and Diamond."

"You mean the Castro. Why doesn't it say that?"

"Because the real name of the neighborhood is Eureka Valley, that's why." He shook his head with a smirk, dismissing the apparent idiocy of the question.

I rolled my eyes. "No one has called this place Eureka Valley since the 60s. It's like referring to Iraq as Mesopotamia."

At the corner of 18th and Castro, we swerved around another homeless person, this one holding a cardboard sign: *Who am I kidding? I'll just use it to buy beer.*

"They're not quite the same," Brendan said as we maneuvered into the crosswalk. "Technically, the Castro is a subsection of Eureka Valley."

"Technically," I echoed, "the word *Castro* scares away straight buyers."

Brendan sighed and started walking faster. "The world is a dynamic place, Charles. You have to learn to embrace change."

"I'm sure that's what the dinosaurs said when they saw the asteroid flying through the air." Somewhere along the way I had become a curmudgeon. "And besides, aren't you the one who was just giving Wayne shit for proclaiming the virtues of change?"

"Well," Brendan said with a dramatic sigh. "Just don't tell him."

We snaked past a line outside the theater and made our way to the corner. Across the street, the enormous rainbow flag, lit from below, ruffled in the wind.

His hand on the door to Twin Peaks, Rafe turned around and smiled at Oscar. "Are you ready for your close-up, Miss Desmond?" he asked.

Oscar sneered and caught the door as Rafe glided through. Following them, I looked back and saw Wayne and John standing by the bus stop, huddled in conversation. They kissed and John made his way to the door.

"Wayne has an early meeting in the morning," he said, "He's going home."

I nodded and, entering the bar, tried to hide any signs of relief on my face.

Twin Peaks was the place you went to when you wanted a cocktail, Brendan had once joked, rather than just a cock. Once known solely as the haunt of gay men past their prime, it had grown more broadly popular recently. Tourists came through with regularity, checking it off their list like Coit Tower or Fisherman's Wharf.

Fortunately, a group was leaving just as we arrived, so we were able to grab a table by the windows. John told everyone else about Wayne, and was met with polite smiles. We were all saved from discussing it by the appearance of the waitress, and within minutes, she laid five nearly overflowing glasses before us. Brendan bent over and sucked the first sip off the rim of the glass.

"Remember how hard it was to cross that threshold the first time?" Brendan asked, delicately lifting his glass.

I laughed. For years, I had passed by the place with disdain, rattling off its many nicknames to anyone I happened to be with. No, I'd said, I'd never be ready for the Wrinkle Room. I'd have to be dragged kicking and screaming into the Glass Coffin. And then, on my own 50th birthday, Brendan and Oscar had bracketed me, one holding each arm, and practically carried me past the plate glass windows, up to the door. "Believe us," Brendan had said, "you're old enough. Officially."

Now this was my go-to place when I wanted to sit at a bar and not be bothered, or have a quiet chat with a friend. And I'd grown ashamed of my youthful arrogance. Aging, I'd come to understand, was all about losing your arrogance. Along with everything else. Now this bar struck me as an oasis; though its huge windows looked out on a constantly changing world, the place itself seemed frozen in time.

"Guess what I got in the mail last week," Oscar announced, placing his glass carefully on the table.

"The latest International Male catalog?"

"Close," he said. "My AARP card."

When my own card had arrived a couple of years ago, I'd practically jumped out of my skin, as if the envelope had been full of anthrax.

"How do they even know I'm 50?"

"They know all," Brendan said.

"Well, anyway," Oscar said, lifting his glass, "thank you for all sharing in my encroaching decrepitude."

I grimaced. "I should have baked you a cake."

He laughed. "Maybe we can just stick a candle in my cocktail."

"That'd set the place on fire," said Rafe.

"So would 50 candles on a cake."

Maybe it was the alcohol, but suddenly something heavy settled over me. I put my chin in my hand and gazed out at the sidewalk. Young men laughing, falling onto one another's shoulders, lesbians in baseball caps, a couple of thirtyish guys with thick beards and plaid shirts nearly bursting with muscle. No drag queens yet, but the night was young.

The light changed, and a gaggle of people dashed across the street, toward the subway. "What happened?" I asked, as if the night would answer.

"Where?"

"Here," I said, turning back to the table and lifting my glass. There were still a couple of sips left. "To us."

"To us." Four other glasses rose into the air, and I laughed.

"No, I wasn't toasting. I was asking: what happened *to us*?"

Brendan shook his head. "Oh hon, I don't have that much time. So much has happened. Most of which I can't remember. What are you getting at?"

"How did we go from *that*," I said, gesturing out the window, "to *this*?"

"To what? Sitting in God's Waiting Room in anticipation of the undertaker?" Oscar asked.

"Well, I wasn't feeling quite that morbid, but…yes. When did we become middle-aged?"

"I don't know," John said. "It just happens. It creeps up on you. One day you're out and about, running around, thinking about the future. And the next you're counting gray hairs in the mirror."

"Just like that. So I didn't miss anything? It's not like I slept through the moment?" I sat back in the chair. "I guess I always thought it would be like driving through the Robin Williams Tunnel, you know? You're in this darkened space between worlds, and suddenly you emerge out the other end and—boom—there's the Golden Gate Bridge in all its glory."

"You thought middle age would be glorious?" asked Rafe.

"I thought it would be something."

Brendan chuckled. "Oh, it's something all right. Ask my aching back." He laughed and turned toward Oscar with an ironic smile. "Not to scare you, hon, but this one's different: 30 and 40 are fabulous, the entry points for exciting new phases of life. But 50?—50 is the beginning of the end."

"Gee, thanks, guys, you're really making this a fun birthday." Oscar fished the cherry out of his drink and bit it off the stem.

"We just want to prepare you," I said.

"Prepare me? It sounds like you're more upset about my age than I am."

I guess I was, in a way. Oscar was the youngest one in our group, so if he was old, it meant we all were.

The waitress came back. With remarkable dexterity, she laid more brimming glasses on the tabletop and took away the empties.

"Where did this come from?" John asked, looking at the new glass before him as if it were Macbeth's ghostly dagger.

"Magic," Brendan said. "Just drink it."

"Well, I have patients in the morning, better have my wits about me."

"Yes," Oscar said with a laugh, "an optometrist can't show up for work blind drunk."

John dutifully nursed his drink, but was the first to call it quits. As we stood to say good night, Oscar and Rafe used the opportunity to leave, as well. And just like that, the evening was over.

As the door thwacked shut behind them, Brendan and I sat back down and looked at each other. He raised his eyebrows.

"Now what?" he said, pushing his own empty glass toward the center of the table.

"Now what what?"

"It's barely 11:00. I say we go somewhere else."

"I couldn't," I said. "Not tonight." I was picturing crisp sheets, the latest David Leavitt on my bedside table.

"Come on," Brendan coaxed. "Just one more drink."

In the old days, I could be easily persuaded. In the old days, I would say *yes* before the question had even been asked. I'd gotten a lot better at giving *no* for an answer, and Brendan, surprisingly, had gotten better at accepting it. "Just walk me to 440," he said.

We crossed the street together and stopped in front of the bar. A burly man in leather pants sat on a stool just outside the door, checking the occasional ID while a few stragglers smoked at the edge of the sidewalk.

"You're sure?" Brendan said, nodding toward the doorway. Loud music blared into the night. The place was crowded. I had once liked crowds.

Two slender boys emerged from the bar. "Screw this place," one of them said loudly. "Too bearish for my blood. Let's go to Box."

"Box?" said his friend. "Where's that?"

"Up on Market. Next to that seafood restaurant." And they were off.

"Oh my lord," Brendan said, rolling his eyes.

"What?"

"*Box?*" he repeated. "They mean Beaux."

"Education is wasted on the stupid." I laughed and kissed him good night.

Brendan slipped past the bouncer—no need to check for ID—and vanished into the crowd. I smiled and made my way down the street.

It had usually been Oscar who directed our evenings out. He had a fail-safe itinerary, a specific order for the pub crawl. We would start at the Midnight Sun—cocktails over music videos and old *Designing Women* clips to loosen us up for the evening. Next, Badlands—before its hip reinvention. We'd huddle in the back, where we could easily scope out the crowd if we were in the mood to cruise, or otherwise simply enjoy one another's company. The evening could easily end there, but if anyone felt like giving in to a darker impulse, there was always the Detour, the Edge, Daddy's. There were ample choices. All that was before Grindr and the like replaced bodies with headless images.

I tried to remember what this street had looked like then, when it was all new to me, as new as it was for the kids who now skidded past with an enthusiasm I could barely recall. Several bars had been replaced by stores, but I could no longer picture where they'd been, nor how many restaurants had changed hands on the corner we'd come to think of as cursed.

I'd met Oscar at Badlands, Brendan at the Sun, Peter and Barry and Jake at one place or another in the neighborhood. It all blended together after a while, but now and then I could still feel it—the excitement of novelty. We were young and free and just figuring out who we were. And most of all, who we wanted to become. We thought in the future and lived in the present.

Now, it was all in the past. As I stepped onto the rainbow-striped crosswalk, I remembered the potholed black one it had replaced. I saw Barry standing in front of the pizza joint, grabbing a mid-evening slice of pepperoni to absorb the beer and give him energy to keep going. I heard Oscar singing a few bars of "Don't Leave Me This Way" when anyone threatened to call it a night.

The crowd thinned out after Harvey's, and I made my way toward 19th Street on a nearly empty sidewalk. I was halfway up the block before I spotted the flashing lights. There was an ambulance parked near the corner, a couple of EMTs by the storefront. They were loading someone onto a gurney.

When I got closer, I saw that the person was entirely wrapped up, like a mummy.

A few people hovered around, and I spotted my neighbor near the curb. She was twirling a strand of hair around her finger, staring absently at the body.

"What happened?" I asked, sidling up next to her. We backed out of the way as the EMTs steered the gurney toward the open back door of the ambulance.

"I don't know." She was staring ahead. I had no idea whether she recognized me or thought she was responding to a random stranger on the street. "I was just getting back from dinner. When I got out of the Uber, the ambulance was pulling up."

"Was it the homeless guy who sleeps there?"

"I think so." She looked shaken, her brow wrinkled in confusion. I suspected she'd never seen death before.

We watched as the EMTs climbed into the ambulance, one in the driver's seat, the other in back with the body, and pulled away. No siren, no flashing lights. No hurry.

"That was terrifying," she said, and looked me in the eye for the first time.

"Poor man."

"I passed by him every day," she continued, "and I knew nothing about him. And now he's gone. I didn't even know his name."

I let the silence hang between us for a long moment. "I'm Charles," I said at last.

Her forehead smoothed out a bit, her eyelids drooping. "Kayla," she said. As she spoke, her jaw darted forward and I noticed for the first time the sharpness of her chin.

We walked uphill together, back to the building, footsteps clicking on the pavement. Once you turned the corner, you could barely hear any noise from below. I'd bought the condo partly because of the quiet. It was close enough to the center of things to make going out easy, and coming home even easier.

"How was dinner?" I asked as we entered the lobby.

She sighed, flat shoes scuffing against the linoleum. "Terrible. It was a first date, an awful first date. I didn't stay for dessert."

I smiled gently, sympathetically. I'd had enough of those.

For a moment I thought she might want to talk about it, but she quickly shook her head and moved toward the stairs. I followed, keeping several steps behind her. On the second floor, I turned and headed for my door while Kayla continued slowly up, her flats making a squishing sound as she climbed.

I hung my coat in the closet and looked around the room. The dining table was a mess—wine glasses empty but stained red at the bottom, crumbs everywhere, wadded-up napkins, candle wax pooling into a hard medallion on the tablecloth. I carried glasses, two crisscrossed in each hand, into the kitchen.

Twenty years ago, I'd fallen in love with this place at first sight. It was all potential then, of course. I'd had the carpet ripped up and replaced with a hardwood floor, repainted all the walls. And over the years, as each appliance broke down one by one, I'd replaced them with the latest model. For a time, nothing had matched—the new stainless steel refrigerator calling attention to the gold porcelain stove that belonged to another era, the dishwasher that rattled so loudly I would run it only during the day, while I was at work. Looking around now, I realized that Brendan was right: what had first attracted me to this place was the bones. I had added the flesh myself, over time.

I'd had a few apartments over time—the Mission, Diamond Heights, the Lower Haight, circling the Castro until I'd finally found the right spot. And now, 20 years filled this place, 20 years of people and life. They were evident everywhere. Barry had helped me pick out the bed—and break it in, of course. Giuseppe, who was spending a summer in the city between semesters at art school in Milan, painted a portrait of me that still hung beside the bookcase. I could barely recognize myself in the image now—35, with a full head of hair and a slim build. The credenza held an eclectic assortment of souvenirs from various trips—a cheap vase from Mexico, a tiny replica of the Colosseum, a collection of stones from a beach in Maui.

I was older than I'd ever expected to be; maybe that was part of it. When I'd first moved to San Francisco, there were no 50-year-olds in the Castro.

I craved a glass of brandy, but decided against it. I'd had enough to drink for one night. Instead, I brushed my teeth and shut out the lights.

I'd just crawled into bed when the voices emerged. I hadn't heard them for weeks, the straining a capella of the boys on the street. They would march through the neighborhood now and then, a small group of black teenagers, singing pop songs—Whitney, Beyoncé, Mariah. I'd watched them from the window once or twice. They couldn't have been more than 16 years old—just kids, playing, trying to outdo one another with the high notes. There were no black families in the neighborhood, hardly any families at all, so clearly they'd come from elsewhere—Bayview, perhaps, the Western Addition, places where it wasn't so safe to call each other "girlfriend" and sing in harmony. Oscar, visiting one evening a few months ago, had christened them the Dreamgirls. Sitting in the window, he sang softly along with them in a lovely, whispered falsetto.

If you like it, then you should have put a ring on it, they sang tonight, in delicious counterpoint. I put my book down on the bed, leaned back against the headboard, and closed my eyes. I let the music swim around me. I wanted to hear every note.

THE SULTAN'S PALACE

ARIADNE BLAYDE

It's fun to be the big spoon," Landon giggled from between James' shoulders. They had just woken up and were cuddling in bed.

James sat up and groaned at the sudden throbbing in his temples. "Ow."

"Are you hungover?" Landon asked.

"Yeah. You're not?"

Landon shrugged. "Not really. I am a lot younger than you, though."

James shot him a look and rubbed his eyes. "What did we even do last night?"

"We started at that bar with your tour guide friends, then went to the Corner Pocket, then the Phoenix. Remember?"

"Oh, right." Images of dancing, drinking, smoking. He let himself fall back onto the pillows next to Landon. "And there was some twink you knew?" James vaguely remembered a young man about Landon's age, some sort of Asian mix with a blond mohawk, the blurry shapes of the two young men grinding on the dance floor. A little ball of jealousy fluttered into being in his gut.

"Yeah, Jax. I introduced you, remember?"

"*Jax?* God, what kind of name is that."

"He's just a friend, you don't need to be catty about it."

Catty! The audacity. "I don't care if he's your friend, friend with benefits, hookup, whatever. You do you," he said, sprinkling just a little disdain into his voice. He had told Landon time and time again that they were not monogamous and never would be. Why should they be? Landon was young and attractive enough that he could have whoever he wanted whenever he wanted, and James was generally able to find plenty of interested parties himself. Just last weekend he had hooked up with a big hulk of a man from Grindr. He assumed Landon fooled around with other people, too, and he didn't—shouldn't—have a problem with it. Not that he needed to know the details.

"I don't want anybody but you," Landon said, brushing his toes against James' under the covers. Their faces were just a few inches apart and Landon's eyes were deep, deep brown, like a dairy cow's. James found himself gazing into them for just a little too long. He got out of bed and pulled on his jeans.

"You're not leaving, are you?"

"Well, yeah, I wanted to hit the gym before the Senior Center."

"Not before you open your present!"

He caught sight of Landon's perfect 21-year-old body in the mirror behind him, holding a box wrapped in shimmery paper and done up with ribbon. "Happy Valentine's Day," the boy smiled.

"Oh…"

"It's okay if you didn't get me anything."

"No—I did. It's in my car."

James had forgotten today was Valentine's Day, wouldn't have spent the night if he'd remembered. Luckily, he did have something for Landon, just a little thing he'd picked up on a whim a couple weeks ago. He went down to get it, pulled the price tag off, stuffed it into an empty paper bag he found in the backseat. He briefly considered just getting into his car and driving away. But his shirt was upstairs.

When James returned, Landon was sitting cross-legged on the bed and patted it for James to join him.

"I hope you like it," he said, handing over the fancy box. James unwrapped it and pulled out a vintage camera. It was a Kodak Duaflex II, a cute little rectangle of a thing with a flip-up viewfinder, a detachable flash, and a neck strap.

"It works," Landon smiled. "And I got you some film too, see?"

Shocked and pleased, James examined the camera. Landon had listened, it seemed, when James had told him photography had been a hobby in college, that he'd loved spending hours in the art department's darkroom listening to Death Cab for Cutie and developing photographs. "This is amazing," James said, forgetting to disguise the sincerity in his voice. "Where did you get it?"

"Ebay. Got into a bidding war," Landon smiled. "I probably paid a little too much but no way was I gonna let 'eatprayknit22' get her flabby mom-hands on it."

James laughed and leaned forward to kiss him. "This is so cool. Thank you. Really."

"My turn?"

"Oh…sure," James said, handing over the paper bag. He found his cheeks flushing hot as Landon pulled out the plushie sparkle-eyed panda, embarrassed by how stupid and inadequate it was in comparison. What right did Landon have to buy him such a thoughtful present? He'd gotten the stupid stuffed animal at a fucking *Walgreens* and it made him look like an asshole, or worse, an idiot. He wanted to say something defensive, sarcastic, even mean, as the top of its fluffy head emerged from the bag. But Landon squealed with honest delight and hugged it to his chest as soon as he pulled it out.

"Oh my God, how adorable!"

"It just…I dunno. Reminded me of you," James shrugged self-consciously. But it had. The stupid panda had been so sweet and cute and sparkly that he'd wandered away from the toothpaste aisle to pull it off the shelf, had known right away that it was for Landon. "You can hug it when I'm not around."

"I will. I love him." Landon picked up the Kodak and held it up to the panda's sparkly eyes. "See? He's a photographer too. Just like you."

"Aww."

"I do, you know."

"Do what?"

"Love him," he said meaningfully.

"You're cute," James laughed, and stood. "I'd better get to the gym. Thanks for the amazing present."

"Don't you want to stay for breakfast? I could make us pancakes."

"Wish I could. I'll text you later, yeah?" He gathered his things and was out the door a few minutes later.

"Bye! Happy Valentine's Day!" Landon blew him a kiss from the top of the stairs.

James could always tell when the boys he dated were about to use the L-word and had gotten pretty skilled at shutting it down. Usually he broke things off a few weeks after the word entered the picture. Landon was sneaky, though; he'd said it in a way that wasn't really saying it at all, which meant that maybe James could let him get away with it—for now, anyway. In a week or two he'd end things with the boy, he'd told himself at Christmas. He was still telling himself the same thing nearly two months later. Another two weeks, after Mardi Gras. Well, maybe three weeks. A month. Surely for another month it could be just this, something easy and uncomplicated.

James' gym had been around since the late 1800s and was something of a New Orleans institution. Rows of fancy touchscreen ellipticals sat under dim sconces and filigree crown molding like you'd find in some noir-era smoking parlor, and the club's puce green walls were decked in black-and-white pictures from the 30's and 40's, portraits of important old men and fading team photos of gymnastics and tennis teams in diaper-like booty shorts. One of the pictures, a portrait of a mustached old man who looked like Warren G. Harding (how James even knew what Warren G. Harding looked like he wasn't totally sure), was on the wall directly across from James' favorite treadmill. The man looked vaguely pissed off, and when he'd first joined the gym, James had teased him in his mind as he ran—*What's wrong, Daddy, you mad there's fags and blacks and women in your fancy athletic club? Why don't you come on up to the steam room, let's see if your balls are as weird and tiny as your spectacles.* Over the years, though, the angry mustached man (whose name, James learned from reading the plaque beneath the photo, was J.J. Gottschmidt), had become a sort of workout buddy, a confidante.

Today Gottschmidt was giving James shit as he ran on the treadmill. *Why are you so unkind to that boy?* his tiny, frustrated eyes seemed to ask. James did feel bad for blowing Landon off that morning. They'd been messing around together for how long now, four months? Five? Last week, Landon had asked James to be his boyfriend, and he had almost said yes. He liked him. Very much.

But it's not simple, he told Gottschmidt. *He's so much younger. They all are.*

So?

You like to keep it that way, don't you? Ever since—

Shut up.

He upped the speed of the treadmill. He was still young enough, mid-thirties, but his body was changing; drinking to excess, as he often did, would swell his gut if he wasn't careful. And damn if he'd become one of these balding, fat old bears who all the twinks laugh at behind their backs. Just a few nights ago one of them had practically begged to suck James' dick in the bathroom of a little hole-in-the-wall club in the Quarter, and he'd had to force himself not to laugh in the man's pathetically hopeful face. Terry and Cleve, a couple of pretentious old married queens who owned lots of real estate in the neighborhood, had noticed and started snickering audibly over their Chardonnay about it and that had annoyed James, annoyed him so much that he almost wanted to take the man by the hand to the bathroom and let him do it, close his eyes and pretend it was Elliot. He tried not to think too much about Elliot, had stopped masturbating about him years ago, but that could be an exception, couldn't it? He wondered who Landon thought about when they fucked. Probably Jax, the blond Asian kid. James' insides knotted in jealousy again and he nearly laughed aloud of the stupid hypocrisy of it. He recalled his encounter with the Hulk, as he'd been mentally calling the guy from Grindr. Why did he care if Landon hooked up with other sweet stupid young boys? Let them have their fun. What did any of it matter.

None of the supervisors at the Senior Center gave a shit what he did, so James had long made it his personal mission to make Arts and Crafts class "lit as fuck," as he liked to describe it. At Halloween time he'd announced that they'd be "bedazzling Satan's wicked little fingers" and had the old people trace their hands on orange construction paper, adding ghastly veins and long pointed nails and rhinestones, lots and lots of rhinestones. At Christmas they made "Gay Elven Wonderlands" with piles of glittery cotton-ball snow. Today they were finishing up their papier-mâché Valentine's Day hearts.

"And when we finish, we'll be starting our Mardi Gras Masques of Transgression," he said, holding up the one he'd made. "See, now I'm in disguise. Once you put these on, I won't recognize any of you, which means you can get away with whatever you want, any of the seven deadly sins. Except probably murder, don't murder anybody. I'm looking at you, Irene."

"Murder's not one of the seven deadly sins," Irene groused back. She was a fat and sharp-witted old woman who no one really liked. Most of the old folks were vacant and cooperative, but he and Irene often heckled each other.

"Maybe not, but that kerchief has got to be," he said, gesturing to her garish orange scarf. It was patterned with purple flowers that looked like puckered assholes.

"Burn," chuckled the woman next to her. Some of them had picked up James' millennial slang. It was cute.

"Well, not too long from now, *he'll* be burning in hell," Irene muttered sourly under her breath.

"I heard that. Not too long from now? What's that supposed to mean?" James said, his hands fluttering to his cheeks. "Do I need a different moisturizer, Irene? Am I wrinkly?"

Homophobia was not something James had to deal with on a daily basis, and in situations like this it felt humorous and quaint, creating in him a sort of nostalgia of disgust for his adolescence in rural Kentucky. His parents, not particularly political one way or the other, had accepted his queerness with the same lack of interest they took in his photography and track meets. Of course, there were the same school bullies and dumb jocks that every gay teen has to endure, but James was generally able to shut them up. He had a killer sneer and knew exactly what to say and do to make anyone feel powerless and insecure. It was a skill he prided himself on, and he honed it constantly by keeping a cynical running commentary in his mind, a never-ending inner monologue of condescension towards everyone and everything around him. He had to be careful, especially when drinking, not to let these cruelties slip to the surface and come out of his mouth, to keep his playful negging from crossing the line into real hurtfulness. It did happen, and he knew what it looked like on each of his friend's faces. That momentary flash of shock and hurt, so quickly replaced by a blank smile and minutes, hours, even days of keeping him at emotional arm's length. *Whatever*, he always told himself. People shouldn't be so sensitive.

"Okay, everybody," he said at the end of the class hour. "Leave your hearts on the rack to dry. Everybody except Irene, whose heart is already as dry as a ten-day old dog turd."

There it was, that momentary flash of pain and vulnerability across the old woman's face. He didn't care.

Anthony, a sweet old man who James was pretty damn sure was a homo too, took him aside after class as he packed up the supplies.

"You should try to be gentler with Irene," he said. "Her daughter just died, you know."

"Was her daughter a homophobe too?"

"Oh, she doesn't mean those things she says. She just wants attention. You know, she doesn't get any visitors."

James watched Irene as she shuffled over to the rack to put her heart out to dry. "LOVE! LOVE! LOVE!" it said in glittery all-caps. He'd watched her painstakingly letter the words with her shaking hands. She really did work hard on the art projects. Apart from her shitty attitude, she was probably the best student in the class.

He got in his car and drove home in a foul mood. Why had Irene's daughter died, he wondered? Probably overweight like her mother, a victim of high cholesterol or something like that; James didn't understand people who didn't make an effort to stay in shape. But still, to lose a daughter. He thought again of Irene and her shaking hands. Her scarf hadn't really been that ugly. At least she made an effort to be different, at least she wore something other than the plain scrubs so many of the residents showed up to class in. If he was in a boring-ass nursing home, he'd probably wear weird shit too. He pictured himself, old and infirm, wearing his by-then-threadbare leopard-print trucker hat just to get attention from the staff who didn't even like him. Irene never had any visitors, Anthony had said. James' anger began to soften, a gloomy knot of sadness blooming in his chest. Surely when he got old he'd be alone too, abandoned in some nursing home with no one to visit him. Most of the other residents had spouses who'd died, but he was fairly sure Irene had never had a husband to begin with. She was too much of a cunt to find love. Like him.

In his sudden despair, James allowed his mind to come to rest on Elliot. Just for a moment, he told himself, just until the feeling passed. He pictured Elliot at his desk in Cambridge, surrounded by books and papers and telescopes. Not that a quantum physicist needed telescopes, but it was a nice image. One of his students would be there with him and Elliot would be animatedly explaining some convoluted mathematical concept, slipping into the lisp that sometimes crept into his voice when he was excited. James had loved listening to Elliot talk. They'd spent whole days lying on a blanket on the Loyola quad, drinking cheap beer under the autumn sun while Elliot talked about quarks and string theory and James listened, his head in his lap. Elliot was a genius. His hair had been fine and soft like brown cotton candy, an amorphous fuzzy mass upon his head, and his eyes were deep green. He had a nice dick, too, but his hands had been what James found most sensual—they were as expressive in gesture, gentle in touch, the nails always neatly trimmed. James and Elliot had dated through most of college. Then Elliot had gone away on a graduate scholarship to Harvard.

They'd kept in touch at first. Mostly through letters—Elliot had been such a romantic—but gradually the letters ceased, and when they did, James was sure Elliot had found someone new, some fellow genius with ambition and drive and talent, who would show him all the devotion and kindness and love he deserved. Surely they'd be married by now, with two or three beautiful children and tenure-track professorships. Elliot deserved all that and more.

James' basic-bitch roommates were in the living room when he got home from the Senior Center, two young medical students who clearly thought of him as their sassy gay friend. He didn't even like them.

"Oh hey girl!" one of them said as he walked in.

"Hi," he sighed. They didn't seem to notice his dejection.

"We're going out tonight!" the other one exclaimed. "Wanna come?"

I'd rather put rocks in my pockets and walk into the river than hang out with your sorry basic asses, he thought, but feigned disappointment. "Darlin' I can't, I have to go to my other job."

"Oh right, your little ghost tour thing. Funnn!"

"*So* fun," he spat. "It's *adorable*."

"Well, we'll be thinking of you!"

"You're gonna *kill* it in that outfit. Slay!" Whenever James was feeling particularly hateful towards the girls he punched up the queerness to comic extremes, just to see if they'd call his bluff, but they never did.

"Thanks girl! Tonight's gonna be so lit."

"Yas kween! Praise Beyonce!" he said and slammed the door of his bedroom.

He checked his phone: a text from Landon, *"How's ur day?"* with three blue hearts and a rainbow. He started typing about his workout at the gym, about the seniors and their crafts and Irene's bad attitude, about his stupid roommates and how sad he was feeling and how much he wanted to take Landon in his arms and kiss every inch of his body and hold him and be held by him until everything felt better, and by the time he was finished he'd written a chunk of text two or three inches long. Then he parked his thumb on the backspace key and deleted it all.

"Fine," he sent. And then, four minutes later, added:

"U?"

After dinner he drove to the French Quarter, found a parking spot, and walked the few blocks to St. Peter Street, waving hello to a few acquaintances as he passed the gay bars. He wrinkled his nose at the acrid smell of piss on the block of St. Peter approaching Bourbon, where drunk idiots always ducked around the corner to relieve themselves. Sometimes there was shit, too, and tonight a new pile of orange vomit had appeared next to somebody's front stoop. James pursed his lips and tried not to inhale as he made his way through the crush of humanity on Bourbon Street. There were packs of drunken bead-wearing bros hollering at the strippers smoking on the balconies, basic bitches with fresh blowouts and hand grenades trying not to trip in their stilettos, dumpy middle-aged couples clutching each others' hands, looking simultaneously ecstatic and terrified.

Finally he reached Madame Livaudais' Curiosity Shop, outside of which the Tour of Lost Souls departed nightly at 8 p.m. The shop was cluttered and homey, stuffed with charms and voodoo dolls and incense, and the green paint on the shutters outside was old and peeling in the quaint, authentic way that always made people ooh and aah over the old-world charm of the 300 year old city. James had been giving ghost tours a few years now, to supplement his income. For the most part, it was a delightful gig. The stories were fun to tell and working in the Quarter fulfilled some masochistic desire in James to surround himself with chaos. "You'd think I'd be tired of it after three years, but what can I say, I just truly love the sound of my own voice," he told people who asked why or how long he'd been doing it.

8:00 arrived and the manager wobbled down the sidewalk to send out the tour guides. He split the waiting gaggle on the sidewalk into two groups, one departing towards Bourbon with another guide, and one heading in the other direction with James, toward the Cathedral.

"This better be cool," he heard the young woman directly behind him say to her boyfriend. They were sort of trashy looking, with bland spray-tan faces and matching sports jerseys. The girl was in cheap and uncomfortable looking heels and the man's pants were sagging stupidly below his ass.

"Are we gonna see ghosts?" the boyfriend said, somewhat aggressively, to the back of James' head.

"Well, you know what they say," he drawled, tired of having to make this joke. "The more spirits you drink, the more spirits you see."

The girl laughed, but the boyfriend was not placated. "What we paid 25 bucks for if we're not gonna see any ghosts?"

James braced himself for a difficult tour and tried to warm them up with small talk. "So where y'all from?"

"We go to Alabama," the first guy said disinterestedly. *"Roll tide!"* the one in the back yelled. James rolled his eyes so hard it hurt and hoisted his pimp cane higher in the air to lead the group as they turned the corner onto Royal. He hoped the Alabama bros and their girlfriends would be sucked into the crowd as they crossed the street and vanish from his tour. But such miracles were rare.

In the shadow of the Cathedral he gathered his group close around him and delivered his introduction. "Good evening, everyone! My name is James, and I'll be your tour guide this evening. But before we get started, just a bit about what to expect. First of all—and I hope you all know this already—this is a walking tour. We'll be strolling around the French Quarter, stopping at several different spots that are all important in New Orleans history and also—you guessed it—haunted." Most of the crowd was nodding along pleasantly.

"Now I'm sure you're wondering, are we going to go into any of these haunted places? I'm afraid the answer is mostly no, but a little bit yes—halfway through the tour, we will be stopping into the city's oldest and most haunted bar."

"Fuck yeah," one of the Alabama bros grunted.

"Another question I get asked all the time—James, are we going to see any ghosts on this tour?"

"We better!" one of the bros yelled again. James took a deep breath.

"Well it's certainly possible. Bit of a disclaimer though, I personally cannot summon ghosts and spirits at will. If I could, I probably would not be a tour guide working for tips on the streets—I would be in a very nice haunted mansion, with my own TV show, surrounded by handsome scientists."

The bros snickered and muttered to each other. He ignored them and focused instead on a smart-looking middle-aged lady up front, who had laughed at the joke and was smiling. He finished going over the rules—don't stand in the street, don't lean on the buildings, et cetera—and then began the tour.

"Alright, folks. I want y'all to imagine what this city was like in the early 1700s, when La Nouvelle Orleans was a little baby colony of France. Bienville put us right here on at this big ol' curve at the mouth of the Mississippi river, because of course in those days whoever controlled the mouth of the river controlled what went up and down the river. Great place to put a city, right? Not so much. Because back then, this whole area was a nasty swamp. Bienville got to work draining it, but even after that, nobody really wanted to live here—because New Orleans was gross. I mean, it kind of still is…" That always got a laugh. "But in those early days, if you came down here from somewhere else and you weren't used to this climate, oh honey. Any given summer, you would probably just…*die*." The group laughed again. James went on to describe how, in the early 1700s, Bienville had begged King Louis to send settlers to the swampy new colony, and how the King's response had been to open the Bastille, put the heretics, drunks, murderers and crazies on ships, and send them to New Orleans. "Kind of explains a lot, doesn't it?" This type of humor about New Orleans, playing up its debauchery, always went over well with the tourists. It was lowest-common-denominator type stuff, but you had to pull them in somehow.

He talked about the transfer of Louisiana from France to Spain, the French coup, the hanging of the rebels in this alley and the ghosts of the French priests who stealthily took the bodies down during a hurricane and buried them. The women up front were nodding and smiling kindly, the way middle-aged women sometimes did, and this always made him feel surprisingly warm and grateful in some deep, oft-inaccessible part of his heart.

These women fell into step with James up front as he led them to the next stop, asking how long he'd been a tour guide, where he was from, whether he liked giving tours, and so on. The Alabama bros and their girlfriends were at the back of the group and he could hear them shouting dumb nonsense.

"You must get tired of dealing with tomfoolery like that," one of the nice ladies said, leaning towards him confidentially.

"Oh, it's constant," he said. "You learn to manage it."

They crossed Jackson Square and he stopped at Muriel's, the imposing restaurant on the corner, to let the group peer in the window at the table that was always set for its resident ghost. Then they continued down Chartres, James' favorite street in the

Quarter. It was usually quiet on Chartres, and darker; some blocks were illuminated only by dimly flickering gas lamps, which the tourists always loved. He liked this part of the walk, the entrée to the Lower Quarter, where the streets weren't so bright and smelly and the beautiful old buildings weren't covered in signs and you could actually breathe a little, away from the crowds. He could always hear the group murmuring about how pretty it was around this point in the walk, and he usually fielded a few questions about the architecture, the unending row of two and three story buildings lining the street, their facades uninterrupted except for gated alleyways to hidden courtyards. A chilly wind blew up Dumaine Street from the river, and James zipped his jacket. Since when was New Orleans this cold? There were always at least a few nights in December and January when the temperature dipped into the 30's, but this year the winter weather seemed to be much worse than usual. New Orleans wasn't built for cold, he thought, glancing around at the unhappy tropical plants that hung from the wrought iron balconies over the street. Someone should have brought them inside.

He told the group briefly about the vampires in the Ursuline Convent, then led them up the block to the house where he always told the story of the Swamp Witch. She was a beautiful young girl seduced by a degenerate who broke her heart and betrayed her, but who lived on to develop witchy powers and exact vengeance upon him and everyone he held dear. The women liked it, but he could hear the Alabama group snickering at the back of the group, making fun of his voice.

"So she moves to the Swamp and begins to communicate with the birds and insects—"

"And *butterflies*," one of the bros whispered with an exaggerated gay sibilance. His friends laughed.

James made meaningful eye contact with the guy as he spoke his next words. This asshole wanted to have a dick-measuring contest? James was happy to oblige.

"And in the swamp, she realizes just how much better off she is without that idiot who laughed at her and cast her aside. From her servant Labasse, Kate learns hoodoo and begins to make gris-gris and potions by hand. In fact, she starts to realize that many things are better when done with her own hands. You see, her former lover's income wasn't the only thing he had that was positively...tiny."

He flicked his eyes downward to the Alabama bro's crotch as he said this, and everybody—Mister Bigshot Bro's friends included—snorted in laughter. The guy tugged self-consciously on his big "A" hat and looked away, his cheeks reddening. His girlfriend was still laughing when James finished the story and led them away.

Later, at the bar break, he took a deep breath of the cool night air as the group dashed into the bar to pee and buy overpriced beers. With groups like this, the break was key to his sanity. Just a few minutes to himself, to breathe a little and look at his phone and—

One of the Alabama hoes tumbled out of the bar and into James' personal space.

"So is this all, like, true?" she asked aggressively, puffing out her tits at him like some kind of threatening bird. He took a step away.

"The history is."

"What about the hauntings or whatever?"

"Well, I suppose that depends on whether or not you believe in the paranormal."

"I'm a Christian," she said disdainfully.

"And?" he said.

"It means I think there's certain stuff that God, like...*frowns upon*."

"Like coming to a city full of addicts and queers and sinners to get wasted and have premarital sex and party?" She opened her mouth to say something, then glared at him and wandered away.

Oops. Having directly insulted two of them, James was certain that she and the rest of the Alabama cretins would fail to rejoin the group after the bar break, but he was surprisingly mistaken. All six of them re-appeared, fresh beers in hand, and though Bro #1 and Hoe #3 looked cranky about it, the others seemed excited to continue. He told a story at the Andrew Jackson Hotel, which was haunted by the ghosts of prank-playing orphans, then took them down the street to the Bourbon Orleans Hotel, where he described the famed Quadroon Balls of the 1800s.

He checked his phone: it was almost 10:00, time to wrap up the tour. He always saved his favorite story for last. He pulled up his group in front of the big pink building at the corner of Dauphine and Orleans and began the tale of the Sultan's Palace.

"Take a look at this beautiful rose pink building behind me, y'all. This building was the home of a wealthy antebellum plantation owner called Jean Baptiste LaPrete. After the Civil War, though, when slavery was ended," (he half-expected a *boooo* from the Alabama kids, but none came), "LaPrete found himself running out of cash. No longer able to afford this place, he was forced to rent it out. But because it was so large, and because nearly everyone in the South was hurting financially after the war, he had a hard time finding a renter for it.

"But finally, in 1872, LaPrete was in a bar bitching and moaning about his unhappy situation to anybody who would listen when a handsome dark man in a turban introduced himself. Think Arjun Rampal—" he said, looking around at the blank faces. "—No? You don't know Arjun? Guess all those hours I spent watching shirtless Indian guys dance around in Bollywood movies for research were a waste of time, darn." That got a laugh. "Anyway, this man claimed to be Prince Suleyman, a Turkish Sultan, and told LaPrete that he was looking for a place to stay with his large family. LaPrete didn't know whether this guy was legit or not, but he agreed to rent the house to him on the condition that he pay two full years' rent up front. Believe it or not, the man presented the money the very next day, and LaPrete skipped off to spend it.

"So Prince Suleyman moved into the mansion with his 'family.' But it becomes evident pretty quickly that they're not family at all. They're friends. Special friends. In fact, what we have here is Prince Suleyman's *harem*, dozens and dozens of beautiful, sexy, young people, both women and men."

One of the hoes wrinkled her nose and went "Ew." James ignored her.

"And then he began to party. The Prince's household feasted, drank, and enjoyed a never-ending supply of opium and hashish, 24 hours a day. This party just never ended. Now, I don't know about y'all, but uh…where's my invitation?" Everybody chuckled.

"It went on for a month. Then another month, then six months, then a year. This house becomes a world unto itself, a world where pleasure is the only pursuit. The Sultan has everything he could possibly want. He's surrounded by beauty, sex, and every kind of drug known to man. What goes on in this house makes the rest of the city look like a convent. It's neverending ecstacy, or neverending sin—I guess it depends how you feel about that sort of thing. But no one from around town is invited to join the Prince in his revelry. He keeps bodyguards around the perimeter and stays locked up inside his mansion, alone with his harem.

"This went on for 18 months straight. The Prince and his household remained shrouded in mystery until one day in 1873, when a young lady walking by the house felt a drop of something wet on her shoulder. Looking up, she realized in horror that blood was dripping steadily from the gallery above. She also noticed a thick pool of blood oozing out from under the door, spilling down the stairs.

"When the police arrived and entered the house, they found a nightmarish scene unparalleled in New Orleans history. Dismembered body parts were strewn all over the house. The floors were covered in a layer of blood so thick the police couldn't walk in it without slipping and had to hold onto banisters and mantelpieces to help them move through the house. It quickly became clear that every person in the house had been brutally murdered, dismembered, and decapitated. The police had to do a "head count" to assess the number of victims, and by that I mean they're picking up severed heads off the floor and putting them in a row. But after all this counting, one person seemed to be missing—the Sultan himself. Finally the police went out to the courtyard, where they saw a stiff hand poking out of the dirt, as if trying to claw its way up. Some digging revealed the body of the Prince himself, whose face was covered in horrible disfiguring cuts and whose throat was so crammed with dirt that it was clear he had been buried alive."

He noticed that one of the bros' jaws had fallen stupidly slack at this detail, and felt a bump of pleasure.

"The massacre at the Sultan's palace is the largest mass murder in New Orleans history. Nearly 70 people were killed here. Now, at the time, people around town suspected it was the work of pirates. But today we have a different theory. It turns out that in the 19th century, middle eastern countries had a rather gruesome custom. Whenever a new Sultan rose to power, he would send assassins to kill all of his male relatives, to ensure that no one except his direct descendants could ever ascend the throne. We think that Prince Suleyman was not actually the Sultan, but the *brother* of the Sultan, who had fled to New Orleans to get to safety. But alas…his brother, the real Sultan, sent emissaries to track him down. And of course, when they found him here in New Orleans, they murdered him and his entire household in cold blood.

"Today, the Sultan's Palace has been broken up into six smaller apartments. Are the tenants here aware of what happened in 1873? You bet. Many report hearing strange sounds in the night—the sound of fleshy thuds, as if body parts are hitting the floors around them. And every so often, someone will report seeing a pool of fresh blood in the foyer, only to vanish an instant later.

"And if you live here, you might someday turn the corner from one room into another, and there you'll see, clear as day, the entire massacre—as fresh as it was in 1873, with blood sprayed across the walls, piles of arms and legs, and a few disembodied heads gaping at you, their mouths twisted in screams of agony. Because here in New Orleans, history always rises to the surface. The Sultan's brother tried to run from his past, tried to conquer his fear with debauchery. But your past always catches up with you, doesn't it? And it'll bury you alive, if you're not careful."

He took a dramatic pause. "And that's the end of the tour."

There was a smattering of applause, mostly from the middle-aged ladies. The group began to disperse, some of them handing him bills before they went.

"Hey," one of the now-very-drunk Alabama bros said, staggering towards him with his chest puffed up. He made a sudden threatening movement towards James, but then clasped him by the arm all the way up to the elbow.

"That was awesome, dude. You're cool." He handed James a ten.

"Isn't that generous of you. Now run along," he said, shooing them away like a mother dismissing her toddlers. "Go have fun on Bourbon Street! Alcohol, mmm." He waited until the corner was empty of tourists, then sighed heavily.

James usually went to the bar after tours to socialize with the other guides, but tonight the thought of bitching about his group to anyone who'd listen made him feel deeply, inexplicably tired. He went back to his car. Settling into the front seat, he pulled the wad of tips out of his pocket and counted them. Sixty bucks—not terrible for such a weird tour. He wanted to be proud for bringing the Alabama group around, for shutting down their bullshit and earning their affection, but he couldn't muster anything but apathy. Fuck those people, honestly. Fuck straight privilege, fuck ignorance and plain-old stupidity, fuck everyone who came to New Orleans to get wasted and trash their Airbnb's and piss in the street. Yes, he'd force-fed them some substance and history, but only by beating them into submission with shame and derision. He wished he could wipe the whole experience from his memory.

He stuffed his tips into his wallet and pulled out his phone. A text from Landon: *"Hey! I miss u, wanna get into some trouble?"* Yes, he thought, yes I do want to get into some trouble. I want drugs and I want alcohol and I want to forget, I want to fuck off and forget about all of this, everything.

But not with Landon. Landon wasn't trouble. Landon was something else entirely, James thought, the boy's big dairy-cow eyes swimming in his mind.

He leaned back in his seat and gazed out through the windshield at the gay bar across the street. There were a few people outside drinking and laughing, their breath little puffs of white in the cold night air. He closed his eyes.

A minute or two later, his phone buzzed in his hand. It was a notification from Grindr. ADM.

"*Hey.*" The DM was from someone named Troy. Peering at the picture, James realized that it was the Hulk, last week's fling, the big muscly brute he didn't think he'd ever hear from again. Another message came a second later.

"*I'm free tn if you want to hook up again.*"

The first time James had been to New Orleans was with his parents and sister on a family vacation, decades ago. And although they'd spent most of their time wandering up and down Bourbon Street with the other bland out-of-towners, 12-year-old James had gotten enough glimpses at the weirdos and queers on the side streets that he'd understood what kind of place the French Quarter really was, understood that it wasn't really *for* people like his parents, but for people like him. And he'd dreamed of living in the Quarter, where whole blocks flew rainbow flags, where he could be safe and happy and surrounded by all the other gay misfits of the world who'd found this place to belong. And of course in the fantasy he had a boyfriend, a soulmate, a person to share it all with. And on a Friday night like this, they'd go to a bar like the one across the street, socialize for a few hours, and then walk back home to their perfect decrepit little apartment hand in hand, laughing and tipsy and in love.

He looked at his phone again. "*I'm free tn if you want to hook up again.*"

James knew where he lived. He remembered the way.

"*I'll be right over.*"

CONTRIBUTOR BIOS

GANIA BARLOW teaches at Oakland University in Michigan. Her creative work has previously been published in journals including *AGNI*, *Fourteen Hills*, *Smokelong Quarterly*, and *Mythic Circle*. Her fiction has been nominated for a Pushcart Prize, awarded as Runner-Up for the Calvino Prize and finalist for the Sequestrum New Writer Awards, and adapted for the stage at Tulane University.

RICH BARNETT's humor column in the magazine *LETTERS from Camp Rehoboth* just celebrated fifteen years and his most recent book, *Fun with Dick and James,* was published in 2016. Rich's work has appeared in a variety of publications, including *Best Gay Stories 2017, Chelsea Station, Delaware Beach Life,* and *Saints and Sinners: New Fiction from the Festival*. Rich and his partner Michael reside in a 99-year old seaside cottage in Rehoboth Beach, Delaware, surrounded by boxwoods, hydrangeas, and a coterie of colorful friends and neighbors.

ARIADNE BLAYDE is a playwright and novelist. Her plays have been finalists for The Arts and Letters Prize, the Tennessee Williams Playwriting Contest, Lark Playwrights Week, and more. Her play *The Other Room* won the VSA Playwright Discovery Award and has had more than 300 productions around the world. Ariadne lives in New Orleans and moonlights as a ghost tour guide in the French Quarter. "The Sultan's Palace" is an excerpt from her (as yet) unpublished novel, *Ash Tuesday*.

MATTHEW CHERRY earned his M.A. in English with an emphasis in creative writing at the University of Central Oklahoma in 2014. He is a Marine Corps veteran and has taught English composition at various colleges and universities. He is currently the Director of the Academic Success Center at Northwestern Oklahoma State University in Alva, Oklahoma, where he lives with his wife and two daughters. His short fiction has been published online and in print.

LEWIS DESIMONE is the author of the novels *Channeling Morgan, Chemistry,* and *The Heart's History*. His work has also appeared in *Jonathan, Chelsea Station, Christopher Street, Saints + Sinners: New Fiction from the Festival 2019, Not Just Another Pretty Face,* and *My Diva: 65 Gay Men on the Women Who Inspire Them*. After spending most of his life on the coasts— first Boston, then San Francisco—he currently makes his home in Minneapolis, where he's honing his skills as a snow shoveler. www.lewisdesimone.com.

MATTHEW HAYNES is the author of the novel *Moving Towards Home* and novella, *Friday*. He was State of Idaho Literary Fellow in 2010, Lambda Literary Fiction Fellow in 2017, and 2018 Lambda Literary Fiction Writer-in-Residence. His short stories and essays have appeared in *Hawaii Pacific Review*, *West Branch*, and *The Normal School*, among others. He has recently completed a new novel and collection of short stories. He lives in his hometown of Butte, Montana.

K.W. HOLLAND lives in Virginia with his husband, two dogs, and too many books, board games, and bicycles. A native of Maryland's Eastern Shore, he was raised in a conservative Evangelical family, and graduated from Washington College. His career has been in business communications, but he now focuses his energy on fiction, which is both more interesting and more true.

DAVID HOLLY lived thirty years in rural Florida before buying a house under tall trees by a tempestuous river on a snow-capped mountain in Oregon. He teaches college English, writing, humanities, literature, and mythology. Once he owned a plant nursery and later a book shop. His tastes run to literature, speculative fiction, strong coffee, and red wine. His novels range from *Kissing Behind the Bathhouse* (romantic comedy) to *Slaves of Greenworld* (SF fantasy) to *A Radical Gynocracy* (dystopian transsexualism) to many collections of sizzling gay erotica.

MORGAN RAE HUFSTADER is a romance and thriller author and book marketer. She studied Creative Writing at Sarah Lawrence College and completed a writing intensive in Bath, England. She has since published seven paranormal and two queer contemporary romance novels. This native New Yorker is currently growing roots in New Orleans, where she lives with her lovely, patient wife and two eccentric dogs. She enjoys exploring dark themes and morally ambiguous characters, and takes her iced coffee shaken, not stirred.

MIAH JEFFRA is author of *The First Church of What's Happening* (Nomadic 2017), *The Fabulous Ekphrastic Fantastic!* (Sibling Rivalry 2020), *The Violence Almanac* (Black Lawrence 2021), and co-editor, with Arisa White and Monique Mero, of the anthology *Home is Where You Queer Your Heart* (Foglifter 2020). Miah is founding editor of queer literary collaborative, Foglifter Press.

JOHN KANE is a playwright and novelist living in Los Angeles. Novel: *Best Actress*, published in six languages and made into a TV movie; short stories on the blog *Hollywood Dementia*. Plays: short plays, including *Are You David Mamet?* and *Long Story* and *Ben and Rachel Get Married* produced all over the U.S. at Fusion Theatre (NM), Empire Stage (FL), Theatre Three (NY), and many others. Kane's play *The Eleven O'Clock Number* won the best play award at the Saints and Sinners Festival (2010) and his short story "Fat Hands" was first runner up in the short story competition (2015). He is a former film publicist. Contact him at JohnKaneLA@aol.com for further information.

GAR MCVEY-RUSSELL's first novel, *Sin Against the Race* (gamr books, 2017) was listed on *The Advocate*'s Best Books We Read in 2018: LGBTQ Novels. His fiction has also appeared in *Sojourner: Black Gay Voices in the Age of AIDS* (1993) and *Harrington Gay Men's Fiction Quarterly* (vol. 7, Num. 3, 2005). Non-fiction has appeared in *Chill Magazine* and *The Good Men Project*. Gar is married and lives in Oakland, California, where he listens to a lot of jazz.

SCOTT POMFRET is author of *Since My Last Confession: A Gay Catholic Memoir*; *Hot Sauce: A Novel*; the *Q Guide to Wine and Cocktails*, and dozens of short stories published in, among other venues, *Post Road, New Orleans Review, Fiction International*, and *Fourteen Hills*. Scott writes from his tiny Boston apartment and even tinier Provincetown beach shack, which he shares with his partner of nineteen years. He is currently at work on a *Know-Nothing* novel set in antebellum New Orleans.

EJ ROBINSON is a freelance tour guide and life-long writer based in London. In 2010 and 2011 she had stories shortlisted in the 17-25 age category of the Wicked Young Writers' Award chaired by Michael Morpurgo and completed Faber Academy's novel writing course in 2014. On most days she's to be found in the taverns and halls and parks of London telling the city's history to people from all over the world, always with a corner of her heart wishing she was at home writing.

GARY SMITH has had numerous stories published in such magazines as the *James White Review, Amethyst, The Evergreen Chronicles, Ball State Forum,* among others. He has also had over a dozen plays produced by Mid-America Playwrights Theatre. One of his short plays was selected by Actors Theatre of Louisville for a workshop production during their Humana Festival. Smith was named 1988 Writer of the Year by Friends of Lincoln Library in Springfield, IL where he lives with his partner, Larry, and their cat, Mercedes.

MICHAEL H. WARD published his memoir of the early AIDS epidemic in Boston, *The Sea Is Quiet Tonight,* in 2016. His short story, "Omaha," was a runner up in the 2019 Saints and Sinners short fiction contest and is anthologized in *New Fiction from the Festival, 2019.* Michael is currently working on a series of nine interrelated short stories set in the Midwest. He lives on Cape Cod with his husband, Moe, and cat, Jack.

ABOUT THE EDITORS

TRACY CUNNINGHAM retired after 25 years in education, having taught English, creative writing, and journalism, and entered the field of non-profit event planning and management. She holds a B.A. in English Education, a Master's degree in English, and a Master's degree in Educational Leadership. She has been a national speaker and writing workshop leader for the National Writing Project, and is the Co-Director of the New Orleans Writing Marathon. She is managing director of the Tennessee Williams/New Orleans Literary Festival. Her writing has appeared in *Louisiana Literature* and in various anthologies and radio shows from the New Orleans Writing Marathon.

PAUL J. WILLIS has over 24 years of experience in non-profit management. He earned a B.S. degree in Psychology and a M.S. degree in Communication. He started his administrative work in 1992 as the co-director of the Holos Foundation in Minneapolis. The Foundation operated an alternative high school program for at-risk youth. Willis has been the executive director of the Tennessee Williams/New Orleans Literary Festival since 2004. He is the founder of the Saints and Sinners Literary Festival (established in 2003). Willis received the Publishing Triangle Award for Leadership (2019). This nationally recognized award is for service to the LGBTQ literary community and was presented at The New School in New York City. Current fascinations include LSU Football and Gymnastics, Baby Yoda, and the artwork of Timothy Cummings.

OUR FINALIST JUDGE

DON WEISE has twenty-five years publishing experience, the majority of which has been devoted to LGBT literature. Among the many authors he has worked with are Gore Vidal, Edmund White, Samuel R. Delany, James Purdy, Leslie Feinberg, Christopher Bram, and Ann Bannon. He was named by Publishers Weekly as one of twelve annual industry "Change Makers" and listed among *Out Magazine*'s "100 Most Intriguing Gay Men and Lesbians" of the year. Weise is currently the founder/publisher of Querelle Press.

OUR COVER ARTIST

TIMOTHY CUMMINGS, represented by Catharine Clark Gallery in San Francisco and Nancy Hoffman Gallery in New York, journeyed to a French Quarter pied-à-terre over-looking Armstrong Park in the Fall of 2017 as part of a My Good Judy Residency. The My Good Judy Foundation provides residencies for artists seeking to produce a body of work or performance in New Orleans that address culture making from an LGBTQ perspective. The residency was established to also honor the work of author and activist Judy Grahn. The subjects of Cummings' work are often children and adolescents struggling with issues of sexuality and sexual orientation in an adult world. In 2013, he was an artist-in-residence and subject of a solo exhibition at Transarte in Sao Paulo, Brazil. His paintings are also part of the collections of Whoopi Goldberg in Los Angeles, CA and Tomaso Bracco and Sara Davis in Milan, Italy.

He enjoyed his time in New Orleans where he received inspiration from the spirits of his favorite writers Tennessee Williams and Truman Capote. "They shaped my early adolescence. They offer a magical telling of the spirit of this place. The darkness and humor of life and the queer Southern aesthetic shows up in my work as well. Williams' "garrulous grotesque", replacing the bleak mundane of the world with a lush queer poetic eye for the shadows is part of my focus," Cummings said. He resides alongside the Rio Grande River in Albuquerque, New Mexico. You can see more of Timothy's work at: timothy-cummings.com. We're excited that Timothy created an original painting of Tennessee Williams to be used as the cover art for the 2020 Tennessee Williams/New Orleans Literary Festival.

Saints + Sinners Literary Festival

The first Saints and Sinners Literary Festival took place in May of 2003. The event started as a new initiative designed as an innovative way to reach the community with information about HIV/AIDS. It was also formed to bring the LGBT community together to celebrate the literary arts. Literature has long nurtured hope and inspiration, and has provided an avenue of understanding. A steady stream of LGBT novels, short stories, poems, plays, and nonfiction works has served to awaken lesbians, gay men, bisexuals, and transgendered persons to the existence of others like them; to trace the outlines of a shared culture; and to bring the outside world into the emotional passages of LGBT life.

After the Stonewall Riots in New York City, gay literature finally came "out of the closet." In time, noted authors such as Dorothy Allison, Michael Cunningham, and Mark Doty (all past *Saints'* participants) were receiving mainstream award recognition for their works. But there are still few opportunities for media attention of gay-themed books, and decreasing publishing options. This Festival helps to ensure that written work from the LGBT community will continue to have an outlet, and that people will have access to books that will help dispel stereotypes, alleviate isolation, and provide resources for personal wellness.

The event has since evolved into a program of the Tennessee Williams/New Orleans Literary Festival made possible by our premier sponsor the John Burton Harter Foundation. The NO/AIDS Task Force of New Orleans provides volunteer and special event support. The Saints and Sinners Literary Festival works to achieve the following goals:

1. to create an environment for productive networking to ensure increased knowledge and dissemination of LGBT literature;

2. to provide an atmosphere for discussion, brainstorming, and the emergence of new ideas;

3. to recognize and honor writers, editors, and publishers who broke new ground and made it possible for LGBT books to reach an audience; and

4. to provide a forum for authors, editors, and publishers to talk about their work for the benefit of emerging writers, and for the enjoyment of readers of LGBT literature.

Saints and Sinners is an annual celebration that takes place in the heart of the French Quarter of New Orleans each Spring. The Festival includes writing workshops, readings, panel discussions, literary walking tours, and a variety of special events. We also aim to inspire the written word through our short fiction contest, and our annual Saints and Sinners Emerging Writer Award sponsored by Rob Byrnes. Each year we induct individuals to our Saints and Sinners Hall of Fame. The Hall of Fame is intended to recognize people for their dedication to LGBT literature. Selected members have shown their passion for our literary community through various avenues including writing, promotion, publishing, editing, teaching, bookselling, and volunteerism.

Past year's inductees into the Saints and Sinners Literary Hall of Fame include: Dorothy Allison, Carol Anshaw, Ann Bannon, Lucy Jane Bledsoe, Maureen Brady, Jericho Brown, Rob Byrnes, Patrick Califia, Louis Flint Ceci, Bernard Cooper, Michael Cunningham, Jameson Currier, Brenda Currin, Mark Doty, Mark Drake, Jim Duggins, Elana Dykewomon, Amie M. Evans, Otis Fennell, Michael Thomas Ford, Katherine V. Forrest, Nancy Garden, Jewelle Gomez, Judy Grahn, Jim Grimsley, Tara Hardy, Ellen Hart, Cheryl Head, Greg Herren, Kenneth Holditch, Andrew Holleran, Candice Huber, Fay Jacobs, G. Winston James, Raphael Kadushin, Michele Karlsberg, Judith Katz, Moises Kaufman, Joan Larkin, Susan Larson, Lee Lynch, Jeff Mann, William J. Mann, Marianne K. Martin, Stephen McCauley, Val McDermid, Mark Merlis, Tim Miller, Rip & Marsha Naquin-Delain, Michael Nava, Achy Obejas, Frank Perez, Felice Picano, Radclyffe, J.M. Redmann, David Rosen, Carol Rosenfeld, Steven Saylor, Carol Seajay, Martin Sherman, Kelly Smith, Jack Sullivan, Carsen Taite, Cecilia Tan, Noel Twilbeck, Jr., Patricia Nell Warren, Jess Wells, Edmund White, and Paul J. Willis.

For more information about the Saints and Sinners Literary Festival including sponsorship opportunities and our Archangel Membership Program, visit: www.sasfest.org. Be sure to sign up for our e-newsletter for updates for future programs. We hope you will join other writers and bibliophiles for a weekend of literary revelry not to be missed!

"Saints & Sinners is hands down one of the best places to go to revive a writer's spirit. Imagine a gathering in which you can lean into conversations with some of the best writers and editors and agents in the country, all of them speaking frankly and passionately about the books, stories and people they love and hate and want most to record in some indelible way. Imagine a community that tells you truthfully what is happening with writing and publishing in the world you most want to reach. Imagine the flirting, the arguing, the teasing and praising and exchanging of not just vital information, but the whole spirit of queer arts and creating. Then imagine it all taking place on the sultry streets of New Orleans' French Quarter. That's Saints & Sinners—the best wellspring of inspiration and enthusiasm you are going to find. Go there."

—Dorothy Allison, National Book Award finalist
for *Bastard Out of Carolina*, and author
of the critically acclaimed novel *Cavedweller*.